In Bad Company

In Bad Company

By
Clint Symons

NOTICE
Mention of specific companies, organizations, or authorities in this book does not imply endorsement by the publisher, nor does mention of specific companies, organizations, or authorities imply that they endorse this book.

Symons, Clint.

ISBN 1449562949 – paperback

In Bad Company

For mom

Preface

Would Bing Crosby, who gave us "White Christmas", also produce a blue movie as propaganda against a Communist regime? Could a Pope assist in smuggling Nazi war criminals from Europe to South America after World War II? Has the United States military assisted in delivering large amounts of heroin and cocaine into American cities? Have cities within the United States been exposed to biological agents without their knowledge from members of the U.S. Army? Did our government give unwitting participants narcotics such as LSD, and expose healthy people to electronic shock treatment to alter their mental state? Would a President of the United States authorize the recruitment and training of assassins with the expressed consent to neutralize foreign leaders opposed to a democracy? Can the U.S. government conceal evidence; overthrow democratic governments; work with organized criminal enterprises; and launder money from illegal transactions including narcotics and bank fraud? Was the free press manipulated to disseminate disinformation to the American public? Have certain government agencies spied, murdered, blackmailed and used extortion against American citizens? Is it possible that all of these actions were the directive of the Central Intelligence Agency?

In pop culture the CIA is often attributed as the shadowing organization behind most major conspiracy events. The assassination of JFK, harboring UFO's, and orchestrating the attacks of 9/11 are often attributed as CIA hatched plans by conspiracy theorists. Strangely enough, the truth about their involvement in many historical events is stranger than fiction. For several years I researched the actual documented evidence of covert political and direct action of the CIA paramilitary services to illustrate the motive, tactics, successes and failures of specific operations. My intent was too focused on the need for CIA and their primary responsibility to the United States.

What the reader will find is my efforts from years of research has created a comprehensive view of specific covert operations from start to finish carried out by members of the Central Intelligence Agency, while separating reality from popular conspiracy. In Bad Company is a historical retrospective of key political and direct action operations covertly carried out by officers and assets of CIA and authorized by members of the United States government. The book was written to provide a historical timeline from WW II to present day of clandestine operations so the reader may comprehend the extent of involvement and the growth and power accumulated by the largest spy network in the world. Readers should expect to gain both a fear and an appreciation for what our intelligence agency is capable of and the turmoil and danger members of CIA face each day.

Although the title of the book is, "In Bad Company", this in no way is meant to perceive negativity towards CIA, but rather an understanding that to gather and analyze important intelligence members are often required to develop close relationships with a criminal and dangerous element, thus placing them in *bad company*.

Instrumental to the accuracy of the book was the last several years of research including sourced interviews of CIA assets, case officers, political officers, paramilitary specialists and directors. In addition, information was collected by reviewing CIA, FBI, DOD, DOJ, and State Department documents through the use of the FOIA. Other sources used include news paper articles, biographies, and books regarding key individuals or operations. The biggest challenge faced during the research process was wading through the maze of lies and truths; reality and fiction; corroboration and disinformation; and conspiracy theories surrounding the secret nature of CIA and level of their involvement. To maintain the integrity of the book I used multiple sources for specific incidents and was critical of each source by researching their background and credibility.

Although much of my research started in the mid 1990s, the book, In Bad Company, was constructed in a single year. The proliferation has left me with feelings of pride and guilt. We do what we do to preserve the liberty and freedom of what we stand hand-in-hand to protect, but at what cost? Is it righteous to sacrifice either the freedom or lives of a few to change the way others live? The challenge with managing an intelligence organization such as CIA is that oversight is limited and must be to preserve secrecy. This reality is what makes CIA both needed to protect the American people, but also very dangerous.

It is difficult to acknowledge everyone that has both assisted and inspired this effort, but must recognize the support of my closest friends and family. Without their faith and inspiration I would not have been able to survive, much less provide this material to those who wish to read. It is to them that I thank for their love and wisdom and whom I truly appreciate.

Contents

In Bad Company

Foundations for Intelligence

Evolution of the Central Intelligence Agency

In July of 1941 Major General William J. Donovan was appointed by President Franklin D. Roosevelt as the Coordinator of Information (COI) after he drafted a plan "Memorandum of Establishment of Service of Strategic Information," for a United States foreign intelligence service. Donovan was born on January 1, 1883. He was an American soldier, a World War I veteran, Medal of Honor winner, attorney and intelligence officer. At the time, American intelligence

William J. Donovan

had been gathered through the military, Federal Bureau of Investigation (FBI) and the United States Department of State, which they were reluctant to share with other departments. Donovan faced struggles early on in receiving cooperation from other intelligence organizations including J. Edgar Hoover, who was reluctant to yield any power. Donovan recruited Allen Dulles to head up the organizations New York headquarters in Room 3603 of Rockefeller Center, which was the prior MI6 operational location. In 1942 the organization changed their name to the Office of Strategic Services (OSS).

The Office of Strategic Services was established by a President Roosevelt in June 1942, to collect and analyze strategic information required by the Joint Chiefs of Staff. The information gathered would be used to conduct covert operations not assigned to other civilian or military agencies. Through the course of World War II, the OSS played a vital role in training Nationalist Chinese troops in China and Burma, and recruited indigenous irregular forces for sabotage operations against the Japanese Army. The OSS also performed other clandestine activities such as supporting resistance movements, including Mao Zedong's Red Army in China and the Viet Minh in French Indochina. The OSS became very valuable by recruiting spies, using propaganda, conducting espionage and subversion tactics. Donovan returned to active military duty during World War II as a Colonel and leveraged the new organization to conduct clandestine espionage and sabotage operations in Europe and parts of Asia.

The OSS purchased Soviet code and cipher material (or Finnish information on them) from the émigré Finnish army officers in late 1944. Secretary of State Edward Stettinius, Jr., protested that this violated an agreement President Roosevelt made with the Soviet Union not to interfere with Soviet cipher traffic from the USA. Gen. Donovan might have copied the papers before returning them the following January, but there is no record of Arlington Hall's receiving them, and CIA and NSA archives have no surviving copies. This codebook was in fact used as part of the Venona decryption effort, which helped uncover large-scale Soviet espionage in North America. (1)

One of the greatest accomplishments of the OSS during World War II was its penetration of Germany by OSS operatives. The OSS was responsible for training German and Austrian individuals for missions inside Germany. Some of these agents included exiled communists and Socialist party members, labor activists, anti-Nazi prisoners-of-war, and German and Jewish refugees. At the height of its influence during World War II, the OSS employed almost 24,000 people. (2)

In 1943 the OSS organized spy networks in Istanbul, which was neutral during WW II, to conduct Project Net-1, subversive action in the old Ottoman and Austro-Hungarian Empires. The OSS was dismantled after World War II in 1945 due to general census that the intelligence was no longer needed. With concerns of the Soviet's and the beginning of the Cold War, the groundwork that Donovan laid during the development of the COI and OSS was the basis for the formation of the CIA in 1947. The CIA adopted and even took over projects and operations that were still being conducted through other channels that originated by the OSS. Donovan is also widely known as the "father" of today's Central Intelligence Agency (CIA).

Operation Alsos

Nazi Nuclear Weapon Advancement

In 1944 the U.S. and Britain began the execution of Operation Alsos, a sub-operation for the Manhattan Project, in an effort to gain intelligence into the German nuclear energy project. The operational goals were to penetrate France and Germany to locate any information, seize

Otto Hahn and Werner Heisenberg

nuclear resources, materials and personnel prior to their capture by the Soviets. The operation was overseen by former Manhattan Project security officer and major league baseball player, Lt. Col. Boris Pash and physicist Samuel Goudsmit. Goudsmit was responsible for the scientific importance of the operation and had infiltrated Europe by June of 1944.

In late November 1944 it became clear to the scientists and soldiers assigned to Alsos that the German nuclear scientists were nowhere near reaching their goal of an atomic bomb. The German physicists under Werner Heisenberg's command had been evacuated from Berlin to a small village named Hechingen. There they continued their attempt to build a nuclear reactor in the wine cellar of their new home. (3)

In addition to the Soviet threat of discovery, the U.S. also grew concerned that France may intervene and capture the Nazi atomic information. Pash organized a combat engineering group under Operation Big, called Task Force A, and overran the Haigerloch laboratory on April 23, 1945. The invasion led to the discovery of an empty German nuclear reactor, drums of water and uranium cubes hidden in a nearby barn. Subsequently, the reactor, on Pash's orders was destroyed and by May of 1945 the operation was concluded with the capture of many significant German scientists. In 1942 the Norwegian resistance had successfully destroyed the main source of the water needed for the  German nuclear reactor program and the facility was eventually disassembled by members of Operation Alsos.

The operation successfully discovered substantial research and removed several German nuclear research personnel including Werner Heisenberg, Otto Hahn, and Carl Friedrich von Weizsäcker. These scientists were later extracted to England for several months of debriefing as part of Operation Epsilon. Through the debriefing sessions the allies found that Hahn discovered nuclear fission in 1938, thus leading the Germans to believe that the Nazis were far more advanced in their atomic bomb efforts.

The path of discovery that led to fission and nuclear weapons started in the early twentieth century when Ernest Rutherford discovered the composition of the atom. In 1932, Rutherford's disciple James Chadwick hypothesized that the phantom third particle in an atom was a separate elementary particle with a neutral charge that he called a neutron. In 1934 Enrico Fermi had the idea to bombard elements using neutrons, which because of their neutral charge would not be repelled by the elements. When he reached uranium, he viewed a change in the element, and thought he had produced a transuranic (an element more massive than uranium). Unknowingly he actually fissioned or split the element. (4)

Fermi continued this research and in October of 1934 put paraffin wax between the uranium and the neutrons. He discovered that the paraffin acted as a moderator, slowing the oncoming neutrons, and changing the rate at which the nuclear reaction took place. Because he used aluminum shielding to protect from radiation, Fermi was still unable to observe the fission he was creating. The theorist Niels Bohr found Fermi's results interesting and used them to invent a model of the atom. He theorized that the atom acted like a drop of water, and if something interacted with it the atom could lose its shape or even break apart. Bohr's theory was published in 1937, giving physicists a blueprint to explain the fission of an atom. (4)

In 1938 Germany, Otto Hahn was working with Lise Meitner, a physicist, on irradiating uranium with slow neutrons. When Hitler annexed Meitner's homeland, Austria, she was forced to flee because of her Jewish descent. Hahn continued his work with Fritz Strassmann and kept Meitner informed of their discoveries. Hahn expected to find that when uranium was irradiated the product would be an element close to it on the periodic table, such as radium. But time after time his experiments yielded a substance that was chemically indistinguishable from barium which is nearly half as massive as uranium. Hahn revealed his findings to Meitner in December of 1938, and she, along with her Nephew Otto Frisch began to hypothesize that perhaps this fit in with Bohr's water droplet theory of the atom. She wrote to Hahn with their ideas, and together they came up with a working theory. (4)

After the conclusion of debriefings, the allies learned that the U.S. had surpassed the entire German atomic bomb effort by 1942. Compared to the Manhattan Project, Germany was both underfunded and understaffed. Another reason for Germany's loss to the U.S. in the atomic race was their focus on other technology. They had proved to be much more advanced in jet fighters (Messerschmitt Me 262) and the first ballistic missile (V-2). In addition, German scientists also believed that German totalitarianism limited the nuclear project from a political standpoint, thus placing their efforts behind U.S. development.

Operation Paperclip
Vatican Ratlines to Smuggle Nazi Scientists

After the failed German invasion into Soviet territory, the Nazi regime began a recall of scientific members from medial positions to pursue research and development projects. The recall first required identifying the men, then finding them and ascertaining their political correctness and reliability, before their names were recorded on the Osenberg List, kept by Werner Osenberg, a University of Hannover engineer-scientist, head of the Wehrforschungsgemeinschaft (English: Military Research Association). (5)

The list was eventually discovered and provided to the OSS, where they created a search mission to locate and interrogate scientists regarding their Nazi involvement including projects, studies, and research conducted. In time the interrogation plan changed to an evacuation plan called Operation Overcast, which later became Operation Paperclip. The object was the full evacuation of the German scientists and their families who were housed in Bavaria and had intimate knowledge of the Nazi V-2 Rocket Program. The OSS belief was by eliminating the Nazi knowledge from Germany, the information the scientists possessed would not fall into the hands of the Soviet Union.

With the success of Operation Alsos in 1945, the OSS conducted Operation Paperclip, which involved the recruitment of German scientists to the U.S. after VE Day. The operation was authorized by President Harry S. Truman in August of that same year with the exception of anyone who was an active supporter of

Nazism. The OSS rectified this dilemma by clearing any record of Nazi participation from their records, an action that is highly debated to this day. Under new identities, the scientists were able to relocate to the United States and pursue scientific research under OSS and U.S. guidelines.

To accomplish this, the United States needed to smuggle the Nazi scientists from the country covertly. Stalin and the Soviet Union were actively seeking out many of the ex-Nazis for war crimes against Russia and Poland. The United States wished to avoid political embarrassment by the discovery of their assistance in aiding war criminals. Prior to and during World War II members of the Catholic Church in both Italy and South America gained permission from the Vatican to secretly transport Catholics in Western Europe to South America for religious freedom.

As early as 1942, Monsignor Luigi Maglione contacted Ambassador Llobet, inquiring as to the "willingness of the government of the Argentine Republic to apply its immigration law generously, in order to encourage at the opportune moment European Catholic immigrants to seek the necessary land and capital in our country". Afterwards, a German priest, Anton Weber, the head of the Roman St. Raphael Society, travelled to Portugal, continuing to Argentina, to lay the groundwork for future Catholic immigration. (6)

The OSS leveraged contacts that they developed during the war that assisted in resistance against the Nazi regime. The OSS leveraged operatives such as Vincent La Vista who was both a Catholic priest as well as an operative with the Counter Intelligence Corps (CIC). Under a bogus cover of Hungarian refugees, La Vista was able to smuggle out Nazis through the aid of Father Joseph Gallov. Father Gallov provided a letter from his Vatican sponsored refugee camp to obtain false ICRC documents directed to a personal contact in the International Red Cross, who then issued the passports.

Catholic Bishop Alois Hudal was rector of the Pontificio Istituto Teutonico Santa Maria dell'Anima in Rome, a seminary for Austrian and German priests, and "Spiritual Director of the German People resident in Italy". After the end of the war in Italy, Hudal became active in ministering to German-speaking prisoners of war and internees then held in camps throughout Italy. In December 1944 the Vatican Secretariat of State received permission to appoint a representative to "visit the German-speaking civil internees in Italy", a job which was assigned to Hudal. (7)

Hudal used this position to aid the escape of wanted Nazi war criminals, including Franz Stangl, commanding officer of Treblinka, Gustav Wagner, commanding officer of Sobibor, Alois Brunner, responsible for the Drancy internment camp near Paris and in charge of deportations in Slovakia to German concentration camps, and Adolf Eichmann. (6) Some of these wanted men were being held in internment camps: generally without identity papers, they would be enrolled in camp registers under false names. Other Nazis were in hiding in Italy, and sought Hudal out as his role in assisting escapes became known on the Nazi grapevine. (8)

Like Hudal, an additional ratline was operated by an influential network of Croatian priests, members of the Franciscan order, led by Father Krunoslav Draganović. Father Draganović was also a secretive member of the Ustashi, a far-right Nazi-affiliated Croatian fascist organization that was given control of Croatia by the Axis powers in 1941. Draganović organized the chain from Rome, Italy with links to both Austria and ending in Genoa used mainly to aid members of the Croatian Ustashi fascist movement and their dictator Ante Pavelic. Draganović reported to Bishop Giovanni Battista Montini, then secretary in charge of 'extraordinary affairs' at the Vatican's Secretariat of State - he would later become Pope Paul VI. Bishop Montini built a friendship with the head of the OSS unit in Rome, James J. Angleton according to U.S. Intelligence officer William Gowen. Through Father Draganović, stolen World War II treasures by Ustashi were then laundered through the Vatican Bank to help finance, OSS and Nazi ratline evacuations.

In the summer of 1947 US Army intelligence began to use Draganović's established network to evacuate its own visitors who had been in the custody of the 430th CIC and completely processed in accordance with current directives and requirements, and whose continued residence in Austria constituted a security threat as well as a source of possible embarrassment to the Commanding General of USFA, since the Soviet Command had become aware that their presence in US Zone of Austria and in some instances had requested the return of these persons to Soviet custody.

That is, these were suspected war criminals and Quislings from areas occupied by the Red Army — legally U.S. Forces were obliged to hand them over for trial to the Soviets. They were reluctant to do this partly due to their belief that fair trial could hardly be expected in the USSR, and at the same time, their desire to make use of Nazi scientists and other resources. The deal with Draganović involved getting the visitors to Rome: "Dragonovich handled all phases of the operation after the defectors arrived in Rome, such as the procurement of IRO Italian and South American documents, visas, stamps, arrangements for disposition, land or sea, and notification of resettlement committees in foreign lands." (9)

The operation supplied the U.S. and their allies with German knowledge on advancements in nuclear energy project, rocket development, and naval weapons. One of the most significant gains was the evacuation of Wernher von Braun, who was the head of the V-2 program. Later, von Braun would become an icon in NASA and be strongly credited for the U.S. moon exploration.

With its radar-absorbing carbon impregnated plywood skin and swept-back single wing, the 1944 Horten Ho 229 was arguably the first stealth aircraft. The US military made one available to Northrop Aviation, the company which would produce the $2bn B-2 Stealth bomber - to all intents and purposes a modern clone of the Horten - a generation later. Cruise missiles are still based on the design of the V-1 missile and the scramjets powering NASA's state-of-the-art X-43 hypersonic aircraft owe much too German jet pioneers. But, while celebrating the undoubted success of Project Paperclip, many will prefer to remember the thousands who died to send mankind into space. (10)

The operation created controversy years later with the findings that many of the scientists were involved in Nazi atrocities. Wernher von Braun and Kurt Debus were former SS officers; Hubertus Strughold, who designed NASA's life-support systems, overseen human experiments at Dachau and Auschwitz which often resulted in death; and Arthur Rudolph, who was deported in 1984, had run Nordhausen, where 20,000 slave laborers died.

Rudolph, was moved to the Ordnance Research and Development Division at Fort Bliss, El Paso, Texas, where his family finally joined him in April. Since he had been brought into the US without a visa, he and others were sent to Juárez, Mexico where he obtained a visa and officially immigrated to the US on 14 April 1949. During this time, he acted as a liaison to the Solar Aircraft Company, and spent much of 1947 and 1949 in San Diego, California. Rudolph was a rocket scientist for Nazi Germany from 1934 to 1945, and helped develop the V-2 rocket. While preparing for his new career in the U.S. he was debriefed by the FBI where he made the following statement:

"Until 1930 I sympathized with the social democratic party, voted for it and was a member of a socialdemocratic union (Bund Techn. Agst. u. Beamt.) After 1930 the economical situation became so serious that it appeared to me to be headed for catastrophe. (I really became unemployed in 1932.) The great amount of unemployment caused expansion of nationalsoc. and communistic parties. Frightened that the latter one would become the government I Joined the NSDAP (a legally reg. entity) to help, I believed in the preservation of the western culture."

In 1961 Rudolph went to work at NASA, once again working for von Braun. In December 1961 he became Assistant Director of Systems Engineering, serving as liaison between vehicle development at Marshall Space Flight Center and the Manned Spacecraft Center in Houston. He served as the project director of the Saturn V rocket program from August 1963 to May 1968 and then became special assistant to the director of Marshall Space Flight Center. The first Saturn V launch lifted off from Kennedy Space Center and performed flawlessly on 9 November 1967, Rudolph's birthday. In July 1969, the Saturn V helped put man on the Moon. At the end of 1969 Rudolph retired from NASA. During his tenure, he was awarded the NASA Exceptional Service Medal and the NASA Distinguished Service Medal. (11)

The Rudolph's retired to San Jose, California to be near their daughter. Soon after moving, he had a heart attack and a triple bypass. In September 1982, he received a letter requesting an interview by the Office of Special Investigations (OSI). Apparently, Rudolph believed this was one of the series of interrogations he had gone through since his arrival in the US. The first of three interviews, it centered on his attitudes on racial superiority, his early participation in the Nazi Party and a possible role in the treatment of prisoners at Mittelwerk. On 28 November 1983, Rudolph, purportedly under duress and fearful for the welfare of his wife and daughter, signed an agreement with the

OSI stating that he would leave the United States and renounce his United States citizenship. Under the agreement, Rudolph would not be prosecuted, the citizenship of his wife and daughter was not in danger of revocation and Rudolph's retirement and Social Security benefits were left intact. In March 1984 Arthur and Martha Rudolph departed for Germany where Rudolph renounced his citizenship as agreed. Germany protested to the United States Department of State, as Rudolph now had no citizenship in any country. In July, Germany requested documentation from OSI to determine if Rudolph should be prosecuted or granted citizenship. After receiving documentation in April 1985, the case was investigated by Herald Duhn, the Attorney General of Hamburg. In March 1987, the investigation concluded after questioning a number of witnesses and determining no basis for prosecution. Rudolph was then granted German citizenship. (11)

Operation Stella Polaris
Finnish Selling of Soviet Secrets

Operation Stella Polaris was a covert action where Finnish signals intelligence records, equipment and personnel were transported into Sweden in 1944 and led by Colonel Reino Hallamaa, commander of Finland's code-breaking services. Reino Henrik Hallamaa was born on November 12, 1899 in Tampere. After attending college in Helsinki he began working for the Finnish railroad as a signals telegraphist at the Helsinki Central railway station. In 1918, Finland declared its independence, and the Finnish Civil War erupted. Hallamaa joined the whites in Seinäjoki. Hallamaa rose through the ranks to Captain of the Finnish Radio Intelligence program in 1929 and Major by 1939 where the prime responsibility was to monitor radio traffic of the Soviet Red Fleet. The Finnish program also worked on other countries codes and ciphers, cracking for instance the US STRIP code, as well as Brazilian, Portuguese, Romanian, Serbian, Vatican, and Vichy French codes. Hallamaa was promoted into Colonel in 1944 and headed the 1,000 personnel staff during the World War II. In 1944 Hallamaa prepared for a Soviet invasion and began planning for Operation Stella Polaris. Along with Aladar Paasonen, the Finnish Chief of Intelligence, the men devised a project to secretly transfer both materials and personnel to Sweden and selling the encryption codes and ciphers of Soviet Union to the United States and other countries. In September of 1944 Hallamaa ordered the transfer of over three hundred crates to be shipped to Sweden.

Accompanying the crates was between seven and eight hundred radio intelligence operators and their families.

The largest intelligence organization in Sweden was the [American Office of Strategic Services, with a] 75-man OSS station in Stockholm. For most of the war the station had been working closely with the Finns. R. Taylor Cole, the director of secret intelligence from August 1944 through October 1944, wrote, "The resources of the entire Finnish intelligence services have been largely available to the OSS." (12) The Finns provided OSS with a bumper crop of hard intelligence on the German military, and, strikingly, on America's ally, the Soviet Union. Based on their past dealings, OSS assumed that except for the Swedes, they would be the only consumer of the material.

During one of OSS's first meetings with the newly arrived Stella Polaris agents, Colonel Reino Henrik Hallamaa, commander of Finland's code-breaking services, revealed that the Finns had broken over 1,000 codes - including the U.S. State Department's diplomatic codes. The Finns read messages from American embassies in Helsinki, Moscow, Stockholm, Madrid, Tehran, the Vatican, Ankara, and Rio de Janeiro. (13)

General William J. Donovan, founder of the Office of Strategic Services (OSS), received approval from President Franklin D. Roosevelt to purchase the secretive Finnish materials without consent, or knowledge of the United States State Department.

"In connection with the cipher matter which was discussed with you this morning. Permit me to inform you that I have sent a Top Secret cable today to Dick Huber and William Carlson instructing them to arrange for a meeting with our friends and accept delivery immediately of the materials previously rejected. Further, I directed that this material be photostated and that the films be left in possession of Huber in Stockholm.... I authorized Huber to make cash payment of 250,000 kroner." (14)

Despite OSS's best efforts to keep the deal secret, the State Department found out about the purchase. Secretary of State Edward Stettinius protested directly to the president, who ordered Donovan to return the codebooks. A cover story was devised that OSS accidentally obtained the materials with other intelligence it was gathering and offered that "we would immediately make it available to the Soviet Government if they so desire." (15)

In the aftermath of the operation, the OSS learned that not only did they purchase Soviet secrets from the Finnish Intelligence Service, but that the Finnish also sold France secrets about the United States. This enabled the French intelligence service to intercept American radio traffic. This was discovered with recruiting agents within the Finnish Intelligence organization who provided information on the Finnish involvement with both Sweden and France after the war. The Soviet secrets learned were strengthened by the access of Project Venona. The Venona project was initiated in 1943 and continued until 1980 through a secret collaboration between U.K. and U.S. intelligence agencies. In 1946 Meredith Knox Gardner identified ciphers through Soviet transmission on the one-time pads. Although most thought the encryption was impossible, Gardner discovered the Soviets were reusing certain pages of their pads. By 1947 Gardner was deciphering KGB messages proving Soviet espionage in the United States. In the early years of the Cold War, Venona was a key source of information on Soviet intelligence activity and unknown to the public, and even to President Franklin D. Roosevelt and President Harry S. Truman. The project was vital to recognizing espionage activity of the Rosenberg's, Donald Maclean, Guy Burgess, Alger Hiss and Klaus Fuchs. The massive database was so important to both the U.K. and U.S. counterintelligence community - it was looked at as the Rosetta stone of code decryption.

A number of Soviet spy rings in Great Britain, Australia, and the United States were disrupted using this information. However, U.S. Intelligence seldom risked Venona in court. More than 200 Soviet agents were identified, but only 15 were ever prosecuted for fear of blowing Venona's cover in an open court of law. For examples, Judith Coplon was a Soviet spy in the Justice Department but charges against her had to be dropped because the compelling evidence against her was in Venona. William Weisband was a Russian-born American Signals Intelligence expert, but also a Soviet spy. The evidence against his was Venona, which could not be chanced in court. He was sentenced in jail in 1950 for contempt for failing to answer questions about his pre-World War II membership in the Communist Party. This fear of disclosing the extent of Venona allowed the American and European leftists and the media to portray these trials as witch hunts and to strongly suggest the idea of Communist agents in the U.S. government was largely the product of right-wing paranoia and irrational fears. (16)

Operation RUSTY
Nazi Intelligence for Cold War

Reinhard Gehlen, a Nazi turned Knight of Malta, was born into a Roman Catholic family. He joined the Reichswehr in 1920 and entered the German Staff College graduating in 1935 where he was promoted to captain and was attached to the Army General Staff under the Nazi government of Adolf Hitler. Gehlen rose through the ranks and by 1941 was promoted to senior intelligence officer with the German General Staff on the Russian

Reinhard Gehlen

front. In December 1944, Gehlen was promoted to the rank of Major General and was tasked with concentrated intelligence gathering directed at the Soviet Union and its battlefield tactics as Head of "Foreign Forces – East".

In March 1945, knowing the end was near for the Third Reich, Gehlen and a small group of his most senior officers microfilmed the holdings of the Fremde Heere Ost on the USSR and put them in watertight drums. The drums were then buried in several places in the Austrian Alps. Two month later Gehlen surrendered to the U.S. Army Counter Intelligence Corps (CIC) in Bavaria and was subsequently brought to Camp King. During interrogation the United States quickly realized his knowledge of and contacts inside the Soviet Union. Gehlen brokered a deal with U.S. Army Captain John Boker offering the U.S. his intelligence archives and network in exchange for his liberty and the release of his colleagues imprisoned in American POW camps in Germany.

Under secrecy Gehlen's friends were released and he fulfilled his part of the bargain by delivering the archives. The transaction earned him support from U.S. Army Brigadier General Edwin Sibert the head of Army intelligence. Soon William J. Donovan and Allen Dulles learned of Gehlen and his knowledge and he and three of his colleagues were flown to the United States where they were trained under the Office of Strategic Services. Soon Donovan and Dulles learned from Gehlen that certain members of the OSS were also associated with the U.S. Communist Party and realized the significance of Gehlen's unique abilities. Gehlen's background and contacts could potentially provide them key information on Soviet activity in Berlin.

In July of 1946 Gehlen was released from U.S. captivity and flown back to Camp King in Germany to begin his intelligence career for the U.S. Gehlen formed a front organization near Munich called the South German Industrial Development Organization which was comprised of former German intelligence officers. Gehlen handpicked more than three hundred German intelligence agents. Gehlen's spy ring would be referred to as Operation RUSTY and known by the nickname the "Gehlen Organization." Over the course of the next couple years Gehlen's group would be loosely overseen by the U.S. Army Counter Intelligence Corps (CIC), and the Central Intelligence Group (CIG), the precursor to the CIA.

In 1948 the CIA scheduled a fact finding mission within Gehlen's group to determine the viability of the program. The Army felt the program should be disbanded because of inaccurate intelligence gathering. Tasked with determining the feasibility was James H. Critchfield who had joined the Central Intelligence Agency the same year. Critchfield was born on January 30, 1917 in Hunter, North Dakota. He attended North Dakota State University, participating in its ROTC program and graduating in 1939. While serving in the U.S. Army during World War II, he became one of the youngest colonels in the military. As commander of the 2nd Battalion of 141st Infantry of the 36th

Infantry Division, he won the Bronze Star twice, and the Silver Star for gallantry in resisting a German assault on December 12, 1944. The Gehlen Organization employed hundreds of ex-Nazis, among them Alois Brunner, who was responsible for the Drancy internment camp near Paris, which was responsible for the death of 140,000 Jews. Although he would later admit CIA got carried away with recruiting some pretty bad people, Critchfield felt Gehlen and his agents were far from Nazi ideologues and that many sympathized with those who tried to kill Hitler. Critchfield concluded that Gehlen and his agents would be of immense value to CIA during a time when such intelligence was hard to obtain, especially on the ground in the Soviet Bloc nations during the Cold War. This led to the Gehlen Organization's official acquisition by CIA in 1949.

"The reason that I recommended my original report in December 1948 that we accept responsibility for this organization was that we really had no choice," Critchfield. "We had no specialists who had dealt with Soviet forces, so here we had the only instrument at hand that could immediately do this. Gehlen's people had real capability to produce intelligence on East Germany and on the readiness of the Soviet air force to support a ground attack. All of this was real life and death intelligence during this period. And I think that is why there was no question of the value of it in that moment in history." (17)

The Gehlen Organization was successful at carrying out counter-espionage activities directed against dissident German organizations in Europe. The organization also assisted with other operations including the Berlin Tunnel and was also responsible for discovering the existence of the secret Soviet assassination unit known as SMERSH. Originally the main task of SMERSH was to secure the Red Army's operational rear from partisans, saboteurs, and spies; to investigate and arrest conspirators and mutineers, "traitors, deserters, spies, and criminal elements" at the combat front.

On February 3, 1941, the Special Sections of the NKVD (responsible for Military counterintelligence of the Soviet Army) became part of the Army and Navy (RKKA and RKKF, respectively). The GUGB was separated from the NKVD and renamed the People's Commissariat for State Security (NKGB), with the Counter-Intelligence (CI) sections assigned to it. Following the outbreak of World War II, the NKVD and NKGB were reunited on July 20, 1941 and CI was returned to the NKVD in January 1942. As the requirements of war expanded and the Soviet armies began their conquest of previously occupied German territory, the complexities of counter-espionage, counter-insurgency, and occupation were sufficiently large to encourage Stalin to consolidate all of SMERSH under his direct control. On April 15, 1943, CI was again transferred to the People's Commissariats of Defense (NKO) and the Navy (NKF), becoming SMERSH within NKO. The organization was headed by Viktor Abakumov, who was a subordinate of Lavrenty Beria. Therefore, SMERSH belonged to the state security apparatus rather than to the Red Army.

SMERSH was also actively involved in the capture of Soviet citizens who had been active in anti-communist armed groups fighting on the side of Nazi Germany such as the Russian Liberation Army, the Cossack Corps of Pyotr Krasnov, and the Organization of Ukrainian Nationalists. SMERSH was given the assignment of finding Adolf Hitler and, if possible, capturing him alive or recovering his body. Red Army officers and SMERSH agents found Hitler's partially burned corpse near the Führerbunker after his suicide and conducted an investigation to confirm the events of his death and identify the remains which (along with those of Eva Braun) were reportedly secretly buried at SMERSH headquarters in Magdeburg until April 1970. This is when a KGB operation called "Archive", used the guise of searching for long-lost Nazi records, excavated what was by then a garage on a Soviet military base and removed the remains of nine persons, including Adolf Hitler and Eva Braun. The base was about to be turned over to the East German government.) The remains, now a "jellied mass" according to a KGB report, were pulverized, soaked in gasoline, and then

James H. Critchfield

completely burned up. The ashes were mixed with coal particles and then taken 11 kilometers north of Magdeburg, where they were dumped into the Bideriz, and a tributary of the Elbe River. (18)

As the war wound down, the need for a strategic directorate focused on counter-espionage wet operations and counter-insurgency pacification operations that answered directly to Stalin was no longer viewed as necessary. Thus, in March 1946 SMERSH Chief Directorate was resubordinated to the People's Commissariat of Military Forces. HKBC was latter reorganized into the Ministry of Military Forces (soon thereafter, and SMERSH was officially discontinued in May, 1946.

The Gehlen Organization had its share of pitfalls too. The lax style of security made the apparatus vulnerable to moles within the ranks. One such mole far succeeded other double agents with the organization with more than eight years of service. Heinz Felfe was an officer in Hitler's SS who after World War II became a KGB penetration agent, infiltrating Gehlen's group of West German intelligence at the request of the KGB. Heinz Felfe was born in Dresden in 1918 and joined the Hitler Youth in 1931 and the SS in 1936 at age 17. By 1943 he was a commissioned officer with Hitler's SS and assigned to the SS

Foreign Intelligence branch, the SD (Sicherheitsdienst), stationed first in Switzerland and toward the end of the war in the Netherlands. When captured by the British in July 45 after World War II, Felfe was converted and worked for British intelligence, reporting on communist party activities in the Cologne area. In 1950 British Intelligence cut off communication with Felfe due to suspicions that he was also working for the Soviets.

Later statements to the CIA by Soviet defectors and by Felfe's own colleagues suggested that the Soviets after the war systematically hired former SS officers for intelligence purposes, using their criminal records against them for continued leverage.

The spotting of people like Heinz Felfe by the Soviet Union was not accidental, but the result of a well-targeted, well-developed recruitment campaign directed against former police and intelligence officers of the Nazi Reich. The thesis was simple.... Some of these people might be susceptible to a Soviet approach because of their general sympathies. Others, such as former Elite Guard (SS) and Security Service (SD) members, many of whom were now war criminals able to make their way only by hiding a past which had once put them among the elite, would be vulnerable to blackmail.

Felfe and other former SS colleagues from Dresden seem to have been easy recruits thanks partly to their bitterness toward the Allies for the firebombing of that city in February 1945. One of Felfe's Dresden colleagues from the SD, Hans Clemens, began working for the Soviets in 1949. Felfe had given Clemens reports from the West while still working for the British, but seems not to have become a full blown Soviet agent until September 1951 when he received the code-name "Paul."

In November the same year, Felfe secured a job in the Counter-Intelligence section of the Gehlen Organization. Felfe quickly moved up the ladder in the Gehlen Organization, taking charge of counter-intelligence against the Soviets in 1955. Thus the head of the West German office charged with countering Soviet espionage in West Germany was he a Soviet agent. Felfe's superiors in the Gehlen Organization, many of whom had also worked for Nazi criminal organizations such as the Gestapo and Secret Field Police, were themselves Soviet agents, thus making it easier for Felfe to advance in the organization.

"We usually met in West Berlin," Hienz Felfe, former Gehlen member. "There was a little news cinema where we use to meet. We would sit next to each other. I would pass him my information and he would go out quickly and give it to someone else. I would them join him and we would go for a stroll at dusk in the tea garden." Felfe bugged the Soviet embassy in East Berlin prior to the arrival of the ambassador. "The responsibility of the Soviet embassy lay entirely and absolutely in my hands. I was responsible for the installation of the microphones; for the tapping of the phones; and for the evaluation of the recorded conversations. My position gave the KGB the ability to hand out false information. Intelligence work isn't just about gathering information, it's also about deception." (17)

According to CIA officers - Felfe was dangerous because he was in a key position with the Gehlen group that enabled him to tip the Soviets off about CIA counter-intelligence operations involving Soviet espionage in West Germany.

Felfe was arrested on spying charges on November 6, 1961, and put to trial in 1963. He obtained a 14-year sentence, but was released in 1969 in exchange for three West German students who were convicted in the Soviet Union for spying, Walter Naumann, Peter Sonntag and Volker Schaffhausen.

After the war there were thousands of anti-communist Russians occupying East Germany. The Gehlen Group decided to leverage these individuals as assets for intelligence gathering as strategy against the communists.

William Sloane Coffin Jr. had been a friend of George H. W. Bush since his youth, as they both attended Phillips Academy, and he brought Coffin into the exclusive Skull and Bones secret society while attending Yale in Coffin's senior year. A year after graduating Yale, Coffin joined the CIA as a case officer spending three years in West Germany recruiting anti-Soviet Russian refugees and training them how to undermine Stalin's regime. Coffin felt he was doing the work of the Lord by helping "courageous young Russians overthrow a cruel, terrible dictator." "It wasn't hard for me to believe in a resistance movement to overthrow a person who would kill so many millions of Russians in the same way some very dedicated German Christian's plotted against Hitler."

Coffin's recruits were trained on parachuting through a secret CIA jump school and provided elaborate cover stories. The CIA goal was to place these assets equipped with radios at strategically located airfields in East Germany to broadcast Soviet activity. They were flown over the border under the cover of darkness low under radar and dropped near key locations. Assets were also equipped with guns, grenades and poisoned capsules to be used if captured and tortured. Support for the operation was also provided by a Russian exile group in Frankfurt Germany called NTS. Almost all of the assets were both captured and executed. Operation reports showed that Soviet military had been aware of the covert activity of Coffin's assets, leading the CIA to believe that a mole had compromised the operations.

The CIA in retrospect learned that the lax security of the Gehlen Organization lent to the ease of Soviet counter-intelligence through the use of the former SS officers. In a 1963 CIA Memorandum to the Deputy Director of Plans from David E. Murphy, CIA Chief, of the Eastern Europe Division stated that from June 1959 until his arrest on November 6, 1961 Heinz Felfe was the most knowledgeable of all BND officials on CIA operations against the Soviet targets in East and West Germany. With already some 8 years experience as a KGB penetration of the BND, considerably more as a counter-intelligence officer, and a higher degree of native intelligence and cunning, the KGB could only have evaluated his agent performance from that dates as of the highest caliber. His reputation with the BND as a Soviet operations expert deeply ingratiate himself in BND to the point of earning a position whereby he could initiate, direct, or halt and BND operations and later some CIA's to the ultimate advantage of the Soviet's.

As a result of the degree of compromise of operations, personnel and facilities in Germany has been very heavy. The details of more than 65 CIA operations are known to the opposition as is their related M/O including relationships with West German intelligence and police organizations. Over 100 CIA staffers were exposed in either true name or alias. Felfe's influence and manipulation on some members of the BND was of such a degree as to permit him at times to dictate liaison policy vis-a-vis the Americans with respect to Soviet operations.

In 1955, the Gehlen Organization was transferred to the Federal Republic of Germany. There the organization reported under the government of Konrad Adenauer, where in April of 1956 became the core of the newly formed Bundesnachrichtendienst (BND or Federal Intelligence Service) with Gehlen as acting President. Gehlen would remain with the BND until 1968 when he retired at the age of 66 and was awarded Großes Bundesverdienstkreuz am Schulterband.

Historically the Gehlen Organization assisted the U.S., Britain and West Germany with vital Soviet information during the beginning phases of the Cold War. The use of former Nazis was not new to the U.S. military. In 1947, Klaus Barbie became an agent of the U.S. Army Counter Intelligence Corps (CIC) prior to fleeing to Argentina in 1951. The U.S. and CIA over the years have had to protect the identity of many ex-Nazis that have been recruited to provide the U.S. and allies intelligence service.

As early as 1952 the BND knew that ex-Nazi Adolf Eichmann was living in Argentina under the alias "Clemens", yet failed to contact the authorities. This decision was made at the request of Konrad Adenauer, head of the West Germany government, out of concern that Eichmann would publically implicate Hans Globke. Globke was Adenauer's national security adviser, and worked with Eichmann in the Jewish Affairs department helping draft the 1935 Nuremberg Laws. In addition, CIA was concerned that the U.S. could be tarnished with Eichmann's knowledge of Reinhard Gehlen and CIA and U.S. involvement with the Gehlen Organization.

At the request of Bonn (the capital of West Germany from 1949 to 1990) the CIA persuaded Life magazine to delete any reference to Globke from Eichmann's memoirs, which it had bought from his family. By the time the CIA and the BND had this information, Israel had temporarily given up looking for Eichmann in Argentina because they could not discover his alias. The Mossad eventually captured Eichmann in 1960. (19)

Operation GLADIO

Italian Political & Covert Action

Italy was the first country the CIA participated in using political action. In the 1950s William Colby, prior to becoming the Director of CIA, was employed in Rome as a political officer. Colby and the CIA felt their role in Rome at the time was the chance for CIA to defend Western Civilization against Communist rule. The CIA's decision to operate a political campaign in Italy was based on the countries large Communist Party ties. Italy had housed the largest Communist following in Western Europe

Aldo Moro

at that time during the cold war. The party was so strong it could coordinate and mobilize thousands for Communist demonstrations with growing support from the countries industries. In the later part of the 1940s, the Communist Party was increasingly growing to the point that the U.S. believed they had a strong chance at winning during the next Italian election.

To assess the situation and oversee covert action needed to handle the Communist threat, CIA assigned Mark Wyatt as a senior officer to the Rome station in Italy. Wyatt's intelligence network established that the strength of the party was directly attributed to the Italian Communist Party leader Palmiro Togliatti. Togliatti's strength was his ability to seamlessly express the Communist benefits and practices to the needs of the Italian people economically. Togliatti focused on laborers as his core audience - knowing their acceptance of his party would provide him the majority rule when voting took place. Wyatt and others believed that the opposing party lead by Christian Democrats and supported by the Roman Catholic Church would be vital to maintain Italy's free democracy.

The CIA started a grass root movement in association with the Vatican to mount an aggressive propaganda campaign against the Italian Communist Party. This campaign included participation of Italian American's in New York that urged them to write their relatives in Italy of the horrors of Communism. Local publications even offered pre-written letters that could be cut from the newspaper and sent. The CIA placed assets in New York City communities like Brooklyn to work with Italian civic leaders and Catholic leaders to draw support for this action. Parishioners were then instructed at Sunday Mass to consider and support the letter writing campaigns to help in the fight against Communism. Within a couple weeks the U.S. postal service mailed out over one million letters to individuals in Italy from the campaign warning them of the Communist threat. To assist in these efforts Italian American newspapers even included pre-written letters warning of the dangers that readers could simply cut out and mail to their Italian relatives in Italy.

In addition to the letter writing campaigns the CIA also developed propaganda films that were then distributed to civic leaders in Italy through the Vatican and Catholic Church. Poster campaigns were also incorporated in the political action depicting Communists as warmongers. Father Lucio Mulachio was an asset the CIA used during the political campaign. Father Mulachio would regularly meet with Rome CIA handlers to pass intelligence and to Vatican officials. "There was a great relationship of trust," Father Mulachio. "The Americans knew we were quite simply working against Communism. They didn't care what party we worked for. They gave us this aid. We meet around a table for a half hour or three quarters of an hour. We told them what we were doing and sometimes mentioned the political situation. They gave us a sealed envelope and we gave it to the administrators."

The CIA's campaign was a success during the 1948 election as the Italian people rejected Communist rule and elected a Christian Democratic leader. But this was only the first battle in the struggle for Communist rule over Italy. In 1953 with the threat of Communist rule reappeared and Italy again sought assistance. Allen Dulles used former World War II Italian contacts to assist in the political action including the editor of the Italian magazine "Peace and Liberty". Again Togliatti was the target of disinformation and propaganda. Peace and Liberty, through the help and funding of CIA, ran articles that Togliatti had betrayed fellow Communists to the Fascists during Mussolini's regime through released historical military documents. The article was a huge success for the CIA because it went unchallenged by Togliatti and the Communist Party in Italy. Later the CIA found out that the propaganda was so effective that Togliatti's own Communist people isolated him from the party and placed distance between him and his political team.

The political action by CIA had been successful again but also introduced the organization to additional leaders within the country including monarchs, industry and right wing fanatics. The Archbishop of Milan, the largest Italian dioceses, Giovanni Battista Enrico Antonio Maria Montini was a spiritual leader among Catholics in Italy. Montini leveraged CIA handlers such as Wyatt to assist with furthering propaganda campaigns against Communist Rule. In the 1950s Montini requested loudspeaker trucks that would be strategically placed within civic areas to broadcast the Catholic Church's dismay for Communism and encourage a Christian Democratic vote. Montini was provided and funded by CIA to carry out the propaganda efforts. This relationship between Montini and CIA would last for years even after 1963 when Montini became Pope Paul VI.

The CIA had very powerful and influential contacts at the highest level of the Italian government. Due to the clandestine nature of the organization, secrecy was needed to maintain covert activity. This posed a challenge to CIA in Italy. "We would have so called 'cutouts'," William Colby. "We would have people on the outside who had no connection with the American government whatsoever and they would be operating as independent people ostensibly and apparently to their neighbors and even to the Italian leaders they were dealing with."

The CIA also leveraged NOCs to develop contacts and work as liaisons between CIA and anti-communist leaders. In this role they would provide intelligence to CIA from these source contacts in return for financial support. Aldo Moro, General Secretary to the Christian Democrats was a key principle for CIA. In exchange for his assistance with supporting NATO and other American interests and opposing Communism, Moro was compensated sixty million lira each month for his political party paid by CIA handlers out of the Rome station. In 1963 Aldo Morrow became the Prime Minister of Italy.

CIA also participated in covert military action along with the Italian secret police. This program was called Gladio. Operation Gladio was created as a contingency plan for the democratic Italian government and right wing militants as a support apparatus in case of Communist threat. In the early 1950s, the United States began training networks of "stay behind" volunteers in Western Europe, so that in the event of a Soviet invasion, they would "gather intelligence, open escape routes and form resistance movements." The CIA financed and advised these groups, later working in tandem with western European military intelligence units under the coordination of a NATO committee. The CIA provided hidden caches of weapons and explosives that could later be used for paramilitary and espionage activity if Communist rule ever came to power in Italy. Gladio resistance fighters were trained with CIA knowledge and support through the Italian government for paramilitary action.

By the 1970s Italy came under fire by many right wing radicals and some had questioned Gladio's role in the violent acts that occurred. After the capture of a one Fascist radical responsible for the murders of two Italian policemen authorities learned that Gladio had been compromised through infiltration. In addition the Communist Party stood a good chance of being voted in to Italy.

A 'Strategy of Tension'

In 1990, the Italian Prime Minister had confirmed that Italy's "stay behind" army, termed "Gladio" (Sword), existed since 1958, with the approval of the Italian government. In the early 1970s, Italy's communist support was growing, so the government turned to a "Strategy of Tension" using the Gladio network. At a top secret 1972 Gladio meeting, one official referred to making a "pre-emptive attack" on the Communists. As the Guardian reported, links between Gladio in Italy, all three Italian secret services and Italy's P2 Masonic Lodge were well documented, as the head of each intelligence unit was a member of the P2 Lodge. (20)

The Italian government released a 300-page report on Gladio operations in Italy in 2000, documenting connections with the United States. It declared that the US was responsible for inspiring a "strategy of tension." In examining why those who committed the bombings in Italy were rarely caught, the report said, "those massacres, those bombs, those military actions had been organized or promoted or supported by men inside Italian state institutions and, as has been discovered, by men linked to the structures of United States intelligence." (21)

As the Communist Party again increased popularity in the early 70s, Aldo Moro took it upon himself to establish communication with the PCI (Italian Communist Party) and bringing them in under a coalition government. Moro had received warning from the U.S. Secretary of State Henry Kissinger about working with the Communists. Four years prior to his death, in 1974, Moro was on a visit as Italian Prime Minister, to the United States. While there, he met with US Secretary of State Henry Kissinger, who told Moro, "`You must abandon your policy of bringing all the political forces in your country into direct collaboration... or you will pay dearly for it." (22)

On March 16, 1978, Moro was kidnapped, after the murder of his five escort agents, on Via Fani, a street in Rome, supposedly by a militant communist group known as the Red Brigades. Moro was kidnapped on his way to a session of the House of Representatives, where a discussion was supposed to take place regarding a vote of confidence in a new government led by Giulio Andreotti (DC) and with, for the first time, the support of the Communist Party.

In the following days, trade unions called for a general strike, while security forces made hundreds of raids in Rome, Milan, Turin and other cities searching for Moro's location. Held for two months, he was allowed to send letters to his family and politicians. The government refused to negotiate, despite demands by family, friends and Pope Paul VI. The Red Guards initiated a secret trial. Moro was found guilty and sentenced to death. They then sent demands to the Italian authorities, which stated that unless 16 Red Guard prisoners were released, Moro would be executed. The Italian authorities responded with a manhunt. The CIA declined assistance to the request of the Italian government regarding his abduction because CIA was not chartered to assist in domestic affairs.

Steve Pieczenik, a former State Department hostage negotiator and international crisis manager, "claimed that he played a critical role in the fate of Aldo Moro." Pieczenik "said that Moro had been "sacrificed" for the "stability" of Italy." He had been sent to Italy by President Jimmy Carter on the day of Moro's kidnapping to be part of a crisis committee, of which he said was "jolted into action by the fear that Moro would reveal state secrets in an attempt to free himself." The action the committee took was to leak a memo saying that Moro was dead, and to have the memo attributed to the Red Brigades. The purpose of this was to "prepare the Italian public for the worst and to let the Red Brigades know that the state would not negotiate for Moro, and considered him already dead." (23)

In a documentary on the subject, Pieczenik stated that, "The decision was made in the fourth week of the kidnapping, when Moro's letters became desperate and he was about to reveal state secrets," and that, "It was an extremely difficult decision, but the one who made it in the end was interior minister Francesco Cossiga, and, apparently, also prime minister Giulio Andreotti." (24)

After 54 days of detention, Moro was murdered in or near Rome in May of 1978. His body was found in the trunk of a parked car with eleven gun shots to his chest.

The Cambridge Four
CIA/MI6 Soviet Mole Hunting

In the wake of the Cold War, the ability to obtain and manage information was crucial for national defense. The United States had now learned that the Soviets were trying to gather information for the atomic bomb and needed to ensure that the secrets at home were safe. It was CIA responsibility to prevent any hostile or enemy organizations from successfully gathering and collecting state secrets. With the newly

James Angleton

formed CIA a Counterintelligence (CI) division was formed to detect and hunt down espionage activity. James J. Angleton, a University of Yale graduate, joined the Army in 1943 and was recruited into the Office of Strategic Service. He was stationed in London where he was introduced to counter-intelligence training by way of British intelligence. Angleton later became known as the "mother" of CIA because of his profound dedication and counter-intelligence mole hunting skills. Much of this may be contributed to his overall paranoia from his betrayal by friend Kim Philby. Philby and Angleton met during World War II while Angleton was receiving his counter-intelligence training.

In 1949 the FBI, through the Verona Project, discovered messages were being sent to Soviet KGB agents through the British Embassy under the code name "Homer". Through the process of elimination, the FBI keyed in on a short list of suspects including Donald Maclean, an MI6 agent and current Secretary of the Combined Policy Committee on Atomic Development. In the spring of 1951 the FBI started conducting surveillance on Maclean's activities. This information was learned by Kim Philby another MI6 agent and U.S. liaison to CIA. Philby, along with Maclean and Guy Burgess, were all graduates of Trinity College, Cambridge, and more importantly were all double-agents for the Soviet Union. In April of 1951, Philby got word to Burgess that Maclean had been discovered by the FBI and for Burgess to help him escape any capture. The following month Maclean, along with Burgess, defected publically to the Soviet Union. This brought immense suspicion to Philby. Over the years Angleton had suspected his friend of espionage and with the events transpired, Philby was ordered back to London. CIA denied him access and would not allow him to remain as a liaison. Although no criminal charges were made against Philby, he was released as an MI6 agent.

The same year John Cairncross, another school-mate and MI6 companion to Philby, admitted under interrogation to spying for the Soviet Union. He was arrested by MI5 after they had found incriminating documents in his possession. Cairncross was a member of British intelligence and worked with ciphers for MI6 at Bletchley Park and supplied Soviets information from 1941-1945. Cairncross claimed he was only trying to assist the Soviets in defeating the Nazi's and denied passing any atomic or other information that could be considered harmful to Britain. He was released without prosecution and shortly after moved to Rome, Italy. Along with Anthony Frederick Blunt, the espionage group became known as the "Cambridge Four" and later the "Cambridge Five" when Soviet defector Anatoliy Golitsyn identified Philby as a soviet spy in 1961. Philby, who at the time was living in Lebanon, fled the Middle East and defected to the Soviet Union.

Later in 1951, Angleton began building a relationship with Israel's Mossad and Shin Bet agencies. With their cooperation and sharing of intelligence, Angleton could provide a broadened range of human intelligence in the Middle East. In 1954 Allen Dulles promoted Angleton to Associate Deputy Director of Operations for Counterintelligence/ADDOCI, a position he would retain until retirement.

This type of activity was a big reason CIA needed to initiate unorthodox tactics in monitoring and tracking potential communist threats. Project SRPOINTER was created to intercept postal mail arriving from the Soviet Union and China. The program would later change the name to Project HTLINGUAL, and operated from the early 1950s to 1973. Under the program CIA would intercept mail from United States citizens and track their names and addresses. Later the program would intercept and open the letters from individuals including Hubert Humphrey, Jane Fonda, John Steinbeck and Martin Luther King.

Operation DBJOINTLY
The Berlin Tunnel Project

In early 1948 the intelligence community saw promise in the use of wire taps for the Cold War escalation. Through briefings in the 1940-1950's of German scientists, who had been taken prior to the Soviet Union after World War II, CIA learned of voice secrecy devices code named "VHE CHE" which meant high frequency. The devices were used for scrambling Soviet communications. By 1951 the CIA had formulated a plan to

William K. Harvey

target landlines in East Germany with special emphasis on Berlin called Operation DBJOINTLY. A network was built and successfully penetrated the East Berlin Office of the East German Post and Telecommunications network. Through trials and error the CIA was able to locate the correct circuits in 1953 and developed a process to monitor the lines intercepted to West Berlin 24 hours each day. A collateral collection effort was designed to recover communications from the magnetic tape recording. The first material recovered was that of a student teletypist practicing on the "home keys." Although the content was insignificant, the process worked and showed great value.

In 1951 British Intelligence shared with CIA a successful tunnel tapping project they had operated in Vienna called Operation Silver. While sharing the information and process with us in the U.S., the idea sparked the same process for Berlin and by May of 1953 the tunnel process started to take form. The planning stages consisted of review multiple tunnel sites both in the British and U.S. controlled Zones. Water tables, distances, land available and engineering issues were all considered prior to deciding a location. Eventually the decision was reached to build a warehouse under the cover of a "Quartermaster Warehouse" so the new building mystery would not peak German curiosity. Engineers struggled with where to place the dirt while digging the tunnel, and eventually decided to create another hole, and use the dirt to fill that hole in. It was decided early on by CIA director to work jointly with British Intelligence, and use the London office to process the voice recordings. It was decided to use the Army Corps of Engineers for the digging and was requested by Allen Dulles personally.

The security measures were of great concern and CIA placed a number of plans in place to ensure the security of the tunnel project including briefings, security contracts, and debriefings. The most challenging security issue was that of interpreters. Considering that much of the traffic collected would be in native Russian, the personnel to interpret would almost need to be native Russian. Extensive screening was conducted prior to placement of interpreters. During the program there were technical scares as well. While encased in the chamber tunnel, echoing from the microphones would pick up horse and buggy and vehicles near the travelled highway of where the tunnel was constructed. On one morning the sound of loud thuds were picked up, only to learn later the German's had made a checkpoint over a part of the tunnel. The thud sound was that of an East German soldier stomping on the ground to keep his feet warm. When construction was complete the tunnel was approximately 1,476 feet in length.

The tunnel cost $6,700,000 to build and collected data on a possible 1200 communication channels and when completed the project collected 50,000 magnetic reels containing 368,000 conversations that had been fully transcribed. In addition, 13,500 German two-voice reels containing 75,000 conversations fully transcribed. The London office employed 300 people while the Washington office employed 200 to work this project. Small units of three to four people were stationed in Berlin for transcription on what was referred to as "hot" intelligence. CIA finally completed all of the translations collected on September 30, 1958, more than two years after the discovery of the East Berlin tunnel.

Termination

After more than eleven months of operation, the tunnel was discovered on April 21, 1956. The exposure was due to problems with one of the cables. The cable needed to be worked and because of the amount of rainfall in the area of the cable and tunnel, the need to dig the cable caused its exposure. A subsequent finding showed that MI6 discovered an operative in British Intelligence under Soviet control. The operative was privy to the tunnel and had informed the Soviet's of this in 1953.

In 1961 the head of British Intelligence MI6 felt that traitor George Blake had damaged the allied intelligence more than Kim Philby. George Blake was born in Rotterdam, Netherlands in 1922, the son of a Dutch mother and a Turkish/Jewish father who was a naturalized British subject. During his childhood he lived in various locales including The Netherlands, France and Cairo. As a teenager Blake was a runner for the anti-Nazi Dutch resistance. Around his 18th birthday, Blake joined the Special Operations Executive, also known as the Baker Street Irregulars, a World War II organization of the United Kingdom to conduct warfare by means other than direct military engagement. Its mission was to encourage and facilitate espionage and sabotage behind enemy lines and to serve as the core of the Auxiliary Units, a British resistance movement. After the war Blake joined MI6.

In 1948 he was chosen to go to Korea to establish a network of agents. While he was there, as vice-consul in Seoul, the

Korean war broke out and the capital was overrun by the Communist North Korean army. In the company of other diplomats and missionaries, Blake was evacuated north and interned and witnessed what he claimed convinced him that he should work for the other side: "It was the relentless bombing of small Korean villages by enormous American flying fortresses. Women and children and old people, because the young men were in the army. We might have been victims ourselves. It made me feel ashamed of belonging to these overpowering, technically superior countries fighting against what seemed to me defenseless people. I felt I was on the wrong side ... that it would be better for humanity if the Communist system prevailed, that it would put an end to war." (25)

Within months of his arrival in Seoul, on June 24, 1950, the city was captured by the advancing North Korean Army and Blake was taken prisoner by the Communist forces, while he was at the British Legation. After capture by the North Koreans, and after reading the works of Karl Marx during his three-year detention, he became a Marxist. Following his release in 1953, Blake returned to Britain as a hero. In 1955 he was sent by MI6 to work as a case officer in Berlin, where his task was ironically to recruit Soviet officers as double agents. It was here that he made contact with the KGB and informed them of the details of British and US operations. In the course of nine years he betrayed details of some 400 MI6 agents to the Soviets, destroying most of MI6's operations in Eastern Europe. Blake said, "I don't know what I handed over because it was so much". In 1960 a senior Polish intelligence officer defected to the West and uncovered many major spies in the UK, including Gordon Lonsdale and Peter and Helen Kroger. In April 1961 Blake was recalled to London from Beirut where he was learning Arabic and accused of working for the Soviets.

"Assuming it [the tunnel] was compromised by Blake I have no trouble reconciling the operation with the activity with the Soviet knowledge that it is going on," Tom Polgar, CIA Officer. "The Soviets new perfectly well what traffic passes on that channel or on those channels they also knew that since they knew there was not going to be a war that they were not going to attack anybody. All this military intelligence is interesting but basically without value because it's going to be overtaken by time anyway. On the other hand, Blake is such a valuable asset that you want to do everything possible to protect him." (17)

What is unclear to this day is how the Soviet Union reacted internal to the knowledge of the tunnel. CIA speculate that the Soviets didn't press the issue once discovered to save face on the development of the tunnel, citing it could appear that their communist government could be perceived as weak among the world for being vulnerable to such an act. Others in the agency speculated that the Commander of the Soviet Berlin Garrison was absent during the tunnel discover, and acting Colonel Ivan. A. Kotsyuba who personally decided no course of action without advice from Moscow. Many CIA officers were recognized for their accomplishment, including William K. Harvey, who was awarded the Distinguished Intelligence Medal for participation in the successful operation. Over time the tunnel project would be known as "Harvey's Hole". With the exception of Blake, CIA had no reason to believe there was any additional security leaks in PBJOINTLY.

Operation MOCKINGBIRD
25 Years of Media Influence

Cord Meyer

In early 1950, Frank Wisner was the director of Office of Policy Coordination (OPC) a department that worked with counter-intelligence and focused on propaganda. Wisner was directed to orchestrate a program that would influence both domestic and foreign media channels throughout the world. The program, Operation MOCKINGBIRD, was formed and Wisner reached out to Philip Graham, a former Army intelligence officer who was with the Washington Post as an adviser. With Graham's assistance, Wisner had created relationships with a number of high profile publishers including Newsweek, The New York Times, Time Magazine and CBS News. In addition to publishing firms, the operation also employed syndicated writers. This enabled CIA the ability to spread propaganda through a single source, yet be published in a broad range of media formats. Within just two years of the programs origination, Operation MOCKINGBIRD possessed major influence in more than twenty newspaper and wire agencies.

In the 1950s, outlays for global propaganda climbed to a full third of the CIA's covert operations budget. Some 3,000 salaried and contract CIA employees were eventually engaged in propaganda efforts. The cost of misinforming the world cost American taxpayers an estimated $265 million a year by 1978, a budget larger than the combined expenditures of Reuters, UPI and the AP news syndicates. In 1977, the Copley News Service admitted that it worked closely with the intelligence services - in fact, 23 employees were full-time employees of the Agency. (26)

Soon after the operation was created, Allen Dulles recruited Cord Meyer to join CIA and over time he became what many consider the driving force in the operation. Meyer was born on November 10, 1920 in Washington, D.C., where he attended St. Paul School in New Hampshire and graduated from Yale University in 1942 with bachelor's degrees in English and philosophy. Meyer saw military action in the South Pacific after enlisting with the U.S. Marines. With the 22nd Marine Regiment, Meyer participated in the Battle of Eniwetok, and in the Battle of Guam, where he lost his left eye from a grenade attack and was later awarded the Purple Heart and Bronze Star. After World War II, Meyer served as an aide to Harold Stassen for the 1945 San Francisco UN Conference. Once with CIA, Meyer worked under Wisner and formed a friendship with CI James Angleton.

Financing for the operation came from a variety of sources including the European Recovery Program, (ERP), which was the primary plan of the U.S. for rebuilding Western Europe, and repelling communism after World War II. From this fund CIA was able use the money to influence their media contacts into assisting them with their operational goals of propaganda.

Thomas Braden, head of the International Organizations Division (IOD), played an important role in Operation Mockingbird. Many years later he revealed his role in these events: "If the director of CIA wanted to extend a present, say, to someone in Europe—a Labor leader—suppose he just thought, This man can use fifty thousand dollars, he's working well and doing a good job - he could hand it to him and never have to account to anybody... There was simply no limit to the money it could spend and no limit to the people it could hire and no limit to the activities it could decide were necessary to conduct the war— the secret war.... It was a multinational. Maybe it was one of the first. Journalists were a target, labor unions a particular target—

that was one of the activities in which the communists spent the most money." (27)

By 1952 Operation MOCKINGBIRD was cataloged under the newly formed Directorate of Plans, where Wisner and Richard Helms overseen the operations. The project had increased not only the influence, but the power of the Central Intelligence Agency and didn't go unnoticed. Both Joseph McCarthy and J. Edgar Hoover targeted the agency and staff with accusations of communist activities, yet allegations fell on deaf ears. Many felt Hoover was still raw that the agency didn't fall under his authority when created in 1947. Shortly after personal allegations made by McCarthy, he was assaulted in the media with negative press coverage as Wisner flexed the power of Operation MOCKINGBIRD. The program became a staple for CIA coups in years to follow including the Guatemala Operation PBSUCCESS, the Iran Operation Ajax and the Bay of Pigs operation.

Crusade For Freedom was a front organization created in the 1950s to support the agency's Radio Free Europe project for Operation Liberation Theory. With spokes people like former President Ronald Reagan, campaigns for the Crusade For Freedom were promoted requesting donations from U.S. citizens. The radio station was funded by the CIA as a way to spread propaganda in hopes of liberating East Germany from Communist rule.

With spurts of demonstrations and resistance in East Berlin beginning to develop, the CIA used Radio Free Europe as a supporting mechanism in providing hope to those under Communist rule. In 1956 the Hungarians rose up against the Communists in Budapest. Radio Free Europe encouraged the Hungarians through transmissions received in liberated territories to rise up and participate in the revolt. The broadcasts also insinuated that there was U.S. involvement and assistance. This disinformation was use by the CIA to increase motivation among the Hungarian people. The disinformation campaigns were recorded off-air and retransmitted to certain Hungarian territories.

"They were extraordinarily dramatic," expressed Cord Meyer. "They would announce the overthrow of the Communist Party. That the Hungarian secret police were taken care of and that all other towns in Hungary should follow the same example. In other words, they were one after another moving into a position of rejection of the whole Communist system." (17)

The Hungarian people felt that American military involvement would be inevitable even though Radio Free Europe never directly stated the U.S. would come to their aid. Many felt that the American message on the radio for them to resist the Communists was a message from the American government since Radio Free Europe was an American radio station. There was no plan for U.S. assistance and the Hungarian resistance was unsuccessful.

"After the events of the Hungarian intervention by the Soviets we reviewed all the scripts and found a number of them where there was clearly more enthusiasm than that liberation was imminent than really the situation justified."

A March 1958 memo from the German BND agency to the CIA wrote that Adolf Eichmann is "reported to have lived in Argentina under the alias CLEMENS since 1952." However, the CIA did not pass the information on to the Israeli MOSSAD, as it feared revelations concerning its use of former Nazis for intelligence purposes — Eichmann, who was in charge of the Jewish Affairs department, was abducted by the MOSSAD two years later. Among this information that might have been revealed by Eichmann were the ones concerning Hans Globke, CIA's liaison in West Germany. At the request of Bonn, the CIA persuaded Life magazine to delete any reference to Globke from Eichmann's memoirs, which it had bought from his family. (28)

The operation was not full-proof. Although there were attempts to control sensitive material about projects, operations and CIA in general, not all were successful. Mockingbird was first exposed by Random House with their printing of Invisible Government in 1964. When John McCone was CIA Director he failed to prevent NBC from airing an unflattering look at the agency. In 1965, Desmond FitzGerald as the DDP tried to prevent a magazine with publishing an article on CIA funding of National Student Association without success. The article even singled out Cord Meyer as a centerpiece of the propaganda and media machine.

Meyer's role in Operation Mockingbird was further exposed in 1972 when he was accused of interfering with the publication of a book, The Politics of Heroin in Southeast Asia by Alfred W. McCoy. The book was highly critical of the CIA's dealings with the drug traffic in Southeast Asia. The publisher, who leaked the story, had been a former colleague of Meyer's when he was a liberal activist after the war. (24)

In addition to influencing content with the media, CIA had developed extensive partnerships allowing them to infiltrate the press agencies and use their publication, staff and journalistic appeal as cover for clandestine and covert activities abroad. Often the role of a stringer was an actual CIA officer hired by the newspaper or magazine as a writer or cameraman.

In November 1973, after many such shifts had been made, Colby told reporters and editors from the New York Times and the Washington Star that the Agency had "some three dozen" American newsmen "on the CIA payroll," including five who worked for "general circulation news organizations." Yet even while the Senate Intelligence Committee was holding its hearings in 1976, according to high-level CIA sources, the CIA continued to maintain ties with seventy-five to ninety journalists of every description — executives, reporters, stringers, photographers, columnists, bureau clerks and members of broadcast technical crews. More than half of these had been moved off CIA contracts and payrolls but they were still bound by other secret agreements with the Agency. According to an unpublished report by the House Select Committee on Intelligence, chaired by Representative Otis Pike, at least fifteen news organizations were still providing cover for CIA operatives as of 1976. (29)

In 1976, under DCI, George H. W. Bush, the CIA announced: "Effective immediately, the CIA will not enter into any paid or contractual relationship with any full-time or part-time news correspondent accredited by any U.S. news service, newspaper, periodical, radio or television network or station."

Joint Advisory Commission, Korea
CIA Special Activities Division (SAD)

During the Korean War the CIA sponsored activities through front companies called the Joint Advisory Commission, Korea. JACK was headquartered at Tongnae, near Pusan and where Paramilitary Operations Officer operated. The activities conducted were often behind enemy lines and included training for military operations with Korean guerrillas. CIA ran numerous maritime raids and ambushes using the Korean guerillas including executing successful prisoner of war operations. These were the first maritime unconventional warfare units that trained indigenous forces as surrogates. Through JACK, CIA operatives and the U.S. trained guerrillas also conducted covert missions in providing escape and evasion support for downed Air Force pilots. These CIA Special Activities Division (SAD) teams often worked directly with U.S. military commanders for executing operations.

Under the 8th Army, CIA/SAD paramilitary teams along with South Korean commandos were inserted deep inside North Korea to gather intelligence, conduct raids and sabotage operations. In addition, they successfully rescued POWs, recruited & lead guerrilla armies and create confusion to the North Korean army. One of the most successful operations was assisting the White Tigers through amphibious assaults on North Korea, including the landing at Inchon.

The principle warfare and covert training and deployment of indigenous forces became a model CIA/SAD adopted and would later use for other paramilitary operations such as Military Assistance Command, Vietnam-Studies and Observations Group (MACV-SOG).

At the end of Korean War, James Power Carne, a lieutenant Colonel in the British Army was released from Chinese captivity. His battalion of 700 was captured after being overrun by 11,000 Chinese soldiers. Carne, an English recipient of the Victoria Cross, told Sir Esler Dening, the British ambassador in Tokyo what had happened while held prisoner.

"He says that between January 1952 and August this year he was kept in solitary confinement by Chinese communists and subjected to a softening-up process including the use of drugs, result of which was, as he put it, to make his brain like a sponge, capable of receiving any kind of information put into it," Sir Esler told the Foreign Office in a "top secret" category telegram.

The note, which was sent straight to Sir Winston Churchill, in his second term as Prime Minister, went on: "In March of this year, (i.e. about the time when the communists displayed a new interest in concluding an armistice) various thoughts were put in to his mind, and he remains convinced that he was meant to retain these and pass them on to Her Majesty's Government."

Some researchers feel that this story was the inspiration for "*The Manchurian Candidate*" conspiracy and films. Once the CIA became aware of the incident, there was considerable interest in pursuing mind control research.

Project NKNAOMI
Chemical & Biological Warfare

Project NKNAOMI was created to provide CIA with covert support in meeting clandestine requirements. Through the use of the Technical Services Department (TSD), CIA was tasked to research and if possible, develop chemical and biological warfare capabilities. By stockpiling agents that could incapacitate or offer lethal means if necessary, CIA created a number of programs involving research on chemical and biological operation potential.

In 1952, the Special Operations Division of the U.S. Army (SOC), assisted in developing, testing, and maintaining biological agents. The joint CIA and SOC program tested chemicals in weapon formats including guns that fired special darts coated with biological agents. These were tested on guard dogs to determine operational incapacitation. The testing monitored how soon the tests subjects became incapacitated and how long the effect lasted. One exercise consisted of dropping a harmless form of bacteria into the New York subway system and monitoring the time it would take to disburse and measure the effective range. Army special operations officers from Ft. Detrick, under the disguise as transportation contractors, dropped the harmless bacteria into grates above subway tracks, while monitoring operatives gauged the effectiveness. The exercise was created to determine how germ warfare could cripple cities within the Soviet Union.

In addition, the program used other various weapons and researched the potentials for using biological agents against other animals and crops. Frank Olson was a biological weapons engineer for the U.S. Army at Ft. Detrick Maryland. Olson was secretly employed by the CIA to assist in developing chemical and biological weapons covertly under Operation NKNAOMI. Spearheading the operation was Dr. Sidney Gottlieb, head of the top secret CIA Chemical Division. Out of Ft. Detrick, both Olson and Gottlieb worked together developing biological weapons for future agency use with chemicals including Anthrax and The Plague. By 1953 the special operations were overseen by Frank Olson. Olson specialized in aerosol delivery systems yet with CIA his research evolved into germ warfare.

Along with the United States, both Great Britain and Canadian governments also work together to establish scientific research that could assist in winning the cold war. In England the Chemical Defense Experimental Establishment near Arlington Farm is one location where the germ warfare research took place, also known as Porton Down Army Base in Southwest England. Porton Down had been the leading institute for biochemical warfare in the 1930s and 1940s. By May of 1953 the scientists of Porton Down were researching effects on a nerve agent known as "sarin". To establish better intelligence on the research unwitting military personnel were used to conduct experiments. This became known as Operation Top Hat.

"On the board there was a separate notice typed, which said in so many words 'volunteers wanted to help find a cure for the common cold...those who take part will receive extra pay'," Ken Earl, Senior Aircraftsman, Royal Air force. "I knew nothing about biochemical warfare. I was unbelievable naive." (30)

On May 4th, 1953 Earl along with five other young Royal Air force personnel were then placed into a sealed room (makeshift gas chamber) and given respirators. The scientists placed drops of sarin on their arms to monitor the effects of how long the agent took to enter the blood stream and how much of the chemical was needed to be considered fatal. Earl's group became very irritated and found difficulty breathing shortly after the sarin nerve agent was placed on their arms, but were fortunate that there were no long-term effects. This was not the case for Ronald Maddison. The twenty year old Royal Air force candidate died on May 6th, 1953 during the second round of testing after the scientists increased the dosage of sarin nerve agent. Within 45 minutes Madison was dead after what witnesses described as being a horribly violent attack including foaming at the mouth.

On February 14, 1970, under direct order from President Richard Nixon, Project NKNAOMI was discontinued.

Project MKULTRA
LSD & Mind Altering Drug Experiments

In 1949 CIA, under the Office of Scientific Intelligence, started a program called Project BLUEBIRD, which involved special interrogation techniques. The basis for the project was to synchronize the use of narcotics with polygraph machines as a form of interrogation. CIA was attempting to use the psychology methods of soviet interrogation through this project. In 1951 the Agency renamed Bluebird to "Project ARTICHOKE" and incorporated training groups to participate in electric shock and narco-hynosis studies. The project was authorized by Allen Dulles and included both Richard Helms and James J. Angleton in the reporting.

Project ARTICHOKE continued into the 1950s experimenting with drugs and hypnosis as well as "total isolation" techniques for interrogation. In addition, the program conducted several hundred hypnosis experiments to staff members and employee volunteers. CIA logged all of these experiments from 1951-1953. The CIA documented no case of operation usage, but included that SRS utilizing an Agency employee under hypnosis was monitored during social activities. Isolation was also studied and in 1955 the Agency in a joint venture with the U.S. military did test six soldiers with isolation techniques. According to the Department of Defense report, the study was ineffective. In the mid-fifties much of the substances used were classified as "Solution 1" or "Solution 2" in reporting.

Sodium Pentothal and other narcotics were used as well including LSD.

In 1959 a Project ARTICHOKE team used LSD on what CIA referred to as a P-1 interrogation. The Agency had relied on the power of what was learned from the studies and created Project ARTICHOKE teams to be assigned to specific stations through the Western Hemisphere. These teams were called to assist in interrogations on captured enemies, saboteurs, or other individuals who may have information that could pose a threat to national security.

In April of 1953, Richard Helms, DCI approved Project MKULTRA. Similar to ARTICHOKE, MKULTRA was created to determine the effects of narcotics used during interrogations. Again headed by Dr. Sidney Gottlieb, the MKULTRA project was initiated by DCI, Allen Dulles in response to Soviet, Chinese, and North Korean use of mind-control techniques on U.S. prisoners of war in Korea. It was the position of CIA to conduct studies to determine if there could be intelligence gathering benefits when practiced on captured enemies of the U.S. and potential in possibly using to manipulate foreign leaders. In addition, CIA funded academic researchers in hopes of gaining additional knowledge of the use of drugs for interrogation, manipulation and other feasible means.

Dr. Sidney Gottlieb, Chief, Chemical Division/TSS expanded the program to research the effects of LSD. Gottlieb was a military psychiatrist and chemist with a Ph.D. from the California Institute of Technology, who stuttered and possessed a club foot. Ironically he got a master's degree in speech therapy and loved folk dancing. Gottlieb joined the Central Intelligence Agency in 1951 and soon earned the nickname "Black Sorcerer". In a June 9, 1953 memorandum, Gottlieb explained how he intended to extend a subproject of MKULTRA and increased his budget to $39,500.00 for just one test subject. The study was to monitor the biochemical, neurophysiclogical, sociological and clinical psychiatric aspects of LSD. U.S. Army soldiers also volunteered for LSD studies through the Army's Special Operations program. Soldiers at Edgewood Arsenal were given doses of LSD and run through a battery of physical tests including marching, obstacle course training and other physical tasks. The experiments produced results that demonstrated the soldier's inability to stay in sync and were often too distracted or delusional to follow even simple and basic instructions. The objective was for the Army to locate a drug that could incapacitate the enemy without fatality and LSD looked promising. In time the sub-project became much larger and according to CIA documents Gottlieb was conducting experiments on unwitting participants.

Dr. Harris Isbell of the Center for Addiction Research in Lexington, Kentucky was contracted by CIA to conduct experiments on the long-term effects of LSD. The test subjects, volunteer prisoners who were mainly drug addicts, were given daily doses of LSD to monitor the effects the drug had on their personality. In return for their participation they were rewarded with doses of heroin. Dr. Isbell claimed that during one experiment the subjects had been on LSD for seventy-seven straight days making it the greatest display of drug tolerance he had ever seen.

In addition to the volunteer Army personnel, tests were also conducted on unwitting Army Scientists including those of the Special Operations branch at Ft. Detrick. On Wednesday November 18, 1953 Frank Olson and six special operations officers arrived at Deer Creek Lodge in Maryland for a covert meeting with CIA scientist Sidney Gottlieb and his assistant Robert Lashbrook. On the following evening after dinner, all but two of the scientists are slipped doses of LSD without their knowledge into drinks. The goal was to determine if the subjects would freely reveal state secrets if questioned while under the influence of the drug. Frank Olson was one of the unwitting subjects. After a while - Gottlieb shares with the men what he had done and the meeting winds down.

Within one week of his being administered the LSD, Mr. Olsen had crashed through the window of his New York hotel room, falling ten floors to his death. Prior he had been behaving peculiar and in an erratic manner and was directed to a psychiatrist. According to a memorandum dated December 1, 1953 the drug had been administered to the subject without prior knowledge and the IG staff impounded all LSD materials. In an interview years later Richard Helms recognized the fatal incident.

In the 1970s public awareness of the experiments began to surface and Richard Helms, then CIA Director, ordered all records of MKULTRA destroyed. This report triggered Senate Subcommittee hearings which investigated MKULTRA, and exposed Gottlieb's sub-project, Operation Midnight Climax. Operation Midnight Climax, with Gottlieb's guidance, was operated during the 1960s by Narcotics Bureau officer George White, who used the alias "Morgan Hall" for this CIA project. In New York and San Francisco the CIA run safe houses where they monitored effects of LSD through luring unsuspecting individuals with CIA paid prostitutes. The Agency would then view the subjects behind one-way mirrors after the prostitutes would slip them narcotics unwittingly. The program gained valuable insight into mind-altering drugs in field operations.

David Frost asked Richard Helms in a 1978 interview: There is virtually no drug-related MKULTRA material in the files, we gather? In terms of destruction of those files, the seven boxes of progress reports that I think you had recalled from the Archives and destroyed on 31 January, was a booklet called "LSD 25, Some Unpsychedelic Implications." Why did you decide to do that?

"It was a conscious decision that there were a whole series of things that involved Americans who had helped us with the various aspects of this testing, with whom we had had a fiduciary relationship and whose participation we had agreed to keep secret. Since this was a time when both I and the fellow who had been in charge of the program were going to retire there was no reason to have the stuff around anymore. We kept faith with the people who had helped us and I see nothing wrong with that." (31)

After the Church Committee findings, President Gerald Ford in 1976 issued an Executive Order prohibiting experimental drug usage on human subjects without their informed and written consent. In 1953 a joint military experiment between CIA and the U.S. Army called Operation Top Hat was created to test both contamination and decontamination results of specific chemical and biological warfare including nerve agents.

After discovering that CIA used unwitting military personnel in MKULTRA studies, Secretary of Defense Charles Erwin Wilson issued what became known as the "Wilson Memo" mandating only witting volunteers may be used for experimental operations within the U.S. armed forces.

On the Senate floor in 1977, Senator Ted Kennedy said: "The Deputy Director of the CIA revealed that over thirty universities and institutions were involved in an "extensive testing and experimentation" program which included covert drug tests on unwitting citizens "at all social levels, high and low, native Americans and foreign." Several of these tests involved the administration of LSD to "unwitting subjects in social situations." At least one death that of Dr. Olson had resulted from these activities. The Agency itself acknowledged that these tests made little scientific sense. The agents doing the monitoring were not qualified scientific observers."

In his 1978 book "Honorable Men: My Life in the CIA", William Colby talked about the situation regarding Frank Olsen and revealed that Frank was actually an officer for CIA: But on one point the Rockefeller Commission Report did add—unintentionally—to the sensationalism swirling around the CIA. That was on the death of Frank Olsen. Indeed, even the CIA professionals, myself included, were shocked and shamed to learn of the true circumstances around this CIA officer's suicide, as revealed in the report, following his being administered LSD without his knowledge in 1953 in a joint CIA-Army test program. I had been aware that a death had occurred in this program. The program itself, which was designed to determine the effects and possible uses of LSD by hostile intelligence or political forces, was listed among the "family jewels" as one of the CIA's past questionable activities. But the Agency's records indicated that steps had been taken in 1953 to ensure that Olson's suicide was treated as a line-of-duty death and that appropriate arrangements were made to take care of his family.

Thus it came as a shock when the Olsen family, identifying the incident from the published Rockefeller Commission Report, stated that this was the first they had heard of the circumstances and specifics of Olson's death. The official reaction was immediate. President Gerald Ford extended his and the nation's regret and instructed that recompense be made. I made a particular point of contacting the family and extending the CIA's very sincere apologies for the tragedy and did everything I could to push through the appropriate and acceptable recompense. But one of the most difficult assignments I ever had was to meet with his wife and his now-grown children to discuss how to give them the CIA records and thus open up and overcome a twenty-year secret that had had such an impact on their lives. (32)

The CIA had contracted more than 80 institutions for the testing during the project and cost the United States tax payers more than $30 million dollars.

After the termination of MKULTRA, other CIA funded programs emerged in exploring mind control including MKSEARCH. This project focused on research studies for developing the perfect truth narcotic that could be used while interrogating Cold War spies captured during espionage activities. CIA also funded Subproject 54, or *Perfect Concussion*, which was a Top Secret Navy program designed to erase a subject's memory through the use of sub-aural frequency exposure.

The CIA sought assistance in creating a perfect assassin through developing a hypnosis process that could trigger a subject to commit an action with an amnesia barrier to make the subject have no recollection of the incident. 1957 to 1961 Dr. Ewen Cameron was contracted by CIA to conduct research on the possibilities of this type of assassin. Cameron had authored the *psychic driving* concept which the CIA found particularly interesting because of the theory on correcting madness, which consisted of erasing existing memories and rebuilding the psyche completely. After being recruited by the CIA, he commuted to Montreal every week to work at the Allan Memorial Institute of the McGill University. His experiments were typically carried out on patients who had entered the institute for minor problems such as anxiety disorders and post-partum depression. Cameron's work in this field was inspired and paralleled by the British psychiatrist Dr William Sargant, a friend of Frank Olson, and MI6 asset, who carried out virtually identical experiments at St Thomas' Hospital, London and Belmont Hospital, Surrey, also without his patients' consent.

Cameron started his treatment of intense electrical shock therapy to wipe clean the memory. Next, Cameron would lock special helmets to a patients head with a recording devise that plays messages of repetitive statements often times for weeks as a way to program new behavior. The final phase that Cameron used was to remove all memory of the action by drugging them in a comatose state for thirty or more days.

Although the agency never achieved the *Manchurian Candidate* results they were expecting, Cameron's research eventually led to the publication of the KUBARK Counterintelligence Interrogation manual.

Project TPAJAX

1953 Iranian coup d'état

In 1952 the Mossadeq government had been involved in negotiating oil settlements with Western countries. It was clear by the end of the year the Premier Mohammed Mossadeq's tenure had been disregarding the Iranian constitution and reaching a dangerous financial deficit based on his desire for personal power. In addition, he had been cooperating with the Tudeh, the Communist Party in Iran, and had severely weakened the Iranian Army. This made it clear to the Western world

Mohammed Mossadeq

that Iran was vulnerable to the Communist threat and could provide the Soviet government an upper hand in the Cold War struggle. After careful review of options in returning the Shaw of Iran to power and stabilizing the county's power, CIA concluded that covert activity would be their only course of action, thus the formation of Project TPAJAX. The operation called for replacing the Mossadeq with one that would govern Iran in a way to reach oil settlements and become economically sound, while prosecuting those who spread Communist beliefs. Prior to the conflict, CIA had submitted and been approved for the use of a plan called "Executive Action". This plan was created to authorize CIA's Division D, a subsection of the agency's Directorate of Operations, to use covert activities to remove an unfriendly foreign leader from power through staging a coup or assassination.

By June of 1953, CIA had created a plan overseen by Kermit Roosevelt, grandson of American president Theodore

Roosevelt and Chief of Near East & Africa Division and Roger Goiran, CIA Chief of Station in Iran. The plan was presented to British S.I.S. in London and approved for operation on June 19, 1953. The center for operation was determined to be in Cyrus and working out of Tehran and supported by Washington. In a joint effort, CIA and S.I.S initiated a propaganda effort including press manipulation, handbills and influencing Iranian clergy to weaken the Mossadeq government including the Non-support of the United States to shatter any hope the country could rely on U.S. for assistance under the Mossadeq regime. The joint forces selected General Fazlollah Zahedi to be the replacement of Mossadeq upon successful completion of the coup d'état. Zahedi was the only candidate that possessed any significant following within Iran. CIA felt that the Shaw's cooperation was vital to the plan so they leveraged his twin sister Princess Ashraf Pahlavi and friend General H. Norman Schwarzkopf to manipulate him into signing firmans, a royal decree dismissing Mossadeq and appointing Zahedi. By August of 1953, CIA had accomplished the signed decree, used Operation MOCKINGBIRD and planted several propaganda articles in the U.S., which later were carried in Iran, and President Dwight D. Eisenhower publically denounced aid to Iran because of the Communist threat.

The decree was to be announced on August 16, 1953, yet the plan was abandoned due to a security leak involving the Shah's body guard who remained loyal to Mossadeq. The backlash caused the Shah to flee to Baghdad for his safety, while CIA kept Zahedi hidden and secure. The next day CIA arranged a secret press conference working in tandem with propaganda efforts including copies of the Shah signed decree, which announced that Zahedi was the legal Prime Minister of Iran and that Mossadeq had staged and illegal coup. Coupled with the information and knowledge of the Shah's exile for safety from Mossadeq, the Iranian people demonstrated their anger and disapproval for Mossadeq and his regime. CIA worked with the British Foreign Office and persuaded the Shah to denounce Mossadeq publically to gain additional momentum in the movement and continue to sway public opinion and Iranian military might to support Zahedi. By noon on August 19th, the immense support for the pro-shah demonstration rallied the Iranian majority, including military, and Zahedi appeared from CIA hiding and embarked on a leadership role. The revolt was a success and Zahedi had full power as the Prime Minister by the end of the day and the Shah had planned his return. To assist Zahedi in stabilizing the economy, the CIA provided covertly $5,000,000 on August 21, 1953.

In the US, Project Ajax was a success, with "immediate and far-reaching effect. Overnight, the CIA became a central part of the American foreign policy apparatus, and covert action came to be regarded as a cheap and effective way to shape the course of world events". (33)

The project demonstrated to CIA that their communication staff through the use of strategic propaganda was critical in the coup's success, thus concurring "the pen is mightier than the sword". This knowledge propelled CIA to seek out additional media sources that they could partner with to leverage for operation success in the future. The CIA officer to journalist relationship would be beneficial in mass producing vast amounts of propaganda. In addition, the agency learned that leveraging the Shah's sister was productive and felt that favorable results for future projects could be achieved through manipulation and applied pressures. The 1953 coup d'état was the first time the CIA overthrown an elected government, but would not be the last.

Project RAINBOW

The U-2 & Early Stealth Design

In the early 1950s, CIA in association with the U.S. Air Force requested proposals for the development of a new reconnaissance aircraft. CIA had been using converted bombers and was vulnerable to anti-aircraft

artillery, missiles, and fighters. The proposal, code named AQUATONE, called for a craft that could fly at an altitude of 70,000 feet to avoid radar and be out of reach of Soviet missiles and fighters. The goal was to have the aircraft invade a country's airspace and gather intelligence through aerial photographs. CIA would settle on a design through scientists from MIT Lincoln Laboratory and Lockheed Aircraft Corporation's infamous division known as Skunk Works. Project RAINBOW was created to reduce the radar cross section (RCS) of the U-2 through the use of wires, ferrite cores and honeycomb styled wallpaper, which overtime would be enhanced and the basis for "stealth" technology. Approved by President Dwight D. Eisenhower, Lockheed received a $22.5 million contract for the development of the U-2, with the "U" referring to the deliberately vague designation "utility". The design of the U-2 was unique to any other airplane and displayed long glider wings which assisted in the craft's performance. One challenge was the operation since the U-2 possessed a narrow window for stalling referred as the "coffin corner", and CIA knew only the best pilots should be used for flying, which meant the U.S. Air Force. With the purpose of invading foreign airspace, it was decided that CIA, a civilian company, operate vs. the military. To become a U-2 pilot an Air

Force officer had to resign his position with the military and enter employment with CIA prior to any mission status. Since the aircraft operated at 60,000 to 70,000 feet, pilots wore suites that delivered them oxygen supply and emergency protection in case cabin pressure was lost at altitude. Prior to flight pilots would also breath 100% oxygen to decrease the chance of decompression sickness. To capture data on reconnaissance missions, the U-2 was outfitted with large-format cameras and special optics. This process alone was a challenge for CIA because of the altitude and balance of the aircraft. Eventually designers used a split-film process that enabled the U-2 to maintain balance.

The U-2, nicknamed "Dragon Lady", was a single-engine, high-altitude aircraft that could provide surveillance day or night and in all weather. On August 1, 1955 the first U-2 flight took place at the Groom Lake testing site, also known as Area 51. Like any experimental aircraft the U-2 possessed flaws. In a span from May-September of 1956, accidents with the plane due to design and operational flaws resulted in the deaths of three pilots. CIA, in association with the U.S Air Force continued testing and operation of the aircraft flying top secret reconnaissance missions from Groom Lake and eventually other air bases including Laughlin Air Force Base near Del Rio, Texas; and McCoy AFB in Orlando, Florida. The U-2 became an incredible asset to CIA in providing valuable Soviet intelligence for years and remained hidden from public attention due to national security until May 1, 1960 when CIA pilot Francis Gary Powers was shot down over Soviet territory.

In October of 1962 Major Richard S. Heyser flew a U-2 mission from Texas over Cuba and returned to Florida with detailed photographs of the Soviet military installing nuclear warhead missiles in Cuba. In 1963, CIA began Project Whale Tale developing carrier-based take off's for U-2 flights to overcome flight range restrictions. The U-2 was a critical tool in obtaining vital aerial documentation during the Cold War. The same year, CIA would abandon the U-2, which would be managed by the U.S. Air Force, and turn to the SR-71 Blackbird, Project GUSTO as their primary reconnaissance aircraft.

In 1952 the CIA along with the United States Air Force embarked on a nation-wide disinformation campaign with the creation of "Project Bluebook". The project publically undertook the perception of providing resources to determine if UFOs were a threat to national security, and to scientifically analyze UFO-related data. Thousands of UFO reports were collected, analyzed and filed.

The goal, which became an enormous success, was to distract the public both within the United States and nations abroad by embracing the possibility of UFO phenomenon vs. acknowledging the sightings were that of top secret and experimental aircraft. The plan was devised after the Roswell incident and the quick rumors of alien spacecraft. The CIA realized immediately the potential of cloaking their national secrets under the premise of alien invasion and began the propaganda in the late 1940's.

The operation assisted in concealing many air defense projects including the U-2 and the SR 71 Blackbird. From Area 51 (Groom Lake) onlookers in the area as well as other bases would get glimpses of the flights. Considering the SR 71 was able to fly at speeds of over 2,000 miles an hour, their rear thrusts were often misinterpreted as UFO's. In December of 1969 Project Bluebook was terminated after collecting 12,618 UFO reports, and concluded that most of them were misidentifications of natural phenomena or conventional aircraft.

Operation PBSUCCESS
1954 Guatemalan coup d'état

In 1950 Jacobo Arbenz Guzman became the President of Guatemala winning 65% of the vote. Arbenz was an army Captain under General Jorge Ubico during "October Revolution" of 1944, and advocated social, political, and land reforms. While peasants welcomed Arbenz's belief, the landowners and factions of the military accused him of influencing Communism, thus creating tension and civil unrest fueled by the resentment of the United Fruit Company

Jacobo Arbenz

(UFC). By 1953 Arbenz's Agrarian Reform Act of 1952, was costing the United Fruit Company millions through the loss of their land. After the UFC lobbied the U.S. for assistance the U.S. State Department requested Guatemala to pay $15,854,849 for the UFC properties expropriated. Arbenz and the Guatemala government denied, charging violation of its sovereignty. With suspicions of Arbenz communist ties, CIA had been working on planning options for the removal of the leader if called upon.

With the recent success of the CIA coup in Iran, President Dwight D. Eisenhower and the U.S. National Security Council gave the agency the green light for Operation PBSUCCESS. The CIA selected Carlos Armas to lead a rebel army for planning with the coup. Armas possessed military skills and attended the national military academy with Arbenz. The project established headquarters in Florida and began the training of the rebel army. CIA also recruited pilots and setup a radio station to run their propaganda campaign against Arbenz. The goal was to place

Arbenz under an extreme amount of diplomatic pressure so that he would be forced from his position. CIA was aware of how a successful propaganda machine could make or break an operation. Assigned to this was Everett Howard Hunt Jr., or Howard Hunt. Hunt was born on October 9, 1918 in Hamburg, New York and grew up in Buffalo. He graduated in 1940 from Brown University and during World War II Hunt served in the U.S. Navy on the destroyer USS Mayo. He joined the Office of Strategic Services (OSS), and then during the 1947 conversion was picked up by CIA. Hunt, who was also a writer of spy novels, was the CIA station chief in Mexico City working with William F. Buckley.

Hunt and other members of CIA had used rumors, pamphleteering, posters and radio to turn the tide during the Iran operation and planned to replicate the same processes. The radio station, La Voz de la Liberacion, was set up in Miami, yet claimed to be in the jungles of Guatemala and provided a broadcast of music and anti-government propaganda. Rhetoric targeted both the Guatemalan general public as well as the Guatemalan Army of 5,000. On February 19, CIA had organized a covert plan, Operation WASHTUB, which dropped a cache of Soviet-produced weapons off the coast of Nicaragua for Arbenz as a way to demonstrate Communist ties. In addition, the agency leveraged Operation MOCKINGBIRD to increase propaganda efforts including the discovery of Guatemalan assassination squads. Helping the propaganda efforts were warplanes that would drop pamphlets over the capital accusing Arbenz of Communism. CIA recruited student groups to canvas the country with Article 32 posters, constitution that prohibited international political parties. The students posted these on buses, businesses and walls and gained media exposure and also created a weekly propaganda newsletter for distribution. Arbenz outrage became visible when he started arresting students and threatening the Freedom of

Assembly. These actions only strengthened the Agency's goal and helped in turning Guatemala into a repressive regime.

The CIA prevented the Guatemalan government from acquiring arms from both Canada and Germany. With the internal conflict from propaganda and the inability to strengthen his military, Arbenz became desperate. Arbenz had worked a deal with Czechoslovakia who had captured German arms from World War II. The arms were sent to be delivered on a Swedish freighter named "Alfhem". When CIA learned of the deal it was promoted as proof that Arbenz was being controlled by the Soviet's. In May of 1954 the U.S Navy created a sea blockade on Guatemala called Operation HARDROCK BAKER. The Navy stopped all ships using submarines and warships to search for arms. Armas's warplanes flew over the capital dropping leaflets intended to turn the army against Arbenz and Communism.

On the morning of June 18 Castillo Armas's rebellion army of 400 soldiers divided into four groups and crossed the Guatemalan-Honduran and the Guatemalan-Salvadoran border. By splitting the army and invading in different locations along Guatemala, it gave Ardenz and his army the impression of a larger invasion force. With key saboteurs in place to destroy bridges and cut off communication, Armas's troops limited confrontation to the Guatemalan Army to minimize casualties and focus on providing the falsehood of their true size and win over the opponent. Propaganda from radio broadcasts also assisted the invasion of providing false reports of battle victories and massive amounts of locals joining Armas in a revolution. Although the propaganda was beginning to work, Armas's army was not. He had lost several soldiers, which decreased the size of his ragtag operation considerably. Among fears of U.S. involvement and the site of amphibious forces along the coast and rumors that a Honduran landing by US Marines was in progress, the Guatemalan military officers began to lose interest and focus during the battles. When an entire army garrison surrendered to Armas a few days later in Chiquimula In, Arbenz announced his resignation. The 1954 Guatemalan coup d'état of Jacobo Arbenz Guzmán was another success for the Central Intelligence Agency and proof of their ability to conduct large-scale covert operations.

In an interview with CNN for a special on the Cold War, Howard Hunt suggested that United Fruit's lobbying campaign was a contributive factor in making policy; although Hunt suggests that the action was justified by security concerns, he believes that United Fruit's political clout was nonetheless a key factor.

A month after the coup, CIA infiltrated the government to investigate the availability of Communist documents to exploit Arbenz to the Guatemalan people. The scheme known as Operation PBHISTORY was covert and ran under cover with experts from businesses and universities. Overall the operation was a failure in finding any solid ties between Arbenz and the Soviet Union. The work done by the PBHISTORY spun off into addition projects including Operation Kufire and Operation Kugown.

Operation Kufire focused on identifying communist members who attended Arbenz's regime and opened the door to investigating Ernesto "Che" Guevara. This operation also included tracking the members and maintaining intelligence information through surveillance and asset collection. CIA's overall perception through the operation was that communism would spread throughout Latin American. In addition to the operation, CIA also created a new project to manipulate the media through Operation Kugown. This operation was focused on spreading to the Guatemalan people on the extent to which communism had infiltrated Guatemala. Much of the campaign was propaganda and derived from the documents seized by the PBHISTORY. For Operation Kugown to be successful the CIA had to accomplish three objectives: Use the documents seized to inform the Guatemalan people on the extent of communism spread throughout the country. Publicize the communist plot worldwide. Finally, solidify the position of the Comite de Defensa Nacional contra el Communismo within the Guatemalan government.

Operation PBFORTUNE was also created by CIA in 1951 and identified approximately sixty Guatemalans targeted for assassination. The operation was a contingency program for Operation PBSUCCESS. Although PBFORTUNE in its original form did not come to fruition, it was a catalyst for several other CIA sponsored assassination plots. In addition to the assassination, the plan called for the U.S. to support Guatemalan exile Carlos Castillo Armas and his rebel army with arms and funding for his army to overthrow Guatemalan President Arbenz. Nicaraguan President Anastasio Somoza Garcia assured President Harry S. Truman that both Nicaragua and Honduras would supply air support to Armas rebels if an uprising should occur.

CIA/BOB Berlin Operating Base
KGB Assassination Teams

Berlin, Germany in the 1950s was the spy capital of the world often pitting spy vs. spy. Covert activities were commonplace as well as surveillance, counter-intelligence, and assassination. In March of 1954 Nikolai Khokhlov, a captain in Soviet Intelligence and trained assassin, was sent to Frankfurt with two other KGB agents on a secret operation to kill Georgi Sergeyvich Okolovich. Okolovich was an NTS recruiting officer who was targeted by the Communist government for assassination. Khokhlov's parents divorced when he was very young so he didn't know his father well who later served as a commissar in the Red Army. During the battle for Moscow the elder Khokhlov was transferred to a penal battalion because he had made unfavorable remarks about Stalin. Khokhlov's father died in the battalion. His stepfather, an excellent lawyer volunteered to defend Moscow in 1941 and died in action almost immediately too. As Khokhlov later put it "the army needed cannon fodder".

In October 1941, Khokhlov, then 19 years old, was a member of an NKVD quartet and trained to commit a spectacular attack against Nazi officers during their victory celebration in occupied Moscow. The mastermind behind the plan was Mikhail Maklyarskiy, a senior NKVD official. The four young agents would have played a vaudeville group on the celebration. Khokhlov was chosen for his role on his whistling abilities. During the training he had his first great romance with fellow agent singer Tasya Ignatova. After the German retreat from the outskirts of Moscow, the deadly show was cancelled. (34)

Nikolai Khokhlov was a member of a successful military unit that fought behind the enemy lines during World War II. He was disguised as a Nazi officer, after parachuting into German-occupied Belarus. He played a part in the assassination of Wilhelm Kube, the Nazi Gauleiter of Belarus. After the war, Khokhlov became the prototype for the main character in a famous Soviet movie, Feat of a Scout, which was made in 1947. Khokhlov's knowledge and background earned him recognition and faith by KGB administrators in his ability to fulfill assigned tasks. Upon his arrival to Frankfurt, Khokhlov felt uneasy by what he was ordered to oversee. The KGB had tasked him with supervising the assassination which was supposed to be carried out by his two KGB associates. Khokhlov decided to seek out the target immediately alone. He located the building that Georgi Okolovich resided and approached. The door was unlocked so he walked in and proceeded up the stairs to the correct apartment and knocked on the door. Within seconds Okolovich opened the door and Khokhlov was standing face-to-face with the man he was sent to murder. Khokhlov immediately explained, "Georgi Sergeyvich, I have come to you from Moscow. The Central Committee of the Communist Party of the Soviet Union has ordered your assassination. The murder is entrusted to my group... who is very well trained for this operation but I can't let this murder happen." (35)

Both men reached an agreement to meet within a couple days and for Okolovich to use caution and avoid detection until then. Okolovich sought protection with the Central Intelligence Agency Berlin base. There he explained his unusual meeting and that he was planning to meet with his would be assassin Nikolai Khokhlov in a couple days.

"Berlin base evolved into one of the most important CIA installations anywhere in the world. It was the only place where you are up against the Russians belly to belly so to speak," Tom Polgar, CIA Officer. "It was the only place where American officers routinely and daily and continuing basis deal with Soviets;

observe Soviets; and for that matter have the Soviets observe us. But also the operational climate developed made certain things possible there that would not be possible say in London, Paris or home." (17)

CIA officer Tom Polgar and team coordinated with Okolovich for his meet with Khokhlov. The meeting took place near a Frankfurt intersection where Polgar and team had secured. Once Khokhlov approached the vehicle the CIA began to close in on the two men. Khokhlov got into the passenger side and immediately was told by Okolovich that he had requested the assistance of the American CIA. Before Khokhlov could even respond - a CIA officer was standing outside his car.

"We kidnapped him...he was clearly on an illegal errand - you know, and had we told the German police he certainly would have been arrested," Polgar. "I think we saved him from a little embarrassment by putting him up in a nice safe house in a town in the mountains. Where he was certainly kept under humane conditions and uh yes I suppose it was during a period when we trying to establish his benefice his freedom of movement was limited but that was as much for his own security." (17)

In Khokhlov's possession the CIA found him armed with a pack of cigarettes that was designed to fire a cyanide bullet through one of the individual cigarettes. This would have allowed an assassin to kill his target by simply offering him a cigarette. While debriefed by CIA Khokhlov explained that because of his wife Yana, he could not go through with the operation. Khokhlov went on to tell CIA that she said "If this man is killed, you will be a murderer. I cannot be the wife of a murderer." The same year Khokhlov testified during his defection to the United States regarding his knowledge of terrorist activities carried out by the KGB. His defect agreement with the CIA was to include the safe defection of his wife Yana and his son Alek who were in Moscow. Before the CIA could arrange their safe passage both were arrested. Yana was sentenced to four years in prison for her association with Khokhlov.

Khokhlov made headlines again in 1957 when the KGB attempted to assassinate him during his attendance at and anti-Communist conference in Frankfurt, Germany. While attending the conference someone had slipped a dose of a radioactive isotope of thallium, a metal, into his coffee, thus poisoning him instantly. Khokhlov was hospitalized from the attempt and lost much of his hair. In addition, his skin was covered with blood splotches and his doctors felt that his body was going to give up. Instead, Khokhlov miraculously survived the poisoning and survived several years until his death from a heart attack in 2007. After being pardoned by Boris Yeltsin in 1992, Khokhlov visited Moscow and was reunited with his wife and child after 38 years. Prior to the visit he and Yana had divorced, and Khokhlov had remarried.

Khokhlov poisoning is claimed to be the first radiological attack by the KGB. His poisoning is often compared to that of Alexander Litvinenko, the former officer of the Russian State security service (FSB), who died November 23, 2006 from poisoning. Former KGB officer Stanislav Lekarev claimed that Khokhlov was poisoned by radioactive polonium (not thallium), exactly as Litvinenko.

Operation Passage to Freedom

Southern Migration/ Geneva Accords in 1955

After the Geneva Accords in 1955, the United States Navy planned an evacuation called Operation Passage to Freedom which transported more than 300,000 Vietnamese civilians, soldiers and members of the French Army from North Vietnam to South Vietnam. The Central Intelligence Agency leveraged propaganda to overtly expose the transportation to the south. Under Colonel Edward Lansdale, a U.S. attaché in Saigon, the CIA operated the cover campaign. Lansdale was born on February 6, 1908 in Detroit, Michigan where he attended school in Michigan, New York and California before attending the University of California at Los Angeles. There he earned his way largely by writing for newspapers and magazines prior to joining the U.S. Air Force and then recruited to CIA. Lansdale also possessed a great deal of influence over President Ngo Dinh Diem to increase the south population for democratic reasons. The propaganda campaign was heavily comprised of students working on pieces to manipulate northerners to migrate south. To assist in distributing the propaganda, South Vietnamese soldiers disguised in civilian attire, infiltrated the north. The propaganda included rumors of Communist invasion of the northern part of the country from China. Columnists published articles of reported raping and pillaging of the north and detailed other atrocities and that the U.S. had planned to drop atomic bombs on the north. In addition, CIA passed counterfeit Viet Minh leaflets detailing false behavioral expectations under Communist rule.

Lansdale's campaign focused on northern Catholics, who were known for their strongly anti-communist tendencies. His staff printed tens of thousands of pamphlets with slogans such as "Christ has gone south" and "the Virgin Mary has departed from the North", alleging anti-Catholic persecution under Ho Chi Minh. Posters depicting communists closing a cathedral and forcing the congregation to pray in front of Ho, adorned with a caption "make your choice", were pasted around Hanoi and Haiphong. Diem himself went to Hanoi while the French were still garrisoned there to encourage Catholics to move. The campaign resonated with northern Catholic priests, who told their disciples that Ho would end freedom of worship, that sacraments would no longer be given and that anyone who stayed behind would endanger their souls. (31)

The Catholic immigrants helped to strengthen Diem's support base. Before the partition, most of Vietnam's Catholic population lived in the north. After the borders were sealed, the majority were now under Diem's rule. The Catholics implicitly trusted Diem due to their common faith and were a source of loyal political support. One of Diem's main objections to the Geneva Accords — which the State of Vietnam refused to sign — was that it deprived him of the Catholic regions of North Vietnam. With entire Catholic provinces moving south en masse, in 1956 the Diocese of Saigon had more Catholics than Paris and Rome. Of Vietnam's 1.45 million Catholics, over a million lived in the south, 55% of whom were northern refugees. (36)

Once again the use of Operation MOCKINGBIRD proved a successful public relations tool for CIA, who reaped benefits from their propaganda efforts depicting South Vietnam as free haven.

This was enhanced by the comparatively negligible number of people who voluntarily moved into the communist north. The event generated unprecedented press coverage of

Vietnam. Many prominent news agencies sent highly decorated reporters to cover the event. The New York Times dispatched Tillman and Peggy Durdin, while the New York Herald Tribune sent the Pulitzer Prize-winning war reporters Marguerite Higgins and Homer Bigart. Future US embassy official John Mecklin covered the event for Time Life. The press reports presented highly laudatory and emotional accounts of the mass exodus of Vietnamese away from the communist north. Time Life called the mass migration "a tragedy of almost nightmarish proportions …Many [refugees] went without food or water or medicine for days, sustained only by the faith in their heart." (36)

Operation Haik
Political Action in Indonesia

Sukarno, born Kusno Sosrodihardjo on June 6, 1901 was the first President of Indonesia. He helped the country win its independence from the Netherlands and was President from 1945 to 1967, presiding with mixed success over the country's turbulent transition to independence. The spelling "Sukarno" has been official in Indonesia since 1947 but the older spelling Soekarno is still frequently used, mainly because he signed his name in the old spelling. Official Indonesian presidential

Sukarno

decrees from the period 1947-1968, however, printed his name using the 1947 spelling. Indonesians also remember him as Bung Karno or Pak Karno.

Atypically, even among the colony's small educated elite, Sukarno was fluent in several languages. In addition to the Javanese language of his childhood, he was a master of Sudanese, Balinese and of Indonesian, and especially strong in Dutch. He was also quite comfortable in German, English, French, Arabic, and Japanese, all of which were taught at his HBS. He was helped by his photographic memory and precocious mind. Sukarno once remarked that when he was studying in Surabaya, he often sat behind the screen in movie theaters reading the Dutch subtitles in reverse because the front seats were only for elite Dutch people. (37)

In his studies, Sukarno was "intensely modern," both in architecture and in politics. Sukarno interpreted these ideas in his dress, in his urban planning for the capital (eventually Jakarta), and in his socialist politics, though he did not extend his taste for modern art to pop music; he had Koes Plus imprisoned for their allegedly decadent lyrics despite his reputation for womanizing. For Sukarno, modernity was blind to race, neat and Western in style, and anti-imperialist. (38)

Sukarno became a leader of a pro-independence party, Partai Nasional Indonesia, when it was founded in 1927. He opposed imperialism and capitalism because he thought both systems worsened the life of Indonesian people. He also hoped that Japan would commence a war against the western powers and that Java could then gain its independence with Japan's aid. In 1929 Sukarno was arrested by Dutch colonial authorities and sentenced to two years in prison. By the time he was released, he had become a popular hero.

Following the Japanese surrender of World War II, Sukarno, Mohammad Hatta, and Dr. Radjiman Wediodiningrat were summoned by Marshal Terauchi, Commander-in-Chief of Japan's Southern Expeditionary Forces in Saigon. Sukarno and Hatta declared the independence of the Republic of Indonesia on August 17, 1945. Sukarno's government was not universally accepted in Indonesia. Indeed, many factions and regions attempted to separate themselves from his government, and there were several internal conflicts even during the period of armed insurgency against the Dutch. One such example is the leftist-backed coup attempt by elements of the military in Madiun, East Java in 1948, in which many supporters of communism were allegedly executed. (39)

Sukarno resented his figurehead position and used disorder to intervene more in the country's political life, while claiming Western-style democracy was unsuitable for Indonesia. He proposed a government based not only on political parties but on "functional groups" composed of the nation's basic elements, in which a national consensus could express itself under presidential guidance. During this latter part of his presidency, Sukarno increasingly relied on the army and the support of the Communist Party of Indonesia (PKI). This concerned the United States as they had witnessed a steady increase in Sukarno's ties to China and admitted more Communists into his government. More troubling was that Sukarno began to accept increasing amounts of Soviet bloc military aid.

On November 30, 1957, an assassination attempt was made by grenade attack against Sukarno when he was visiting a school in Cikini, Central Jakarta. Six children were killed, but Sukarno did not suffer any serious wounds. In December he ordered the nationalization of 246 Dutch businesses. In February he began a crackdown on the PRRI rebels at Bukittinggi. These PRRI rebels, a mix of anti-communist and Islamic movements, received arms and aid from Western sources, including the CIA. By now the United States concerns had justification of CIA involvement to the point of political action. This involvement, Operation Haik, opened the CIA books to incorporate a number of projects against Sukarno in hopes of his immediate dismissal. In 1957 the CIA commissioned the production of a pornographic film to discredit the leader of Indonesia.

The CIA's basic approach was similar to PBSUCCESS in Guatemala. The United States had made common cause with a band of restless colonels in Sumatra who in February 1958 declared themselves an independent government. Once again the agency looked to psychological warfare to undermine the regime. The agency began to spread the rumor that Sukarno had been seduced by a good-looking blond airline stewardess who worked for the KGB. To document this seduction, the CIA commissioned a blue movie to be made of a Sukarno look-alike in the amorous embrace of a porn actress posing as the Russian spy. To play Sukarno, the movie makers chose a bald Chicano wearing a latex face mask. The CIA wanted the model to be bald because Sukarno was vain about his own baldness and always wore a skullcap, except, presumably, in bed. (40)

The agency had monitored Sukarno closely on a recent visit the United States and then to Russia. There they had learned Sukarno had been in the company of a beautiful blond Russian woman that they had reason to believe was a KGB agent, or at least an asset.

"I was asked if I thought I could get Larry Crosby they knew he was a friend of mine and his brother Bing Crosby to assist me in making a movie in Hollywood," CIA asset Robert Maheu. "I told Bing the exact truth and Bing said that he'd be very happy to cooperate with his government any chance he had and he laughingly said: "Do we have any more movies we can make Bob to get rid of these bastards that are plaguing us in the world?" (17)

The agency made still photos of the film that were clandestinely distributed to Asian newspapers along with specific text.   Unfortunately the effort was a complete flop.   The Indonesian people actually embraced the fact that their leader was having sex with a white woman.

Operation Haik pressed on with the attempts of military coups against Sukarno by funding the PRRI-Permesta rebellion in Sulawesi but produced even greater damage to the CIA. While flying a B-26 during a raid on government forces at the Indonesian port of Amboina, a former U.S. Air Force officer - Allen Lawrence Pope was shot down. Pope had broken his leg during the attack and was captured. The incident was a public embarrassment for both CIA and the United States.

Some other twenty aircraft supporting the Indonesian rebels were reported seen with Nationalist Chinese markings covered over with hasty coats of paint; their pilots were Chinese and Americans from Claire Chennault's Formosa-based Civil Air Transport. Pope claimed he was paid $10,000 month by the rebels, but the operation is widely believed to have been bankrolled by the CIA as Operation Haik to overthrow the Sukarno government which was feared to have communist sympathies. Pope's capture along with a number of incriminating documents led to great embarrassment to the US government. U.S. Ambassador Howard Jones characterized Pope as an American "paid soldier of fortune", and expressed his regret at the involvement of an American. (41)

After the event the U.S. policy shifted, prompting a closer relationship with Sukarno. Sukarno increasingly attempted to forge a new alliance called the "New Emerging Forces", as a counter to the old superpowers, whom he accused of spreading "Neo-Colonialism, Colonialism and Imperialism" (NEKOLIM). His political alliances gradually shifted towards Asian powers such as the PRC and North Korea. In 1961, this first president of Indonesia also found another political alliance, an organization, called the Non-Aligned Movement (NAM, in Indonesia known as Gerakan Non-Blok, GNB) with Egypt's President Gamal Abdel Nasser, India's Prime Minister Pandit Jawaharlal Nehru, Yugoslavia's President Josip Broz Tito, and Ghana's President Kwame Nkrumah, in an action called The Initiative of Five (Sukarno, Nkrumah, Nasser, Tito, and Nehru). This action was a movement to not give any favor to the two superpower blocs, who were involved in the Cold War. Sukarno was forced out of power by one of his generals, Suharto, who formally became President in March 1967.

Project CORONA
CIA & Satellite Imaging

In 1959 the CIA Directorate of Science & Technology with substantial assistance from the US Air Force launched Corona, a U.S. military reconnaissance satellite system to gather photographic surveillance of the Soviet Union, China and other countries deemed a potential threat to national security. The initial project was masked under part of the space technology program named Discoverer. The first successful launch was in 1959, and in June of the same year the CIA used recovered the capsule holding the photographic data. The capsule was collected during its parachuted decent through a specially equipped aircraft. The satellites were named Key Hole (KH) and totaled 144 launches from 1959 to 1972. The Corona satellites 31,000 ft of special 70 mm film to produce the imaging from 165 to 460 km, producing resolution success down to 7 m. Over time scientists and researchers were able to make adjustments thus creating better quality images and providing CIA more detail and accuracy. From the mid-sixties to 1971 the CIA was able to successfully execute more than 30 Corona satellite launches. The program was abandoned in 1972 after a Soviet submarine was located beneath one of the satellites retrieval locations. The success of Project CORONA opened the doors for additional Satellite usage for Recon Imaging including the GAMBIT and SAMOS satellite programs.

Dalai Lama Evacuation

CIA/SAD Tibetan U/W Training

In 1959 a tense political environment began to spread through the Tibetan population. Although the Dalai Lama was viewed as a man of peace and a fighter for justice, he was also an asset for the CIA and frontman for covert operations associated with his Lamaist organization. During the 1960s the organization received $1.7 million annually to fund and train contra forces in the fight against China, while the Dalai Lama was paid $186,000 annually from the U.S. intelligence services. During a major uprising the Dalai Lama suspected that China was going to attempt an assassination. With assistance from CIA, a clandestine escape was orchestrated. The Dalai Lama was safely extracted by from Tibet and transferred to India on March 13, 1959 by CIA paramilitary teams sent from a Special Activities Division (SAD). After the Chinese invasion of Tibet, CIA/SAD teams trained groups of Tibetan soldiers on island of Saipan and even Camp Hale by Anthony Alexander Poshepny.

Poshepny, also known as Tony Poe, was born on September 18, 1924 in Long Beach, California. During World War II he joined the U.S. Marine Corps and saw battle in the Pacific including Iwo Jima where he received two purple hearts. After graduating from the University of San Jose in 1951, Poshepny joined CIA where he put his past paramilitary skills to good use with the agency's Special Activities Division by training refugees for sabotage missions behind enemy lines. In 1958-1960, Poshepny was responsible for various training programs for Tibetan Khambas and Hui Muslims special missions. The Agency continued support until 1972 when President Richard Nixon ordered a cease in assistance due to new China relations.

Gambling Syndicate

Introduction of the Syndicate

Prior to the summer of 1960, CIA had been tasked primarily with schemes to discredit Fidel Castro's Cuban government. Most schemes involved altering his appearance or discrediting him through propaganda. Schemes were hatched to use hallucinogens during his press conferences and methods of making his hair fall out to appear ill. In August of 1960 pressure was mounting for CIA to aggressively handle Fidel

Sam Giancana

Castro either by overthrowing the regime, or assassination. CIA Deputy Director of Plans, Richard Bissell was tasked with the specifics. Bissell assigned the matter to Sheffield Edwards, CIA Director of Security, who the same month consulted with Robert Maheu, private investigator and a former FBI agent, in regards to approaching the syndicate for assistance on the Cuban matter. Maheu advised that he had a contact within the syndicate named Johnny Roselli who lived in Los Angeles. Edwards and Maheu planned to approach Roselli as a representative of business men who wanted to eliminate Castro to recoup their investment and would pay a bounty of $150,000 for the successful elimination of the Cuban leader.

In September, Edwards named James F. O'Connell as the case officer to handle the operation. O'Connell, like Maheu, was a former FBI agent, then acting as a CIA Chief of Operation Support Division, Office of Security. At this time, Bissell, Edwards, and O'Connell were the only CIA personnel that were aware of the mafia being used for the assassination attempt of Fidel Castro. On September 14, 1960 O'Connell and Maheu met with Roselli in

New York. O'Connell was introduced to Roselli as an employee of Maheu's and not an operative with CIA. Roselli, reluctant at first, agreed to arrange a meeting with a contact named "Sam Gold", who possessed contacts in Cuba that might be able to handle the job. Roselli also stated that he and "Gold" would not wish to receive any compensation for their assistance. On September 25, Maheu and O'Connell flew to Miami where Roselli introduced Maheu to "Sam Gold" at Fontainebleau Hotel. "Gold" said he knew a man name "Joe" who would be the Cuban contact to make arrangements. Although not meeting in person, O'Connell was able to identify "Gold" as Salvatore "Sam" Giancana, a Chicago-based crime boss and "Joe" as Santos Trafficante, crime figure in Cuba, through a Miami newspaper article about prominent Costa Nostra members. Although closed for a week, Castro had reopened the Casino's in January 1959 for tourists and Trafficante was making weekly trips between Havana and Miami on behalf of the syndicate.

After the meeting O'Connell had devised plans used for the assassination with Edward's. Edwards's recruited Dr. Edward Gunn, the CIA Chief of Operations Division, Office of Medical Services to assist with the assassination plot. Gunn was provided a box of Cuban cigars that were suspected to be Fidel Castro's favorite brand. The cigars were supplied by Edwards, with the intent of contaminating with a form of poisoning. Gunn used a toxin and virulent poison in hopes of producing a fatal illness hours after the cigar was ingested. After injecting the cigars, the packaging of each wrapped cigar and the box were re-sealed to hide any tampering. The toxin was so potent, that tests showed the cigar only needed to be placed in the mouth for the lethal dose to kill the intended target. The cigars were ready for delivery on February 13, 1961; however, the cigars were never used. O'Connell never considered the cigars as a serious avenue during the operation. According to Gunn, the cigars were then stored in his personal safe, and later destroyed after Edward's retirement in June of 1963. In addition to the cigar toxin method, CIA chemists reviewed four other options of assassination including:

(1) Toxic substance such as Shellfish poisoning to be administered through a needle (similar to what was provided Gary Powers).
(2) Liquid form of bacteria material.
(3) Bacteria treatment for a cigar.
(4) A bacteria treated handkerchief.

Bissell felt that the liquid bacteria were best suited due to Castro's love for tea, coffee and bouillon. Despite the decisions of the liquid form, the method provided would be a solid-based poison in pill or tablet format. The pills were required to be stable, soluble, and undetectable and not take immediate effect, yet provide predictable results. Botulin was the closest poison to meeting the requirements. The Mafia was actually the driving force behind the pill poisoning method, opposing the CIA suggested firearm hit originally planned on Castro. The pill method was thought of because of Trafficante's knowledge of a Castro insider who could gain access for the poisoning. The insider, named later, was Juan Orta, Office Chief and Director General to Castro. According to Trafficante, Orta's motive was money, since he had been getting payoffs from their casinos and with Castro's decision to close, he was losing financially. The pills were tested on guinea pig and later a monkey to confirm effectiveness and then disguised in a concealing device before provided to O'Connell in February of 1961. O'Connell provided six pills to Roselli, who later delivered to Trafficante and reported back to O'Connell that they had been received by Orta in either late February or March of 1961. Unfortunately Orta, who lost his position during the planning of the poisoning, got cold feet and the pills were returned through similar channels to O'Connell.

A month after the Orta loss, Roselli approached O'Connell with a different asset in Cuba that was willing to partake in the assassination attempt. The man's name was Dr. Manuel Antonio de Varona. Varona was involved in the Cuban exile movement, and held the position as leader of the Democratic Revolutionary Front. This organization was already supported by CIA using the military wing, Brigade 2506, as part of the Bay of Pigs invasion plan. O'Connell learned through CIA reporting that Varona was unsatisfied with the extent and support offered to his organization from the agency. The agency learned through FBI reports that the syndicate most likely had been assisting Varona financially for his anti-Castro efforts as means of building a relationship. The FBI felt that the syndicate was trying to secure their organized crime activities if Varona's group overthrew the Cuban leader. Trafficante approached Varona who was receptive to the opportunity. Varona felt the money for the assassination attempt could provide his army with additional guns, ships and equipment for the planned invasion.

According to O'Connell he organized through Roselli a payment to Varona of $50,000 initially. CIA reports this number has been skewed from $10,000 to $25,000 according to requisition records. Edwards was away at the time so O'Connell sought approval through Edward's deputy, Robert Bannerman, who up until then was unaware of the operation. Roselli had also confronted O'Connell and told him that he suspected him as a CIA operative, rather than Maheu's employee. O'Connell denied the suggestion, but felt Roselli knew better and stated that he, Roselli, was a loyal American and would never divulge the operation. The transaction involved the payment to Roselli along with the pills that in return passed to Varona. Varona had an asset in Cuba who worked at one of Castro's favorite restaurants. The plan was for the asset to place a pill in either Castro's food or drink the next time he visited the establishment. The operation never completed and according to Bissell, it failed because Castro had not frequented the establishment during the time frame.

In the spring of 1961, shortly after the Bay of Pigs, O'Connell, on orders from Edwards, contacted Roselli to terminate the operation. Although confident that the poisoned pills were returned to him, O'Connell could not recollect when or by whom. He advised CIA that he most likely flushed them down the toilet. According to memorandum by Edward's there was only six persons with knowledge of the assassination attempt, yet during an internal CIA investigation there was many more involved. The report identifies the following CIA personnel as having knowledge: Allen Dulles, DCI; General C. P. Cabell, Deputy Director of CIA; Richard Bissell, Deputy Director of Plans; Sheffield Edwards, Director of Security; James O'Connell, Office of Security; J. D. Esterline, Chief, WH/4; Cornelius Roosevelt, Chief, TSD and an unidentified Chemist in his department; Edward Gunn, Chief, Operations Division, Medical Services; William Harvey, Chief, FT/D; Sidney Gottlieb, Special Assistant to DD/P; Robert Bannerman, Deputy Director of Security; and J. C. King, Chief, WH Division. In addition, the following outside sources were familiar with the operation: Robert Maheu, private investigator; John Roselli, Sam Giancana & Santos Trafficante of the syndicate; Juan Orta, Antonio Varona and his son-in-law. The report also stated that Varona's son-in-law was not listed in his 201 File.

Congo Independence

Execution of Patrice Lumumba

In December of 1959 the Movement National Congolais (MNC) won a majority in the December local elections in the Congo and offered a declaration of their independence for June 30, 1960. After the May elections, the MNC won their independence of Congo from Belgium and Lumumba became the Congo's first Prime Minister with Joseph Kasa-Vubu as its President. Patrice Emery

Patrice Lumumba

Lumumba was born on July 2, 1925 in Onalua a province of the Belgian Congo. Lumumba was raised Catholic and educated at a missionary school and worked as a postal clerk and travelling beer salesman. In 1951, he married Pauline Opangu and a few years later joined the Liberal Party of Belgium where he was arrested for embezzlement of post office funds. After serving twelve months of a two year sentence, he helped found the Movement National Congolais and became the organizations leader in 1959. Shortly after gaining independence government decisions started a mutiny within the army. Civil unrest began and Lumumba was unable to gain control. In addition, Katanga also declared independence with assistance from the Belgium government. Lumumba reached out for Soviet assistance to repress Katanga through an invasion but failed due to poor communication and terrain issues.

President Dwight D. Eisenhower and DCI Allen Dulles viewed Patrice Lumumba as a potential Communist threat and believed he did not share the best interests of the Congo or the Congolese people. During a special group meeting with President

Eisenhower, Dulles received word for "straightforward" action against Patrice Lumumba was to be taken. In the meeting CIA officer Thomas Parrott outlined efforts to mount an anti-Lumumba campaign in the Congo targeting labor groups to turn their confidence away from the leader. On August 19 CIA Chief of Africa Division's clandestine services Bronson Tweedy received a cable to prepare for Lumumba's replacement with a pro Western Group. The following day on August 26, 1960 Dulles issued a CIA cable to CIA Station in Leopoldville that Patrice Lumumba's removal must be urgent and a prime objective as a high priority of covert action. Dulles specified the station to act on own authority. The CIA and Richard Bissell perceived this as authorization for the assassination of Patrice Lumumba. By September no action had been taken against Lumumba and CIA cabled Station Officer Larry Devlin that Lumumba would remain a grave danger as long as he was not yet disposed of. President Eisenhower stepped up the assassination by authorizing CIA to become more aggressive with plans to remove Lumumba.

Lumumba's decisions lost his good graces with President Kasa-Vubu and he was deposed in September of 1960. Lumumba declared Kasa-Vubu deposed too and a governmental collapse began to form pitting Senate against parliament. By September 14, 1960 Colonel Joseph Mobutu had organized a coup d'état placing both leaders in custody and under U.N. guard.

Dulles sent word to the CIA station to giving the desire to supporting the elimination of Lumumba even though he was in U.N. custody. Dulles had feared that the Congo was working on reconciling with the deposed Premiere and could pose a Communist threat if an agreement was reached. On September 7, 1960 CIA officers met with Congolese officials who shared the United States belief that Lumumba could be more of a threat out of office than when he was in office. They also expressed their desire to eliminate Lumumba physically. Devlin began working as an advisor for the Congolese government to assist them with stabilizing the government and providing arms through CIA. With assistance it was decided that Lumumba must be eliminated permanently. On September 26, 1960, Dr. Sidney Gottlieb, a CIA scientist from Langley arrived at the Leopoldville CIA Station to consult with Devlin and provide him with biological toxins from Gottlieb that could be used to poison and eliminate Lumumba. With Lumumba under U.N. guard Devlin felt difficult to gain access for the assassination and consulted with the Congolese government. Devlin was instructed to use the toxin to be taken by Lumumba orally through food or toothpaste. Devlin had been working one of his assets WI/ROGUE to gather information and recruit intelligence in the area. WI/ROGUE, a former convicted bank robber and forger, had undergone plastic surgery and was disguised in a toupee while in Leopoldville. He had just completed CIA sponsored training on demolitions, small arms and medical immunization, which would be beneficial in the poisoning attempt.

Since Lumumba was still under guard, Devlin offered assassination through shooting Lumumba and although the alternative was not opposed by CIA, it was made clear that no American involvement could be discovered. On October 17, 1960 Devlin cabled CIA headquarters and requested a high powered rifle with a scope and silencer. He advised that he would keep in the Station Office in Leopoldville until the right opportunity. Over the course of October Devlin kept target under heavy surveillance and cabled CIA advising that Lumumba had remained heavily guarded by U.N. and the opportunity to assassinate was unavailable.

With increased pressure from Dulles to eliminate Lumumba and no progress being made by Devlin, DDP Bissell approached CIA officer Justin O'Donnell to travel to the Congo and assist with the Lumumba assassination. O'Donnell rented an observation post near where Lumumba was being held and recruited a U.N. guard to assist him in luring Lumumba out into the open. O'Donnell's plan was to covertly assist Lumumba away from the guarded palace and into the custody of the Congolese authorities where he would be placed in custody and face capital punishment for alleged atrocities. On November 13th O'Donnell requested the use of a QJ/WIN asset, foreign assassins managed by Division D William K. Harvey to carry out the operation and provide the U.S. plausible deniability. O'Donnell's request was for the QJ/WIN asset to assess the operation and requested someone quick-witted to in case the objective needed to divert from original planning. On November 21, 1960 from request of William K. Harvey, QJ/WIN asset Jose Marie Andre Mankel arrived from Luxemburg to Leopoldville to assist in the operation. Devin cabled CIA on November 29 to advise that QJ/WIN was seeking permission to penetrate the U.N. guards in an effort to lure Lumumba from the secure location. Soon after QJ/WIN learned Lumumba had been smuggled from his secure location on November 27th and was heading towards Stanleyville. An additional request to CIA was submitted to pursue Lumumba to Stanleyville location in which CIA authorized. Prior to QJ/WIN intercepting Lumumba, he was captured in Port Francqui on December 1, 1960. The CIA had learned through intelligence gathering that Lumumba supporters were planning to evacuate him from the secure camp and transport him to Stanleyville. The information was shared with the Congolese government prior and road blocks were set up leading to his capture.

By mid-December Devlin grew concerned over WI/ROGUE through learning from QJ/WIN of his actions. Both assets were staying in the same hotel yet unaware of each other's association with CIA and WI/ROQUE had approached the other asset about joining an assassination team or death squad. Distressed over WI/ROQUE's behavior, Devlin cabled CIA and suggested it would be in the operations best interest to have the asset recalled from the Congo and evaluated for future use by the agency.

Although under arrest, Lumumba supporters were gaining ground with parliament and the U.S. feared they would re-open elections and Lumumba would once again gain control. The U.S. also knew this would surely open the door to Soviet population within the Congo. On orders from Allen Dulles and Richard Bissell, Devlin encouraged the Congolese government to take action. On January 17, 1961 Lumumba and two of his advisors were placed on a plane in Leopoldville destined for Bakwanga, but during flight the plane changed course and landed in Elisabethville in the Katanga Province, home of Lumumba's sworn enemies. Reports were publicized that Lumumba had escaped capture and was killed by angry villagers, yet CIA learned later that while in Katanga, Patrice Lumumba was executed by a firing squad on orders from Belgium military officials the same day the plane had arrived.

Project ZRRIFLE

Assassination of Fidel Castro

In January or February of 1961 during the original assassination plans on Castro, Bissell approached William K. Harvey, Chief FT/D, to assist in creating an Executive Action Capability to eliminate Fidel Castro. During this time, Bissell briefed Harvey on Phase 1 of the gambling syndicate operation. After reviewing and approving through DD/P Helms, Bissell and Harvey created the Executive Action program known as ZRRIFLE. The principle

Allen Dulles

asset for ZRRIFLE was an operative codenamed QJWIN, who had been recruited prior for special operations in the Congo and controlled by Justin O'Donnell. The project was funded under CIA general accounting and Harvey was approved a budget of $14,700 with $7,200 for QJWIN's annual salary and the remainder for operation expenses. Project ZRRIFLE was covered under an FT/D operation and was kept separate from Edward's gambling syndicate operation which was already ongoing.

In November of 1961 Bissell approached Harvey and asked for him to take over the contacts Edward's had for the syndicate operation and use the resources for ZRRIFLE. At the same time, Helms tasked Harvey with taking over the CIA Cuba task force, Task Force W. Harvey and Edward's didn't finalize the takeover until March of 1962. Although he now controlled both operations, he continued to run them separately. In April 9 Harvey was introduced to Johnny Roselli through his CIA handler James O'Connell in New York. The meeting was held at the Savoy Hilton and had dinner at the Elk Room and ended up drinking

with Roselli at the Copacabana.
The men arranged to restart the
original plan and in late April
O'Connell provided Roselli with
the poison pills once again and
began Project Gambling Syndicate
Phase II. According to Harvey, he
met with Roselli in Miami on April
21, 1962 and that both Giancana

and Trafficante were no longer involved in the operation. Harvey
felt Giancana should remain outside of the plan, and Roselli
agreed and Trafficante was of no use since the Casino's again were
shut down. Roselli had a new contact for the assassination
attempt only known to Harvey as "Maceo". Over the course of
ZRRIFLE, Harvey explained that Roselli became very involved
and worked directly with Varona and the CIA. Roselli passed the
pills to Varona and communicated his request to Harvey.
According to Roselli, Varona needed guns and additional
equipment for his army. Harvey worked with Ted Shackley, who
was Chief of JM/WAVE Station in Miami, and procured
explosives, rifles, radar and radio equipment and munitions. To
maintain the business cover, Harvey didn't offer items that would
be available to the United States Government that Varona
requested. To transport the equipment, Harvey and Shackley
rented a U-Haul truck under an assumed name and delivered to a
drive-in restaurant where they meet with Roselli and gave him the
keys. Once the truck was emptied by Varona, it was returned to
the designated place and Harvey returned to the U-Haul dealer.
Harvey explained that Shackley had no knowledge of the
operation or the key principles involved, he was only used for
gathering and assisting delivering the materials.

In May of 1962 Roselli contacted Harvey through their
arranged telephone system, Harvey's home and Roselli at Friars

Club, to advise that the pills were at the restaurant again in Cuba. During the months of June through September, Harvey received contact from Roselli advising him of Varona's movements. Varona had sent two three man teams to infiltrate the Castro regime in hopes of recruiting additional assassins for Castro's termination. From September to January 1963 the attempts were all backed off for a variety of reasons. Harvey stated that "conditions inside" there and the Missile Crisis were reasons for delays. During December 22 until January 6, Harvey remained in Miami and met with both Roselli and Varona several times and by the end of the month both Roselli and Harvey agreed nothing was happening. The men believed that Varona's second team never reached Cuba and were probably in the Florida Keys and that the first team obviously failed to meet their objective. In February Harvey left message in Miami for "Maceo" that the operation was over and then echoed this to Roselli in a meeting the following day in Los Angeles. Both men agreed that there was no reason to keep the operation open and was agreed to shut down. The men did agree to keep the lines of communication open between Roselli and Varona, and Roselli would relay any new information to Harvey.

In June of 1963 Harvey met with Roselli at Dulles airport. Harvey in preparation for his transfer to Rome had already sold his house and was staying at a neighbor who was away. Roselli stayed with Harvey as a houseguest and the men went to dinner along with Harvey's wife. During the meal Harvey received a call from FBI agent Sam Papich. Harvey learned that the FBI had Roselli under surveillance. The next morning Harvey met Papich for breakfast and under FBI rules, Papich would have to report the sighting of Harvey and Roselli. Harvey understood and passed the situation to Helms.

Eventually the story would get leaked from someone close to the operation. An article by Jack Anderson broke the original story and prompted an internal CIA investigation.

Operation 40

In March of 1960, President Dwight D. Eisenhower and Vice President Richard Nixon authorized DCI Allen Dulles and CIA to sponsor a covert group whose primary objective was to sabotage the newly formed Cuban government. The group, a ZR/RIFLE unit named Operation 40, operated in the Caribbean, Central America, and Mexico. Alleged members of this group included Tracy Barnes, David Atlee Phillips, Jacob Esterline, Howard Hunt, Frank Bender, and David Sanchez Morales whom had worked with each other prior on Operation PBSUCCESS. In addition, CIA officers Felix Rodriguez, William K. Harvey, Thomas G. Clines, Porter Goss and Ted Shackley would assist the efforts. The group focused on anti-Cuban covert activity by training and equipping Cuban refugees as guerilla army. Operation 40 members recruited mercenaries such as Frank Sturgis and former South American intelligence operatives including Virgilio Gonzalez, Eladio del Valle and Rolando Masferrer. Over time the group had developed relationships with several anti-Castro Cuban organizations and some CIA sponsored groups such as Alpha 66. Alpha 66 was a CIA sponsored paramilitary group ran by Antonio Veciana and trained in the Florida Everglades who many believed to be the brainchild of David Atlee Philips.

Operation 40 sabotage operations claimed the responsibility of bombing the La Coubre, Belgian ship supplying arms to Cuba in March of 1960. The attack killed more than seventy people. Frank Sturgis, allegedly told author Mike Canfield: "this assassination group (Operation 40) would upon orders, naturally, assassinate either members of the military or the

Frank Sturgis

political parties of the foreign country that you were going to infiltrate, and if necessary some of your own members who were suspected of being foreign agents...We were concentrating strictly in Cuba at that particular time."

In May of 1961 George Tanner formed the Anti-Communist Legionnaires, a group of American adventures set to overthrow the Cuban Government. Tanner, who referred to himself as Colonel Tanner, set up training camps in the Florida Keys where members deemed him a psychopath and exiled him from the organization. The group was then headed up by for Air Force control tower operator Gerald Patrick Henning. Hemming was born on March 1, 1937 in Los Angeles, California. He attended El Monte Union High School before joining the U.S. Marine Corps in 1954. He received an honorable discharge in 1958 as the rank of a sergeant. Henning, who had spent a year in Cuba serving under the Cuban Revolutionary Air Force, changed the name of the group to Interpen (Intercontinental Penetration Force). Henning had moved the group of 20 to a camp near Davie Airport in Davie, Florida to prepare Cuban nationals in the U.S. for guerilla warfare in Cuba. By 1961, Hemming was working with other anti-Castro organizations including The Revolutionary Junta of National Liberation, Frente Revolutionario Democratico (FDR), Movimiento Revolucionario Del Pueblo (MRP), and Frank Fiorini, aka Frank Sturgis, International Anti-Communist Brigade. In 1961 Miami Herald article the paper even confused the groups by reporting Henning's organization was the parachuting division of Fiorini's International Anti-Communist Brigade.

Frank Anthony Sturgis was born Frank Angelo Fiorini on December 9, 1924 in Norfolk, Virginia and grew up in

Philadelphia, Pennsylvania. In 1942 Sturgis joined the Marines and served in the Pacific during World War II. After the war Sturgis attended Virginia Polytechnic Institute and then joined the United States Army in 1950 and served until 1952. Sturgis had managed bars and nightclubs including The Whitehorse Tavern and Tophat Nightclub and briefly attended Old Dominion University in Norfolk, Virginia. In 1956, Sturgis moved to Cuba but had spent time in a variety of Latin American countries including Mexico, Venezuela, Costa Rica, Guatemala, Panama, and Honduras. Once Fidel Castro gained control of Cuba, Sturgis formed a paramilitary organization called the Anti-Communist Brigade. He became quite popular in the Miami area and anything but secretive. He would brag to people and reporters that his brigade was 3,000-5,000 man strong. Sturgis had even given interviews and advised media he had underwater demolition training programs in New York and California.

Operation ZAPATA

The Bay of Pigs Invasion

On March 11 of 1961, against CIA suggested operations, President John F. Kennedy selected Operation Zapata, known as the Bay of Pigs, due to aircraft logistics for the invasion plan. Due to the noise of aircraft, the invasion landing was changed to beaches bordering the Bay of Pigs in Las Villas Province, which Kennedy felt would strengthen plausible deniability of US direct involvement. The invasion points were to be located east of the Zapata peninsula near Playa Girón, Playa Larga, and Caleta Buena Inlet. The infantry of the invasion was Brigade 2506, which CIA had sponsored. The Brigade was populated with Cuban-exiles recruited from the Miami, Florida area and trained in various locations including Useppa Island and Fort Gulick, Panama. Addition support came from an airfield constructed near Retalhuleu, Guatemala supplied with U.S. airships showing Fuerza Aérea Guatemalteca markings. In addition, CIA provided amphibious landing and underwater demolition training and used Douglas C-54 transports to deliver the Brigade and their supplies. On April 9, 1961 the Brigade 2506 personnel and other forces began to mobilize and transferred from Guatemala to Puerto Cabezas, Nicaragua.

The CIA continued to leverage their Operation 40 group to carry out sabotage missions in Cuba through bombings and arson in an effort to demonstrate a revolting anti-Castro Government. Propaganda efforts also grew through the use of CIA's Radio Swan, the former transmitter used by Radio Free Europe. Radio Swan was relocated to the Swan Island where Spanish language broadcasts aired as Radio Swan, la Voz Internacional del Caribe, of taped recordings from anti-Castro political groups in exile. After two days of bombing raids using the FAG planes, President Kennedy advised that the United States would not provide any additional air support for the invasion on the following day. This decision was based on guaranteeing that he could hide U.S. involvement from the United Nations. The CIA Brigade 2506 had mobilized and converged approximately 60 miles south of Cuba. The United States Navy at the time was running a dummy mission hoping to draw attention with seven destroyers circling the other side of Cuba.

On April 17, 1961 at midnight CIA covert operatives including underwater demolition teams (UDT) penetrated the Cuban coastline. Poor lighting delayed the additional transport ships and by daybreak the Cuban Army, aware of the invasion, began attaching the transports with rockets. The course of the invasion included a number of downed aircraft losing scores of pilots more than 200 men drown and poor logistics of paratroop drops. Over the course of three days the Brigade and the invasion had failed horribly. The invasion took the lives of twenty airman, 104 Brigade 2506 members, 2,000 Cuban exiles and 1,204 Cubans and 2 Americans captured. Both Americans were then executed. In the days following CIA was able to rescue approximately 30 survivors off the Cuban Coast. The failed invasion embarrassed the Kennedy Administration and resulted in the forced resignation of CIA Director Allen Dulles, CIA Deputy Director Charles Cabell, and Deputy Director for Plans Richard Bissell.

Project AMLASH
Castro Assassination Plot

In March of 1961, CIA met with Rolando Cubela at the Mexico City Station. Cubela had been attending the Latin American Conference on National Sovereignty, Emancipation, and Peace days prior. The meeting was arranged through a long-time friend of Cubela named Carlos Tepedino (AMWHIP-1). Cubela was believed to participate in the 1956 assassination of Lt. Col. Antonio Blanco Rico, who was then the head of the Batista military intelligence. According to a CS report in March of 1959, Cubela, a major in the Cuban army at the time, made comments that he was so upset over Castro's regime in Cuba, he had to flee the country soon or he would kill Castro himself. The initial meeting spawned new meetings that over time formed Project AMLASH. Cubela (AMLASH-1) believed that to take over Cuba, Fidel Castro had to be killed prior and Cubela was on board to overseeing his assassination. He requested special equipment for technical assistance in the assassination attempt and according to Nestor Sanchez, CIA case officer and Cubela's controller, this was provided. Later in the month, the Miami Station, JM/WAVE received a report from one of their asset's that both Rolando Cubela and Juan Orta, poison pill asset from the earlier Gambling Syndicate project, wished to defect to the U.S. and were requesting assistance with their escape. The CIA was very interested in collecting the men, but the ex-filtration plan was aborted when reports that Cuban police were aware of the defect plans.

Rolando Cubela

Tepedino reported that Cubela was attending a French festival later in the month and contacted Tepedino about meeting CIA contacts in the Paris office. The Paris Station was given approval, but the meeting never occurred. On June 15, of 1962 JMWAVE was advised by an asset AMCONCERT-1, that Cubela had traveled on a Czech airline to Prague and later to Helsinki where he was attending the World Youth Festival. On his return, Cubela planned to meet with Tepedino in Paris. In June and July of 1962 Tepedino communicated with both CIA and FBI on the defection of Cubela. Tepedino, who was himself a Cuban-exile, worked as a jeweler in New York and there met with CIA to plan Cubela's defection. The plan was for Tepedino to travel to Helsinki to aid in Cubela's defection. On July 30, 1962 Tepedino arrived in Helsinki where he found Cubela. Over the course of the week, Tepedino, under the guidance of CIA, worked on convincing Cubela to return to Cuba rather than defect. The agency was more interested in leveraging Cubela as an asset than as a defector. With Tepedino's assistance, the recruitment was successful and Cubela desired that if he could assist in the fight against Castro and make a significant difference he would return.

Cubela had plans to bomb an oil refinery; assassinate Carlos Rodriguez, a top ranking Castro member and Soviet Ambassador; and assassinate Fidel Castro if the opportunity was available. CIA advised Cubela that they appreciated his interests, but also cautioned that partaking in these events would take time due to planning. Cubela agreed and planned that future meetings would take place in Stockholm and Copenhagen vs. Helsinki due to the amount of Cuban delegates that could risk the operation status.

During August of 1962 Cubela and Tepedino met with CIA in Copenhagen and later in Madrid, Spain. In Madrid Cubela was provided S/W training and issued appropriate supplies. The same month Cubela was taken to France and provided a demotion demonstration. At this time Cubela was requested to take a polygraph test to be submitted to him in Paris. Cubela emphatically refused, the agency decided that with his refusal to take a polygraph that he would not be used to carry out any physical elimination mission and was agreed by CIA headquarters. On August 29, 1962 Cubela left for Havana from Prague.

CIA case officer Nestor Sanchez again met with Cubela in Porto Alegra, Brazil on September 3, 1963. Cubela advised that he was concerned using S/W because of the unreliability of the Cuban postal service. He discussed possibly approaching a couple of Cuban military officers regarding an assassination attempt, but felt conflicted. He told Sanchez that he knew both men were against a Communist government, but they were also either loyal to Castro due to respect or from fear. Cubela expressed high regard for Ramon Guin Diaz, a CIA asset who was hiding Miguel Diaz Isalgue (AMICE-14). Diaz was sent by CIA to Cuba to recruit Guin in his place. Cubela was instructed he could assist Guin with his intelligence assignments but not to assist with Guin leaving Cuba.

In October 1963 Sanchez arrived in Paris to meet with Cubela. When Sanchez arrived, Station officers, John Stent and Richard Long, were already attending a meeting with Cubela. During the meetings Sanchez discovered that the French had Cubela under surveillance. Sanchez had French authorities contacted and advised that CIA was working with Cubela for defection purposes.

On October 11 Sanchez cabled JM/WAVE and advised that Cubela was requesting to meet with United States Attorney General Robert Kennedy as a show of U.S. moral support to his efforts in Cuba. Sanchez advised that the answer he received could be crucial to his further participation in any CIA relationship.

According to Sam Halpern Robert Kennedy put the CIA under a lot of pressure to arrange the assassination of Castro. Halpern later claimed that "Bobby Kennedy was a bad influence on Des (FitzGerald). He reinforced his worst instincts." Thomas Parrott, the secretary of SGA, claimed that FitzGerald had trouble dealing with Kennedy: "He was arrogant, he knew it all, he knew the answer to everything. He sat there, tie down, chewing gum, his feet up on the desk. His threats were transparent. It was, If you don't do it, I tell my big brother on you." (40)

Sanchez advised that Cubela appeared determine to attempt the assassination with or without U.S. involvement. CIA officer Stent cabled within a couple days of Sanchez relaying the same concerns expressed to him by Cubela in further conversation. On October 29, 1963 Desmond FitzGerald, chief of SAS, flew to Paris to meet with Cubela personally at Stents home, as way to provide him with assurances of U.S. support. FitzGerald had discussed the planned meeting and gained approval through DD/P Helms. FitzGerald used an alias for the trip of James Clark, and was assisted by CIA officer Nestor Sanchez as an interpreter. During the meeting FitzGerald advised Cubela that the U.S. would assist him in any way if successful in neutralizing Fidel Castro's regime. FitzGerald also reiterated that support would be provided only after the coup was accomplished and U.S. involvement was requested. During the meeting FitzGerald also stated that Cubela was seeking for the agency to provide him with a high powered rifle so he could use to assassinate Castro. He told Cubela that the U.S. would not participate in any such action and it was not the policy of the U.S. to have any part of taking Castro's life. On November 19, 1963 a CIA memorandum prepared by Nestor Sanchez stated that FitzGerald approved telling Cubela he would be provided high-powered rifles with scopes if requested and for written AMLASH operations reports to be kept to a minimum.

Both Sanchez and Sam Halpern reported that Cubela was interested in a high powered rifle, preferably with a silencer, so that he could make the shot from a great distance. The men claimed that Cubela, although wanted to assassinate Castro, was not willing to trade his life during the event. Discussion with Sanchez and Halpern discovered that they had approached Dr. Gunn for some alternative method of assassination and was received well by Cubela. Dr. Gunn had worked out a plan to use Black Leaf 40, an insecticide containing nicotine sulphate, which could be a deadly poison if distributed orally or through the skin. The plan reached the action stage on the morning of September 20, 1963 when Gunn advised Sanchez and Halpern the device used for administering the poison would be a ballpoint pen rigged as a hypodermic syringe. The following day, November 21, 1963 Gunn provided the pen to Sanchez, who later advised that Cubela refused to accept the device but has no recollection of the poison pen ever being returned.

On November 22, 1963 Sanchez arrived in Paris and met with Cubela later in the afternoon to review the operation of the poison pen. According to Sanchez, Cubela was not impressed with the device, and although he accepted it he believed that Cubela wasn't taking it to Cuba. During the meeting Sanchez advised that the pen was empty, and suggested the Black Leaf 40 to Cubela because it could be purchased at any hardware store. Cubela was unimpressed and felt CIA could have been more sophisticated in their device.

After the meeting both Sanchez and Cubela were advised that President John F. Kennedy had been assassinated. According to Sanchez's report, Cubela was visibly moved about the news and asked, "Why do such things happen to good people?" Later that evening Sanchez received a cable from FitzGerald advising him that the operation was off.

After the assassination of President Kennedy the FBI reported that Cubela had returned to Cuba through Prague on December 1, 1963. Two months later JM/WAVE Station cabled that 2 caches containing FAL 7.62 automatic rifles were being prepared for delivery for Project AMLASH in March of 1964. Because of size dimensions of the caches, delays were experienced through the usual delivery channels but eventually arrived in April. On May 3, 1964 the Paris Station received word that Cubela had requested a silencer for the Belgian FAL machine gun, which SAS requested the Technical Services Department (TSD) to produce. In June of 1964 Operation ZORRO dropped the AMLASH cache on the north coast of Primar del Rio. According to CIA reports the silencer was not ready yet and not included in the drop.

On August 30, 1964 Manuel Artime was contacted to meet with a group of dissident members of the Castro regime. A meeting was planned and Artime sent an associate on October 7, 1964 to meet with an intermediary Alberto Bianco Romariz. On November 12 the FBI cabled CIA to advise that Maj. Rolando Cubela was attending an International Student Union meeting in Prague as a guest later in the month. Artime agreed to meet with AMLASH-1 to see if he is the leader of the internal dissident group. On December 6, CIA officer Sanchez met with Cubela in Paris where Cubela expressed his frustration for not being able to carry out the assignment. Sanchez advised that the U.S. would no longer provide assistance and Cubela understood that if he wished to continue his efforts he would need to seek help elsewhere. Sanchez reported that CIA didn't feel it wise to provide a silencer directly to Cubela, but if they could work Artime and Cubela together, there would be no direct link. In December of 1964 the two men met together for the first time.

After another meeting in December with Cubela, Artime flew to Miami to discuss the conversation with CIA case officer

Sanchez. According to Artime, Cubela was upset that the Americans couldn't furnish him a silencer, so Artime stepped in. He advised Cubela that he could provide a silencer for the gun he possesses or a different rifle all together. In a February 1965 meeting with Cubela, Sanchez reported that Artime had delivered Cubela a package for his assignment that he would take with him in his personal luggage and that he was satisfied with the arrangement.

On March 15, 1965 a Rafael Garcia-Bango Dirube arrived in Madrid, Spain and contacted a CIA officer advising his contact with a group of Cuban military leaders. Garcia-Bango advised that the group was planning to take over the government and eliminate Castro. The officer realized that the contact Garcia-Bango was referring to was Cubela. Garcia-Bango was the attorney for Santos Trafficante, who had participated in Sheffield Edward's Gambling Syndicate operation phase 1.

Due to increasing concern of outside individuals that were aware of Cubela's plans and association with CIA, the agency decided in June of 1965 to terminate all contacts with members of the Cubela group. In March of 1966 Reuters reported that Cuban security police had arrested two Cuban military officials for counterrevolutionary activities involving the United States Central Intelligence Agency and identified both Rolando Cubela and Ramon Guin. In March the trial began and the FBI shared the testimony made by the defendants. Much of the operation was uncovered and made public and Cubela and Guin received 25 year sentences for their participation in the conspiracy.

Operation MONGOOSE
The Cuban Project

Formed after the Bay of Pigs failure by President Kennedy, Operation MONGOOSE was constructed under the orders of the Attorney General Robert Kennedy and the Directorate of Central Intelligence to take an aggressive approach to eliminate Fidel Castro. During Operation Mongoose, the agency utilized many projects which were started and aborted while seeking out an effective method to obtain operational success.

In early 1963 during the negotiations between Donovan and Castro for the release of Bay of Pigs prisoners, a new Executive Action Plan was created. The plan called for Donovan to present Cuban leader Fidel Castro with a skin diving suit as a gift. The suit was contaminated with a fungus that had been produced in a dust form and lined the inside of the suit. In addition the breathing apparatus would be contaminated with tubercle bacilli. The plan was originated by William K. Harvey and thought to be a good idea due to Castro's enthusiasm of skin diving. According to Sidney Gottlieb, the suit was purchased and the contamination was completed and ready for delivery. According to one of the participants Samuel Halpern, the scheme was abandoned due to Donovan giving Castro a suit prior on his own accord.

In early 1963 Desmond FitzGerald, then Chief, SAS, formed another Executive Action plan involving an explosive-rigged sea shell for the assassination of Fidel Castro. The plan was to place the shell in an area where Castro commonly would go skin diving. The shell would be designed in a way to draw attention to Castro and when lifted, the shell would be triggered to explode killing the Cuban leader. According to FitzGerald, he along with Sam Halpern and Bruce Cheever discussed the planning extensively but brought nobody else into the operational discussions. After reviewing the feasibility the plan was aborted.

Operation NORTHWOODS

Justification for US Military Intervention in Cuba

On March 13, 1963 General Lyman L. Lemnitzer, Chairman of The Joint Chiefs of Staff (JCS), issued a Top Secret memorandum for the Chief of Operations, Cuba Project. The memorandum stated that in the event covert activity doesn't foster a Cuban rebellion, additional action will need to be planned. U.S. unilateral military intervention in Cuba can only be undertaken in the event that the Cuban regime commits hostile acts against US

General Lemnitzer

forces or property which would serve as an incident upon which to base overt intervention. The memorandum, Operation NORTHWOODS, contained an outline of covert actions demonstrating Cuban aggression against the United States to justify U.S. military involvement. The memorandum was directed toward the Robert McNamara, Secretary of Defense and Col. Edward Lansdale, Chief of Operations, Cuba Project and specifically hidden from commanders of unified or specified commands of U.S. officers assigned to NATO, the Chairman, US Delegation, and United Nations Military Staff Committee. A plan objective was to provide adequate justification for U.S. military intervention through the impression of Cuban rashness and irresponsibility on a large scale. The United States believed that planned harassment plus targeted deceptive actions could convince the Cubans an imminent invasion would occur. In return, the United States military posture throughout execution of Operation NORTHWOODS would allow a rapid change from exercise to intervention. Since the United States felt that it was just a matter of time before Cuba became a member of the Warsaw Pact, the following projects were considered for operation status.

CIA had planned to use clandestine radio to implement rumors and drop friendly Cubans in uniform around Guantanamo to stage an attack, capture saboteurs and start riots on the U.S. base. The operation also suggested inflicting damage and chaos within the U.S. compound by staging mortar attacks, burning aircraft and even sinking a U.S. ship off the Cuban Coast and conduct mock funerals. This would enable the U.S. to respond by executing force against the Cuban regime. During planning, CIA considered a "Remember the Maine" incident where they would be able to use an unmanned drone ship and destroy it near Havana or Santiego. The plan would then stage a U.S. rescue to add credibility; US fighters to "evacuate" remaining members of the non-existent crew; and print casualty lists in U.S. newspapers to generate a wave of national indignation.

Through the JM/WAVE Station CIA would develop a Communist Cuba terror campaign in the Miami area and surrounding cities in the U.S. The campaign could leverage Cuban refugees seeking haven in the United States to exploit communist activities. The memorandum even included the notion of sinking "a boatload of Cubans en-route to Florida (real or simulated)". CIA officials felt this would foster attempts on lives of Cuban refugees in the U.S. and publicize the wounded with propaganda including releasing Cuban documents to show their involvement.

Through intelligence operatives CIA learned that Castro had supported subversive efforts against Haiti, Dominican Republic, Guatemala, and Nicaragua. One plan called for simulating a Cuban-based filibuster and offered examples of invading Dominican national air space. By flying Cuban B-26 or C-46 type aircraft and execute cane-burning raids using Soviet Bloc incendiaries. One larger-scaled operation was considered involving the United States flying MIG style aircraft and initiating civil air attacks on surface ships and destroyed a U.S. military drone aircraft to show aggression.

One of the biggest planned undertakings was to create a convincing Cuban attack on a civilian airliner. The plan called for an Eglin ABF aircraft to be painted to duplicate a civilian charter plane with the cover would be college students off on holiday. The plan called for CIA personnel to board an aircraft in Jamaica, Guatemala, Panama or Venezuela and leave en-route to the United States. Once the plane entered Cuban airspace, the craft would dip below radar level and the flight space would be intercepted by an unmanned drone. The drone would possess the same civil aircraft number and log information and be flown from a CIA proprietary organization in the Miami area. The drone would issue distress signals that could be picked up and the drone aircraft could be detonated off the Coast of Florida.

The plan was eventually rejected under the Kennedy Administration and never actually executed. On March 1, 1962, Army memorandum entitled "Possible Actions to Provoke, Harass or Disrupt Cuba," was attached to numerous schemes including Operation Bingo, a plan to fake an attack on Guantanamo Bay; Operation Dirty Trick, a plot to blame Castro if the 1962 Mercury manned space flight carrying John Glenn crashed; and Operation Good Times, releasing decadent faked photos of "an obese Castro" with two women vast amounts of Cuban food and captioned "my ration is different."

Project MOCKINGBIRD
Domestic Wire Taps

On March 12, 1963 Sheffield Edwards, CIA Director of Security, under DCI John McCone, authorized wire taps on two Washington Post reporters who had published articles quoting Top Secret and Special Intelligence materials that were classified by the Central Intelligence Agency. The telephone intercept activity was installed at the office of the reporters as well as each of their homes. Project MOCKINGBIRD was productive in identifying contacts and methods of

John McCone

operation used by the sources of the reporters. During the operation the agency discovered that the reporters were gaining information from thirteen news reporters, twelve senators, six members of Congress, 21 Congressional staff members, and 16 government employees. In addition, key members of the White House, Vice-President's Office and an Assistant Attorney General. The two reporters had acquired more classified information than they could use for their articles, and passed much of the data on to other reporters and news personnel. This indicated that the leads appearing in many publications were actually being funneled through the two reporters. The operation ended on June 15, 1963 and all materials related were maintained under strict security.

Surveillance activity (CELOTEX I) was conducted on Washington Post reporter Michael Getler between October of 1971 and January of 1972. In addition the CIA conducted physical surveillance by using the Statler Hilton Hotel as an observation post to maintain the operation. The location was selected to observe the building that had house Getler's office. The surveillance was put in play and authorized to view and record contacts and sources of Getler's to identify possible leaks of sensitive and classified agency materials. Under direction of DCI, surveillance was also conducted on Jack Anderson (CELOTEX II) and his sources, Britt Hume, Leslie Whitten and Joseph Spear. These activities were conducted from February 15 to April 12 of 1972. The same physical observation location was reserved for monitoring the Washington Post reporter's office. From March to April 20 of 1972, Victor L. Marchetti (BUTANE) was added as a CIA surveillance target due to his proposed book and magazine articles exposing CIA operations. In addition to the domestic American targets, CIA also ran surveillance operations with Soviet defectors and U.S. citizens who received postal communication from Communist sources abroad under Project SRPOINTER, Project AELADLE and Project REDFACE 1.

Project 404

CIA's Secret War in Laos

In 1959 the United States executed Operation Hotfoot and deployed one hundred soldiers of 77th Special Forces Group for an advisory mission into Laos. By May of 1960, the Special Forces Group was renamed the 7th Group and overseen by the legendary Green Beret Lieutenant Colonel Arthur D. "Bull" Simons. In association with CIA, these Green Berets wore civilian attire to fit in with the Laotian community and conceal U.S. involvement as preparation for the Vietnam conflict. The purpose of the mission was to train the Royal Laotian Army, and indigenous Hmong tribes to combat against communist invasion. This effort would be known as Operation White Star until the summer of 1962 when the CIA would oversee the entire program from the U.S. Army and eventually become Project 404 during the Vietnam War.

Anthony Poshepny, also known as Tony Poe, became infamous for his cruel techniques in exploiting physiological warfare to Communist fighters. He started collecting human ears and would pay money for them as a way to establish a bounty. He would also use decapitation as method of intimidation and admitted to dropping human heads on enemy positions. Poshepny believed that these tactics assisted in motivating his Laotian guerrilla fighters and even encouraged them to place the decapitated heads on sticks and spikes to show as trophies. Many have suggested that Poshepny was the inspiration for the character Col. Kurtz in the film Apocalypse Now, yet both Poshepny and director Francis Ford Coppala denied the claim.

"I still collected them, until one day I went out on an inspection trip ... and I saw this little kid out there, he's only about 12, and he had no ears. And I asked, 'What the hell happened to this guy?' "Somebody said, 'Tony, he heard you were paying for ears. His daddy cut his ears off. For the 5,000 kip,'" Poshepny said.

"As for dropping human heads on enemy villages, I only did it twice in my career," Poshepny told the Wall Street Journal - once on a Lao ally who had been flirting with the communists. "I caught hell for that." (42)

Although many considered Poshepny to be crude, drunk, and a Neanderthal, he drew admiration from those who truly knew him. He epitomized what former friend and colleague Ted Shackley referred to as the 'Third Option'. America - to avoid the potential twin options of using nuclear or conventional forces to defend its interests - should instead rely on special, elite clandestine forces to recruit, train and arm indigenous, or tribal forces, to project power, protect its interests and counter guerrilla movements, terrorism or other attacks. Poshepny, although a factor for their success, was not the Hmong operational originator.

The Hmong project was primarily the work of CIA paramilitary specialist James W. (Bill) Lair. A veteran of World War II, Lair had joined the CIA at the outbreak of the Korean war. Assigned to Thailand, he had worked as a civilian instructor with the Thai Police Department in a CIA-sponsored program to enhance the organization's ability to deal with threats from Communist insurgents. Attached to the Border Police, Lair soon encountered the problem of assisting remote border outposts. When police units in outlying areas of Thailand were attacked by Communist guerrillas, it often took a week to get reinforcements to the stations. Lair argued that it would be better to have a parachute-trained unit for such emergencies. Although the Thai Army was not happy about the appearance of a paramilitary police organization, Thailand's government approved its creation. Aware of the Army's sensitivity, Lair selected an innocuous name for the new organization: Police Aerial Reinforcement Unit (PARU). (43)

Project 404 would also be responsible for supporting CIA's Air America who was supplying Royal Lao Army troops, Laotian civilians, Thai military, ARMA and AIRA covertly in Laos.

Air America

CIA's Secret Airline 1950-1973

In 1950 the CIA established a covertly owned American passenger and cargo airline to provide supplies for clandestine operations abroad. The airline was originally called Civil Air Transport, or CAT, and acquired from the founder Claire Lee Chennault who was a Flying Tiger pilot. Over the years the airline added front companies including Air Asia Company, Ltd; Civil Air Transport, Inc; Southern Air Transport; Intermountain Aviation; and Bird and Sons until finally establishing the name Air America. The CIA airline slogan was "Anything, Anywhere, Anytime, Professionally" and flew DHC-4 Caribou and Fairchild C-123 Provider cargo planes. Air America possessed bases all across Asia in countries like Japan, Taiwan, Laos, Cambodia and Vietnam. The CIA recruited pilots by offering them hazard pay, which allowed them to make more money than commercial airliners or military airlines offered. Some hazards that faced pilots included limited radio contact, poor weather conditions and terrain, logistic issues and often carrying overloaded cargo. This meant that the pilots needed to be both skilled and what some considered a bit crazy. The biggest hazard facing pilots was enemy fire. Air America pilots, both airplane and helicopter, were targeted and would come under fire almost daily and overtime the occupation became synonymous with the term "down aircraft".

In the early sixties Air America supported CIA Operations Hotfoot and Project 404, and later provided support through insertion and extraction of both U.S. personnel and Royal Lao Army. Air America was also used for search and rescue efforts of downed U.S. military pilots during the war. Within ten years Air America operated more than 80 aircraft with 300 pilots and became the most versatile air support the U.S. in Vietnam. The diverse group of pilots flew missions transporting everything from food, medical supplies and refugees to spies, commandoes and diplomats.

When North Vietnamese forces overran South Vietnam in 1975, Air America helicopters participated in evacuating both South Vietnamese and American civilians from Saigon. The iconic photograph depicting the final evacuation from the "U.S. Embassy" by Dutch photographer Hubert van Es was actually an Air America helicopter taking people off of the CIA station chief's apartment building. C.I.A. employee, O. B. Harnage landed on the roof in a silver Huey helicopter, some people were panicking. Some junior officers and policemen had been allowed in on condition that they use their weapons to keep a crowd milling in the street outside from storming the building. Stationing himself next to a ladder leading onto the roof, Mr. Harnage tried to help the Vietnamese families up. But the first man who appeared, Mr. Harnage recalled, was a Korean who was hysterical and Mr. Harnage punched him out of the way to maintain order. The Huey, the workhorse of the American effort in Vietnam, normally carried about eight passengers, but Mr. Harnage jammed in as many as 15 Vietnamese, and jumped on the helicopter's skid, standing in the open doorway as it flew to Tan Son Nhut on the edge of the city. Mr. Harnage, who was later awarded a C.I.A. medal, made four or five of these flights to the air base, where larger Navy or Air Force helicopters ferried the families to ships waiting in the South China Sea. At a time when America abandoned many Vietnamese allies and South Vietnam's military and political leaders abandoned their own country, it was a heroic act. (44)

After leaving South Vietnam a failed attempt to keep an Air America presence in Thailand, resulted with the official disband on June 30, 1976.

The CIA came under scrutiny through the use of Air America during the Vietnam War because of the importation of heroine allegedly from sources within the Hmong population. To substantiate the claims individuals involved in the operations during that time, including former pilots and the CIA's own Anthony Poshepny confirmed the allegations.

Although the organization has been shrouded in both secrecy and negative overtones with drug trafficking allegations, it is not without supporters. Don Boecker recounted his experience in July of 1965 after ejecting from a craft in Vietnam due to faulty bombing equipment. Boecker admitted he was scared out of his wits and had remained in the thick jungle overnight trying to avoid capture. On the following day he was rescued, but not by the military, but rather by a pilot of Air America.

"Most people don't even know it occurred. It was a secret society," said Boecker in an Associated Press interview. "They flew in all sorts of danger ... flying every day in terrible wartime conditions. They did a beautiful job."

Capture of Che Guevara
National Liberation Army of Bolivia (ELN)

Ernesto "Che" Guevara was an Argentine Marxist revolutionary guerrilla leader who felt the economic inequalities were the result of monopoly capitalism and imperialism. His radical ideology was to counteract the issues facing Latin America by initiating a world revolution. He assisted Fidel Castro in 1956 to invade and overthrow the Cuban dictator Fulgencio Batista. He rose through Castro's ranks and was considered a prolific poet and warfare tactician. In 1965 Che Guevara left Cuba for South America to incite revolutions in the Congo-Kinshasa and later in Bolivia. By August of 1967, Che Guevara and his guerrillas attack efforts against the Bolivian Armed Forces demonstrated a success rate of 30 kills to 1 loss. Two months prior General Ovando, of the Bolivian Armed Forces entered into an agreement with the U.S. Army establishing U.S.-Bolivian Armed Forces training programs. The U.S. believed that Guevara was operating in the area but didn't possess reliable intelligence.

In June of 1967, Cuban-American CIA agent Felix Rodriguez receives a phone call from a CIA officer, Larry S., who proposes a special assignment for him in South America in which he will use his skills in unconventional warfare, counter-guerrilla operations and communications. The assignment is to assist the Bolivians in tracking down and capturing Che Guevara and his band. His partner will be "Eduardo Gonzalez" and Rodriguez is to use the cover name "Felix Ramos Medina." (45)

Felix Ismael Rodriguez Mendigutia was born 1941 in Havana, Cuba. After the Cuban Revolution he and his family became exiles in the United States where he attended Perkiomen Valley Academy, in Pennsylvania. In 1960 he joined a CIA sponsored paramilitary group of Cuban exiles called Brigade 2506 and was involved in the Bay of Pigs invasion.

While in LaPaz, Bolivia Rodriguez and Gonzalez are briefed by CIA station chief John Tilton and create a CIA sponsored Guevara task force. After a successful battle the Bolivian Army captures one of Guevara's guerilla's José Castillo Chavez. Within a week he is interrogated by CIA and the lean that Guevara's health is deteriorating. In September Guevara is tracked to the village of La Hiquera where a battle with the Bolivian Army ensues. Guevara's guerilla's escaped, but not before losing vital members of his group. The CIA suggests for the Bolivian Army to order the newly formed U.S. training Ranger Battalion to Vallegrande. After cordoning off escape routes, the Ranger Battalion began to close in on Guevara's guerilla forces. On October 8, 1967, tips led the Bolivian Rangers to a ravine in Queered del Yoro where they located and engaged the guerilla fighters. Although claims were dispatched of Guevara's death across the Bolivian Army radio, he was alive. He had been struck numerous times in the arm and legs from enemy fire. According to friend Ricardo Rojo, once the Bolivian Rangers started closing in Guevara shouted, "Do not shoot! I am Che Guevara and worth more to you alive than dead."

The following morning CIA's Rodriguez arrived by helicopter in La Higuera. Upon landing Rodriguez photographed documentation including Guevara's diary. Held in a school house, Rodriquez witnessed Guevara tied up on the dirt floor. In one interview, Rodriguez states that, "I had mixed emotions when I first arrived there. Here was the man who had assassinated many of my countrymen. And nevertheless, when I saw him, the way he looked....I felt really sorry for him." (46)

After contacting the CIA station in Brazil, Rodriguez spends time talking to Guevara and even poses for a picture with him. According to Rodriguez, the CIA desired to keep Guevara alive, yet Bolivian high command issued an order for his execution to avoid a trial and possible support for Cuban sympathizers. After advising Guevara of his fate, he passes word to Rodriguez to be delivered to his wife and Fidel Castro. Although there are several accounts of who actually killed Guevara, the Department of Defense report states: "When Sgt. Terán (the executioner) enters the room, Guevara stands up with his hands tied and states, "I know what you have come for I am ready." Terán tells him to be seated and leaves the room for a few moments. While Terán was outside, Sgt. Huacka enters another small house, where "Willy" was being held, and shoots him. When Terán comes back, Guevara stands up and refuses to be seated saying: "I will remain standing for this." Terán gets angry and tells Guevara to be seated again. Finally, Guevara tells him: "Know this now, you are killing a man." Terán fires his M2 Carbine and kills him."

Shortly after the execution, Rodriguez and senior army officials fled La Higuera, while Che's body was flown to Vallegrande to be fingerprinted. The following day Guevara's death certificate was filed stating his cause of death was multiple bullet wounds to the thorax and extremities resulting in hemorrhaging. On October 14th officials of the Argentine Federal police visited Bolivian military headquarters in La Paz and identified the two amputated hands in formaldehyde through fingerprinting as those of Che Guevara. Thirty years later his body was returned to Cuba, where a ceremony attended by Castro and thousands of Cubans, celebrated his return.

Operation BLACK SHIELD

Lockheed's A-12 & SR-71 Blackbird

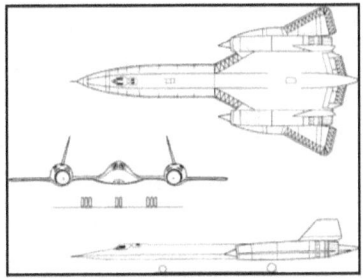

In the 1950s preliminary work began from Lockheed's Skunk Works on a project called "Archangel", which would be a successor for the CIA's U-2 program, known as "Angel". Through the next few years designer Clarence "Kelly" Johnson's team progressed with multiple designs including Archangel-1, Archangel-2, etc. By the late 1950s the design references where cut down to single letters referred to as A-1, A-2 until they completed their twelfth design A-12. In 1960 the CIA approved the design and ordered production of the A-12 through a project code named OXCART. The Lockheed A-12 reconnaissance aircraft, the precursor for the SR-71 Blackbird, was produced at the Skunk Works, in Burbank, California. Upon completed production, the A-12 was transferred to Groom Lake test facility in late April of 1962. The first test flight took place on April 30th with pilot Lou Schalk and in May 1962 the A-12 reached supersonic speed with a test flight that reached a speed of Mach 1.1. The original A-12 was equipped with Pratt & Whitney J75 engines enabling the craft to reach speeds of Mach 2.0, but changed in 1963 to newly developed J58 engines. The J58 engines obtained speeds of Mach 3.2 and would remain the engine for the remainder of production. By the summer of 1964 the last of the CIA ordered A-12's were delivered where they recorded over 2,500 test flights from Groom Lake.

Although the craft was originally designed to replace the U-2, with the advancements of satellites the CIA no longer felt the plane was needed to penetrate Soviet airspace. Three A-12s were deployed to Kadena Air Base, Okinawa, Japan in May of 1967 where the units formed Operation BLACK SHIELD. For the next two years Operation BLACK SHIELD flew several missions over Vietnam providing image analysis through photographing Surface-to-Air Missile (SAM) sites. The design of the A-12 earned the nickname "Habu" by the locals in Okinawa due to the craft's resemblance to a cobra viper snake. In 1966 the CIA closed down the A-12 program prior to the craft's first mission. In 1968 the A-12 was retired and replaced by the SR-71 Blackbird. The pilots of A-12 during Operation BLACK SHIELD were presented the CIA Intelligence Star for valor.

In March of 1968 the SR-71 arrived in Kadena Airbase, Okinawa, Japan and soon started reconnaissance missions over North Vietnam under the program "Senior Crown." Prior testing for the SR-71 was conducted out of Air Force Plant 42 in Palmdale, California in 1964 and later Beale Air Force Base, California in 1966. The design of the SR-71 was unique due to many factors including the use of titanium. The craft was also the first to use stealth technology. Some of the added features to reduce radar absorption included saw tooth shaped sections of the craft's skin and cesium-based fuel additives reducing exhaust plumes. Since the SR-71 was a black project for national security reasons, it was often targeted through the senate. In the 1970s the program was closed due to costs associated and the refusal to share the entire programs ability in fear of tipping the hand to the Soviet Union. The program was reinstated in the 1980s for a short time and an attempt was made to use in Operation Desert Storm. The program and the SR-71 Blackbird were retired in 1998.

Although the SR-71 lost many crafts throughout the years, none were ever recovered by an enemy and only one crew member, Jim Zwayer, was killed during the program. The SR-71 had flown more than 3,500 sortie missions, 11,000 flight hours, and logged over 2,700 Mach 3.0 mission hours during its activation. Through its activation the SR-71 Blackbird remained the fastest and highest operating manned aircraft in the world. From an altitude of 80,000 ft (24 km), it could survey 100,000 square miles (260,000 km2) per hour (72 square kilometers per second) of the Earth's surface. On March 6, 1990 SR-71 set a coast-to-coast aircraft speed record traveling from Palmdale, California, to Chantilly, Virginia in 67 minutes 54 seconds, at an average speed 2,125 mph. In 1974 the SR-71 flew from New York to London in 1 hour 54 minutes and 56.4 seconds and still holds the record for that flight.

With the enhanced ability of Satellites, CIA had limited use for craft such as the SR-71, although there are current uses for targeted locations where intelligence is needed. Many speculate the new craft as many different versions, with the most popular being the Aurora, CIA for national security purposes has not yet declassified any information.

Phoenix Program
CIA/MACV-SOG Covert Action

In 1964 through the Civil Operations and Revolutionary Development Support, or CORDS, the U.S. had begun training indigenous soldiers and building a peasant militia. After the TET offensive the United States policy makers and military officials realized Vietnam could not be won through conventional warfare but rather through the people and at a political level.  Vietnam would be fought on two fronts with a formal military and guerrilla tactics. The CIA philosophy was to remove the VC threat by making the Vietnamese people resist the VC guerrillas so they in time prove ineffective and fade away. This was to be accomplished by embarking on the largest CIA operation in its history and creating their guerrilla army.

Within the program CIA used counter terror teams for seek and destroy missions of National Liberation Front of South Vietnam (NLF or Viet Cong). By 1967 the CORDS group was 500,000 strong and the counter terror group broke-off into the Phoenix Program. The primary objective was to gather intelligence of the Viet Cong infrastructure (VCI), which was a secret network that provided the direction and control of the war within the villages, tunnels and hamlets of South Vietnam. CIA believed that by 1967 there was 100,000 VCI members and had strategically placed personnel in most every village in South Vietnam. VCI's most powerful asset was their spy network across the entire country. The VCI gained information from cab drivers, bartenders and prostitutes on a regular basis providing bits and pieces of information learned from American soldiers. VCI members provide the information to their selected operator, who in return would pass up the chain and transmit orders from the Lao Dong Party Central Committee in North Vietnam. The VCI was a vital support arm for the NLF by providing caches of food and equipment for troops. The plan was to identify, capture, interrogate and if necessary kill the people running the undercover war - the Vietcong command structure. For this to succeed, CIA decided to enter the war at a village level. This decision was also supported because it would cause less death and destruction than conventional warfare tactics.

The CIA sponsored program was formed as a military intelligence operation, but soon added internal security to its list of tasks. The program was carried out by Republic of Vietnam security, Navy SEALS, and U.S. Army Green Berets. Eventually the program would be carried out also by MACV-SOG to identify and neutralize civilian infrastructure supporting the NLF insurgency. MACV-SOG, Military Assistance Command, Vietnam - Studies and Observations Group, was a classified U.S. special operations unit that conducted covert action using unconventional warfare both prior and during the Vietnam War. The unit was modeled after the Central Intelligence Agency (CIA) Special Activities Division (SAD) developed prior, including paramilitary and indigenous trained commando teams. Created in 1964, MACV-SOG conducted strategic reconnaissance missions in South Vietnam, North Vietnam, Laos, and Cambodia using clandestine agent team activities and psychological operations.

The CIA created and advised the Phoenix Program to be carried out by South Vietnamese teams. A Vietnamese peasant Tran Ngoc Chau had gained valuable intelligence as a province chief in his village. CIA William Colby was impressed with his tactics of obtaining information and met with Chau in Vietnam. Chau believed in trying to convert communist peasants into nationalists whenever possible but if unsuccessful implement strong measures. Those measures included Chau creating three man terror teams to assassinate communists in his province. The CIA provided weapons, explosives and communications for the teams. In addition CIA provided Chau money to reward his teams including 20 pounds for killing a Vietcong village official and 30 pounds for killing a district officer. Teams were trained at the Vung Tau training camp. The CIA had overseen the training and built originally more than fifty three man teams. Each three man team was comprised of a team leader, a psychological warfare specialist, and an intelligence officer. The camp was run by CIA Robert Komer with training provided by both CIA and U.S. Special Forces. Once graduated from training the teams would be deployed to operate in the countryside.

Once intelligence was gathered, often through interrogation, the VCI member would become a prisoner of war or killed. U.S. involvement was to be the intelligence part of the equation, leaving the South Vietnamese security and police to handle the wet work. Neutralization was not expected to be arbitrary but rather to take place under special laws that allowed the arrest and prosecution of suspected communists, but only within the legal system. To avoid abuses such as phony accusations for personal reasons, or to rein in overzealous officials who might not be diligent enough in pursuing evidence before making arrests, the laws required three separate sources of evidence to convict any individual targeted for neutralization. If a suspected VCI was found guilty, he or she could be held in prison for two years, with renewable two-year sentences totaling up to six years. (47) This practice soon fell by the wayside as the program grew and became more of a death squad than intelligence apparatus. The program was to provide daily intelligence to all available CIA resources and assets to identify targets for capture or assassination. Critics opposed to the program felt the CIA quotas initiated to the teams were a major downfall to the accuracy of captured and murdered targets. To increase accuracy CIA recruited Asian American Special Forces soldiers whom could pass as Vietnamese to assist with Phoenix teams.

During the TET Offensive in 1968, CIA fully understood the power of the VCI. In a short period of time the NLF had organized simultaneous attacks on over one hundred strategic targets including villages and U.S. bases. This raised a red flag among the military and urged CIA to step up the Phoenix Program to assist in destroying the VCI. Villages that were loyal to the Saigon government were subject to elders assassinations by North Vietnamese forces or NLF guerrillas. A clear message was sent that anyone supporting the Saigon government would be executed. In 1969 over one thousand South Vietnamese citizens were targeted and assassinated including three hundred village leaders.

"We had quotas for absolutely everything," CIA Director, William Colby. "Phoenix, like other programs, was issued quotas. We ran much of the war on numbers. And as a way of stimulating the local officers into paying attention to the matter that was the way we stimulated them. There was an enemy that was several tens of thousands and we'd like to see people captured or defect or if necessary killed." (17)

"The problem was how do you find the people on the blacklist? It's not like you had their address and telephone number," explained Vincent Okamoto. Okamoto was born to an American family of Japanese origin. In 1968, Lieutenant Okamoto was assigned as the intelligence-liaison officer for 2 months for the

Phoenix Program while attached to Company B of the 2nd Battalion, 25th Infantry Division.

"The normal procedure would be to go into a village and just grab someone and say, 'Where's Nguyen so-and-so?' Half the time the people were so afraid they would say anything. Then a Phoenix team would take the informant, put a sandbag over his head, poke out two holes so he could see, put ammo wire around his neck like a long leash, and walk him through the village and say, 'When we go by Nguyen's house scratch your head.' Then that night Phoenix would come back, knock on the door, and say, 'April Fool, motherfucker.' Whoever answered the door would get wasted. As far as they were concerned whoever answered was a Communist, including family members. Sometimes they'd come back to camp with ears to prove that they killed people."

One former Phoenix member stated, "We were assassination squads. We would go to their homes in the middle of the night and either abduct them or assassinate them. In general we were a death squad. We were to be sure about the elimination of our target. If we were not sure we would take the next hut to the right and the next hut to the left. Sometimes we would hit the wrong village. If our mark was tagged for extermination it would be identified with a red stripe on the dossier - he was a walking corpse. As soon as you walk in you start shooting. You kill everyone whether they're armed or not. I'm going god I'm playing god here." (17)

"First we would get a photo of the man or drawings. The kind of drawings they have in police stations and if we couldn't find this person we would get someone that looks like him and bring him back. And most of the time you cannot really carry a corpse for miles at a time so one of the most sadist Asian things to do was to just bring the head back to prove that you got him. Intimidation was what Phoenix was all about shock and intimidation. In a sense we were terrorists. Instead of being counter terrorists we were terrorists."

"I consider myself a warrior born on both the Chinese side and apache side. I'm a warrior from warrior stock but there was no honor in my war. It's kind of hard to accept from being a soldier to being an assassin for hire...and from being an assassin for hire to being a murderer. The playing cards were like a warning sign. Almost like a calling card just to let them know who did it. My favorite card was the Ace of Spades."

The CIA desired for the program to perform a surgical strike vs. a broad military action. Unfortunately through the program there was often extensive use of firepower. In addition, the civilian population became very indifferent to the U.S. due to random searches and long detentions of non NLF personnel. Intelligence was the key to the program so interrogation and torture was often a key role in gathering information.

"The CIA was tolerant of torture in Vietnam it also participated in it on occasion in some of the interrogation centers," John Stockwell, CIA. Stockwell was awarded the CIA Medal of Merit for keeping his post open until the last days of the fall of Saigon in 1975. "As a matter of policy it had to deny it. In my own experience when I moved to Tay Ninh I found the police chief using are safe house to carve up prisoners who didn't have family protection. I reported in a discreet memo to Tom Polgar the Chief of Station and his response was to have me down for a cocktail party and quietly in the garden, a nice man, explained to me that he couldn't close the post down that it was to important. He couldn't get the man transferred because that would be interfering in Vietnamese affairs so all he could think to do was to transfer me and he pointed out that would seriously damage my career. So I went back to Tay Ninh and closed the safe house down put out the word to my staff that I vigorously disapproved the torture so no one mentioned to me again for my two years in country. By suppressing it so that no one would talk about it I could pretend I had stopped it or maybe curtailed it and proceeded to work with this monster the next two years on a very intimate basis." (17)

"You know I thought I was with the first team," CIA officer Orrin DeForest. "Plenty of money, logistics support anything I needed to accomplish the effort of developing spies. That's the name of the game. I was appalled when I realized my inquires along the line had nothing. No spies no evidence or indication that they understood where the enemy was and if you don't know this you can't effectively interrogate anyone."

Forty four provincial interrogation centers or "PICS" were designed and created by CIA. Interrogators often used electric shock to inflict pain and terror to extract information. Clips would be attached to ears, lips, nipples or other body parts and currents of electricity would be increased and decreased often to the point of the subject losing consciousness from pain.

"None of the PICS worked, "explained DeForest. "All that we ever got of them was - I don't know. I don't know. I don't know. They denied everything. In fact I never found one that was identified as a class A VC from a village. I never found one in any of the PICS in military region three. Useless. Totally useless." (17)

According to one view, Phoenix was a clear success. Between 1968 and 1972, Phoenix neutralized 81,740 NLF members, of whom 26,369 were killed. This was a large section taken out of the VCI and, between 1969 and 1971; the program was quite successful in destroying the infrastructure in many important areas. By 1970, Communist plans repeatedly emphasized attacking the government's pacification program and specifically targeted Phoenix officials. The NLF also imposed quotas. In 1970, for example, Communist officials near Da Nang in northern South Vietnam instructed their assassins to "kill 400 persons" deemed to be government "tyrant[s]" and to "annihilate" anyone involved with the pacification program. Several North Vietnamese officials have made statements about the effectiveness of Phoenix. In the end, it was a direct conventional North Vietnamese military invasion, not the guerrilla insurgents that defeated the South Vietnamese. (47)

Some feel the program was a failure due to its inability to eradicate the VCI to the point of rendering non-effective. Others feel the program was corrupt and violated human rights through the assassinations committed and the vast amounts of people exterminated over the course of the program. Although the Phoenix Program did assist in gathering important information, it came at a point too late to turn the tide of the war and concluded official operation in 1972.

In 1969 Frank Snepp was tasked to put together hit lists of VC for Phoenix to target while working at the U.S. Embassy in Saigon. Smith seen first-hand how Phoenix PRUs would turn what was supposed to be a surgical strike assassination into a public blood bath with many innocent victims.

"I remember totaling up the amount of kills we had made with Phoenix operations and had discovered that the number of kills far exceeded the shrinkage of the communist apparatus," CIA officer, Frank Snepp. "In other words we were killing somebody but they weren't communist cadre. The sin is that once we realized we were hitting the wrong people we didn't stop." (17)

The CIA occupied the top three floors of the U.S. Embassy in Saigon. This made the location at one time the largest CIA station in the world and the last building abandoned at the end of the war. Through CIA issued diamond radios many Vietnamese were requesting help. According to CIA officer Smith, the primary radio room in the Embassy during the evacuation was haunted by the radio traffic of pleas coming from those around Vietnam.

"Americans are not good losers and planning for a loss is not part of the American mentality," Tom Polgar, CIA chief of station. "There was no contingency plan for giving up Vietnam. In fact we had no plan to evacuate any Vietnamese at all. When a person decides to work for CIA that doesn't mean CIA assumes the role as guardian over his future fait. It's an adult person and he makes a conscious decision and knows there are certain risks connected with the decision. We didn't have a bunch of innocent virgins here we seduced." (17)

During the afternoon of the final evacuation day classified documents of CIA that had been shredded had broken from the bags they were placed and blown across the exterior of the Embassy. The material, some sensitive, was later pieced together by Communist VC. In addition, files naming CIA officers and assets were also left behind and intercepted from Vietnamese intelligence allies.

"When I joined the Agency I was a right winged cold warrior and looked at the Communist movement as an anti-Christ out to destroy the world," CIA Officer Ralph McGehee. "However, when I came out to Vietnam my own ideological set of cards collapsed and I began to see the program from a new perspective. It was a murder program an assassination program designed to force the people to accept an American controlled government." (17)

Operation MHCHAOS
Domestic Surveillance and Eavesdropping

Operation MHCHAOS, also known as Operation CHAOS was the Central Intelligence Agency's domestic espionage project. Although officially established in 1967, the origins of the operation can be traced to 1959 when President Dwight D. Eisenhower used the CIA to "sound out" the

Richard Helms

exiles that were fleeing Cuba after the triumph of Fidel Castro's revolution. Most were wealthy educated professionals looking for a sympathetic ear in the United States. The CIA sought contacts in the exile community and began to recruit many of them for future use against Castro. This U.S.-based recruiting operation was arguably illegal, although Eisenhower forced FBI Director J. Edgar Hoover to accept it as a legitimate CIA function concealed from Congress.

According to Verne Lyon, a former CIA undercover operative, the CIA's Office of Security was monitoring other groups at this time and had recruited agents within different émigré organizations. The CIA considered this a normal extension of its authorized infiltration of dissident groups abroad even though the activity was taking place within the U.S. Increased use of the CIA's contacts and agents among the Cuban exiles became commonplace until mass, open recruitment of mercenaries for what was to be the ill-fated Bay of Pigs invasion was no longer a secret in southern Florida or Fidel Castro.

This activity led the CIA to establish proprietary companies, fronts, and covers for its domestic operations. So widespread did they become that President Lyndon B. Johnson allowed the then CIA Director, John McCone, to create in 1964 a new super-secret branch called the Domestic Operations Division (DOD), the very title of which mocked the explicit intent of Congress to prohibit CIA operations inside the U.S. In the classified document creating the DOD, the scope of its activities was to "exercise centralized responsibility for the direction, support, and coordination of clandestine operational activities within the United States...." One of those was burglarizing foreign diplomatic sites at the request of the National Security Agency (NSA). The CIA also expanded the role of its Domestic Contact Service (DCS), an operation designed to brief and debrief selected American citizens who had traveled abroad in sensitive areas of intelligence interest. Because the interviews took place in airports between the aircraft and customs and immigration control, the operations were not technically considered domestic. The DCS also helped with travel control by monitoring the arrivals and departures of U.S. nationals and foreigners. (48)

In April 1965, Johnson appointed Vice-Admiral William Raborn CIA Director (DCI, or Director of Central Intelligence) and Richard Helms Deputy Director. Since Raborn's days at the helm of be CIA seemed numbered from the outset, he never really became involved in the nuts and bolts of domestic operations; that was left to Helms, a career intelligence officer who had come up through the ranks (he had been Deputy Director for Plans (DDP) since 1962 and Deputy DCI from 1965-66) and who could be trusted. Helms became DCI in June 1966. As Deputy Director, he had allowed the CIA slowly to expand its domestic intelligence operations and understood his orders from President Johnson were to collect intelligence on college and university campuses with no governing guidelines other than "don't get caught." Helms now had a free hand to implement Johnson's orders and, by August 1967, the illegal collection of domestic intelligence had become so large and widespread that he was forced to create a Special Operations Group (SOG). The SOG was imbedded in the DDP's counterintelligence division and provided, data on the U.S. peace movement to the Office of Current Intelligence on a regular basis. (49) By the end of 1967 President Johnson continued efforts with the project to expose foreign influences to the U.S. anti-war movement in universities. CHAOS was then overseen by DCI Richard Helms and the chief of counter-intelligence James J. Angleton. The CIA continued to gather intelligence from stations abroad through the use of physical surveillance and electronic eavesdropping.

As campus anti-war protest activity spread, the CIA reacted by implementing two new domestic operations. The first, Project RESISTANCE, was designed to provide security to CIA recruiters on college campuses. Under this program, the CIA sought active cooperation from college administrators, campus security, and local police to help identify anti-war activists, political dissidents, and "radicals." Eventually information was provided to all government recruiters on college campuses and directly to the super-secret DOD on thousands of students and dozens of groups. The CIA's Office of Security also created Project MERRIMAC, to provide warnings about demonstrations being carried out against CIA facilities or personnel in the Washington area. Under both Projects, the CIA infiltrated agents into domestic groups of all types and activities. It used its contacts with local police departments and their intelligence units to pick up its "police skills" and began in earnest to pull off burglaries, illegal entries, and use of explosives, criminal frame-ups, shared interrogations, and disinformation. CIA teams purchased sophisticated equipment for many starved police departments and in return got to see arrest records, suspect lists, and intelligence reports. Many large police departments, in conjunction with the CIA, carried out illegal, warrantless searches of private properties, to provide intelligence for a report requested by President Johnson and later entitled "Restless Youth."

SOG was being directed by Richard Ober, a CIA person with an established record of domestic intelligence operations in academia. When Ramparts magazine disclosed the relationship between the National Student Association and the CIA in early 1967, Ober was assigned to investigate the magazine's staff members, their friends, and possible connections with foreign intelligence agencies. In July 1968, Helms decided to consolidate all CIA domestic intelligence operations under one program and title. The new operation was called CHAOS and Ober was in charge. Its activities greatly expanded from then on at the urging not only of President Johnson, but also his main advisers Dean Rusk and Walt Rostow. Both men were convinced that Hoover was right and foreign intelligence agencies were involved in anti-war protests in the U.S. Johnson was not convinced and wanted the CIA's intelligence in order to compare it with that provided by the FBI.

After President Richard D. Nixon took office in January 1969 he expanded the domestic surveillance activities funding CIA to increase man power of both case officers and assets. These individuals increased their efforts to include infiltrating antiwar groups through informants. In addition to Students for a Democratic Society and Black Panther Party, the program evolved over the course of a couple years to include left-wing groups with no connection to the Vietnam War. In addition to CHAOS, CIA purged intelligence gathered from other programs such as HTLINGUAL.

Helms continued operations with the assurance that nothing would ever be leaked to the public. But he began to face pressure from two opposing factions within the CIA community. One wanted to expand domestic operations even more, while the other reminded him that Operation CHAOS and similar activities were well "over the line" of illegality and outside the CIA's charter. To put a damper on this internal dissent, Helms ordered Ober to stop discussing these activities with his direct boss in counterintelligence, James J. Angleton. The internal protests continued, however, as White House aide and staunch anti-Communist Tom Charles Huston, pressed for ever increasing domestic operations.

Huston was eager to expand Operation CHAOS to include overseas agents and to "share" intelligence with the FBI's intelligence division, directed by William Sullivan. There were more than fifty CHAOS agents now, many receiving several weeks of assignment and training positions to establish their covers as radicals. Once they returned to the U.S. and enrolled in colleges and universities, they had the proper "credentials."

In June 1970 Nixon met with Hoover, Helms, NSA Director Admiral Noel Gaylor, and Defense Intelligence Agency (DIA) representative Lt. Gen. Donald V. Bennett and told them he wanted a coordinated and concentrated effort against domestic dissenters. To do that, he was creating the Interagency Committee on Intelligence (ICI), chaired by Hoover. The first ICI report, in late June, recommended new efforts in "black bag operations," wiretapping, and a mail-opening program. In late July 1970, Huston told the members of the ICI that their recommendations had been accepted by the White House.

John Dean replaced Tom Huston as White House aide in charge of domestic intelligence, and at his urging a Justice Department group, the Intelligence Evaluation Committee, was established to study domestic groups, over Hoover's protest. Deteriorating relations between the FBI and the other intelligence agencies, especially the CIA, caused Hoover to fire William Sullivan. At that time, Sullivan was the liaison officer between the FBI and the other intelligence agencies and he strongly favored the expansion of domestic operations.

Even Helms began to have second thoughts about how large CHAOS had grown, but Nixon made it clear to him that the CIA was a presidential tool he wanted at his disposal. Helms got the message, yet he also understood the growing uneasiness in other government circles. In 1972, the CIA's Inspector General wrote a report that expressed concern about Operation CHAOS in the following way: "... we also encountered general concern over what appeared to be a monitoring of the political views and activities of Americans not known to be or suspected of being involved in espionage ... Stations were asked to report on the whereabouts and activities of prominent persons ... whose comings and goings were not only in the public domain, but for whom allegations of subversion seemed sufficiently nebulous to raise renewed doubts as to the nature and legitimacy of the CHAOS program."

Helms was being squeezed by White House demands to expand Operation CHAOS and the fear that the whole question of domestic operations was going to become public knowledge, as Hoover feared. Helms found himself constantly shoring up one lie with another and then another. He found himself deceiving Congress and lying to the public as well as CIA employees. In March 1971, a group of young CIA executives known as the Management Advisory Group (MAG) protested Operation CHAOS and similar domestic operations by issuing a statement saying, "MAG opposes any Agency activity which could be construed as targeted against any person who enjoys the protection of the U.S. Constitution ... whether or not he resides in the United States." (50)

The operation began to unravel in the summer of 1972 when Howard Osborn, then Chief of Security for the CIA, informed Helms that two former CIA officers, E. Howard Hunt and James McCord, were involved in a burglary at the Watergate complex in Washington, D.C. Helms appointed CIA Executive

Director William Colby to handle any investigations into the Agency's domestic operations prior to his termination at Camp David by President Nixon. In July 1973 William Colby took over as DCI and decided that Operation CHAOS and Project RESISTANCE should be terminated.

In 1975 the CIA underwent public investigation and scrutiny by both the Church and Rockefeller committees. These investigations revealed considerable evidence showing that the CIA had carried out its activities with a tremendous disregard for the law, both in the U.S. and abroad. After the Rockefeller Commission the DCI, George H. W. Bush acknowledged that the program and CIA had improperly accumulated domestic data on the American people.

During the life of Operation CHAOS, the CIA had compiled personality files on over 13,000 individuals including more than 7,000 U.S. citizens as well as files on over 1,000 domestic groups. The CIA had shared information on more than 300,000 persons with different law enforcement agencies including the DIA and FBI. It had spied on, burglarized, intimidated, misinformed, lied to, deceived, and carried out criminal acts against thousands of citizens of the United States and violated its charter and may have contributed either directly or indirectly to the resignation of a President of the United States.

Project SCANETE
Clairvoyance and Psychic Phenomena

In 1970 CIA started a number of programs that explored the potential of military and domestic applications through the use of psychic phenomena. Under the operational name Stargate Project, the U.S. Federal Government tapped the CIA to investigate the reality of remote viewing,  the alleged ability to psychically vision events, sites, or information from a great distance. The CIA had interests in the subject during World War II after rumors surfaced of Nazi's developing ESP (Extra-sensory perception) capabilities. Both MI6 and CIA felt that ESP existed but could be either understood or controlled. Interest surfaced again in 1970 when SRI discovered a Soviet video of a man moving inanimate objects with his mind. The video was shared with CIA and the relationship and Stargate Project was born. The CIA piggybacked on research that had been conducted from The Stanford Research Institute (SRI) and The American Society for Psychical Research. Dr. Harold Puthoff and Dr. Russell Targ of (SRI) and Ingo Swann of (ASPR) worked towards developing the Coordinate Remote Viewing (CRV). Although skeptical, CIA and military intelligence sources pursued research into the origins of psychic capabilities by sponsoring the researchers for $50,000 under Project SCANETE. Annually the agency would review and research sub-projects to determine feasibility. Work results were reviewed, and remote viewing was demonstrated with the results being kept secret from the "viewer". It was thought that if the viewer was shown they were incorrect it would damage the viewer's confidence and skill. This was standard operating procedure throughout the years of military and domestic remote viewing programs. Feedback of any kind, back to the viewer was very rare. It was kept classified and secret. (51)

Through establishing protocols, the CIA practiced remote viewing attempts through subjects to sense unknown information about places or events. Most commonly the practice is for current events, but intelligence purposes were to see if subjects could sense or visualize situations in the future, referred to as precognition. The CIA focused on separating the science from the hokum to minimize the chance of false clairvoyant accusation. The project possessed numerous labs and was considered a last resort for actual live or mission status. Stargate was only used when conventional intelligence practices had been exhausted.

The program included approximately twenty viewers during its heyday, and CIA found that the accuracy level of results offered fell into the 20% realm. This meant that 80% of the time the viewers were wrong and depending on the information could greatly jeopardize the safety, time and cost of an intelligence operation if weighed in on through this process. The project did produce successful results including Joseph McMoneagle's predictions of launch dates for newly constructed submarines in 1980. His prediction was made several months prior to the actual launch. In addition, Keith Harary offered vision of the hostages released in the Middle East weeks prior to their decision and the early release of hostage Richard Queen due to illness.

One viewer Pat Price was given the coordinates to a Soviet facility that CIA was familiar with. The goal was to see if Price could provide details of the facility and demonstrate how accurate his visions. Price viewed a USSR map after given the logistics and then proceeded to view the area. While he accurately targeted a crane and described it in some detail, he completely missed the oil derricks, which the Agency new existed.

Despite the failure to reveal the derricks, it was decided to continue the experiment with Price. Price now met with a CIA official for the first time: Dr. Kenneth Kress, an engineer with OTS who had worked intimately on the project. Kress asked Price why he had not seen the derricks. Price responded that they used to be there but had since been dismantled. New reconnaissance of area was done. It was shown that the derricks were in fact still there.

Again, despite this setback experiments continued. Price was then asked to view the interiors of certain embassies of which the CIA had knowledge. Again and again Price provided some exceedingly accurate details combined with a number of errors. Unfortunately during these experiments Pat Price passed away of a heart attack. (52)

Based upon collected findings, which recommended a higher level of critical research and tighter controls, the CIA terminated the 20 million dollar project, citing a lack of documented evidence that the program had any value to the intelligence community with three full-time psychics were still working on a $500,000-a-year budget out of Fort Meade, Maryland, which would soon close up shop. (53)

Although the 20 years of research has produced split decisions on whether the program was truly a success, the CIA felt that the results didn't produce enough accuracy to maintain the cost and resources needed for the project to continue. Project SCANETE spawned other agencies to invest into psychic research including the Defense Intelligence Agency (DIA) with operations including Sun Streak, Grill Flame, and Center Lane. The United States Army continues research today under a private company they fund called Psi Tech.

Operation Tailwind

Covert Diversion Action in Laos

In an attempt to turn the tide on the Vietnam War and exert pressure on the occupied forces of the People's Army of Vietnam (PAVN), the CIA planned a covert incursion into southeastern Laos. The plan, called Operation Tailwind,  called for U.S. Army Special Forces and CIA SAT forces, of MACV-SOG, accompanied by indigenous forces to form a Hatchet Force and create diversions for a Royal Lao Army offensive. Hatchet Forces were special operations teams of American and South Vietnamese members who carried out small covert operations such as search and destroy missions; sabotage operations and in locating MIA's in Laos, Cambodia and North Vietnam. Hatchet Force usually consisted of three American Special Forces soldiers and twenty to thirty indigenous soldiers whose primary goal was to seek out the enemy and pick a fight.

Operation Tailwind consisted of a Hatchet Force in size of sixteen Americans and 110 indigenous Montagnard tribesmen whom were inserted by helicopter 60 miles west of Dak To to an LZ. This was 20 miles beyond the authorized military operating area. The teams were led by Captain Eugene McCarley and focused on seeking out enemy troop dispositions and calling in air strikes to U.S. Air Force Pathfinders. To remain as undetected and mobile as possible, the teams continued to move through the nights and on day three encountered heavy opposition resulting in more than 140 PAVN soldiers' deaths. After the engagement, the team located a bunker containing maps and documents in two footlockers and realized they had just discovered a PAVN headquarters. With North Vietnamese closing in on the team's position, McCarley ordered the group to split into three smaller teams and established separate extraction points. This action was productive in confusing the enemy. During a firefight with approximately 140-150 of the enemy, nine U.S. soldiers were injured and the evacuation was delayed due to weather. Combat continued throughout the evening and during one rescue attempt a CH-53 helicopter was shot down by B-40 rocket rounds resulting in a failed medivac. During the extraction the U.S. Air Force used chemical agents similar to tear gas against the North Vietnamese to provide cover. When the extractions were completed the Hatchet Team had lost three Montagnards and sustained several injuries, including all of the American Forces. Later the SOG medic Sergeant Gary Rose was recommended for the Medal of Honor.

Year's later accusations would become public that the gas used on the extraction was sarin nerve gas, which would have been a breach of international treaties through NATO. Witnesses stated that gas was used but it was a form of tear gas rather than nerve gas. CNN and Time magazine accused the U.S. of using sarin nerve gas on both Vietnamese and American soldiers in Laos who had been deserters and the result was the death of over one hundred men, woman and children. After separate Pentagon and CNN investigations, the media company retracted their story claiming that the reporting had been flawed using sources that were not in their best mental state of mind. The producers were later terminated.

Project FUBELT

1970 Chilean Coup Attempt

Concerned over elections of the Chilean government, President Richard D. Nixon authorized a ten million dollar covert operation to the CIA to prevent the placement or overthrow leadership to Chile of Salvador Allende. The operation,  called Project FUBELT, was ordered to be carried out without coordination with the Department of State or Defense. The operation was headed by the DDP Thomas Karamessines in association with operational leadership including CIA's chief William Broe of the Western Hemisphere Division. Prior to the operation Karamessine had learned that General Roberto Viaux Marambio had plans for a coup and were already viewed by the agency. Viaux, who had attempted a coup against President Eduardo Frei Montalva the year prior, had planned his second aimed at Salvador Allende. The CIA sent word to Viaux that after review of his plan it was to be called off. The CIA felt that there was only a 5% chance that the coup could be pulled off successfully and decided to abort the original plan. The agency advised Viaux to maintain assets and that the U.S. would offer support when the time was right. Karamessine, on direction from Henry Kissinger, increased agency assets in Chile to procure intelligence for future plans.

In September of 1970 the CIA established a task force in Chile and withdrew four CIA officers from their selected outposts. The officers were selected because of their appearance, language and experience and ability to masquerade as foreign nationals in the country of Chile. The officers were briefed in Washington, D.C. and individually inserted into Chile within three days. The only CIA contact was the station chief in Santiago where at the chief's residence planning with current Chilean military support met in the coup planning stages. The CIA embarked on pressuring the Chilean government to support Jorge Alessandri through mobilizing an extensive propaganda campaign against Allende. In addition, CIA worked with the military to increase pressure against Allende through rumoring a military coup would be eminent if he were to come to power.

The propaganda campaign was designed to increase fear among the Chilean people with Allende participating in media intimidation through assassination threats, takeovers of worker organizations and ultimatums to radio and newspapers as means of smothering any opposition and strong arming his position to power. The CIA worked with "El Morcurio", the most popular Chilean newspaper, and produced news articles that Allende had been attacking the freedom of the press. "Freedom of the press is strangled by Communist and Marxists forces." Additional cables were dispatched to other press outlets including the Associated Press for World coverage. By September 28, 1970, CIA used 23 different asset journalists from 15 separate countries to spread the disinformation for the propaganda campaign. Unfortunately the tactics ceased by the end of September and CIA was faced to create new propaganda efforts. Additional resources were used including the funding of an underground press for direct mailings; the financing of a small Chilean newspaper; creating an anti-Allende radio program; political rallies and advertisements. U.S. journalists were also briefed to influence U.S. media, although a Time cover story that provided much of the back story actually drew public outrage by Allende stating the magazine was calling for an invasion of Chile.

The CIA goal was to create a panic to President Eduardo Frei Montalva to realize that both the people of Chile and military would up rise against Allende's appointment on November 3, 1970 if he were to win the election. CIA orchestrated additional efforts to plea on Fei's intervention including Christian organizations denouncing Marxism and pleading for Frei's intervention. The United States also encouraged Frei by offering any support needed for him to maintain office since Alessandri support was less than desired. Unfortunately Frei never asserted himself even with all of the support and influence thus leaving CIA to go scrap Operation Track I and move forward with the planning of the military coup, which was named Operation Track II.

By early October of 1970 the CIA faced a number of issues regarding the military support. Much of the military was loyal to serving the Chilean Constitution and feared Chile's Army Commander, General Rene Schneider. There were also pro-Allende supporters and those in the military who believed that his acceptance of office would have little effect on their positions.

In an effort to remove General Schneider from power, CIA sponsored a kidnapping attempt to be carried out by loyal General Viaux supporters. After a clandestine meeting with two Chilean military officers, a Chilean CIA asset expressed confidence in the abduction plans. Two contacts loyal to General Roberto Viaux had failed in prior attempts due to intelligence blunders but were confident they could carry out the mission. On October 21, 1970 three sterile .45 caliber grease guns requested by the asset arrived at the Chilean CIA Station in Santiago through normal courier service. After providing the arms to the asset, they were delivered to the two Chilean officers who prepared for the attempted kidnapping. On the evening of October 22, the plotters ambushed General René Schneider's vehicle in the capital city of Santiago. During the attempted kidnapping, Schneider made an attempt to defend himself by pulling his sidearm and a firefight ensued. The Viaux plotters fired on Schneider several times at point blank range and fled the scene. General Schneider was rushed to a hospital but died three days later on October 25, 1970 from multiple gunshot wounds at the age of 56. The failed kidnapping turned assassination created outrage among the Chilean people and backfired for CIA by solidifying overwhelming support for Allende resulting in his election victory. Afterwards the United States with no true military support, made efforts to have Chile expelled from the Organization of American States. In addition, a call for removing economic and military assistance on human rights grounds, but were overruled by the Ambassador and officials of The Pentagon and Treasury Department.

With no support or recourse, the operation was aborted failing in a coup attempt against Allende, only to see his government topple three years later. In September of 1973 the Chilean military executed a coup and stormed the Chilean palace, where President Allende committed suicide prior to capture.

In 1976 the U.S. State Department investigated the murders of two U.S. journalists that were in Chile during the 1973 coup. In the case of Charles Horman, made famous through the 1982 film "Missing", the state department suspected that the Government of Chile sought Horman out believing he was an American intelligence agent and ordered his immediate execution and believed he could be killed without negative fall-out from the U.S. The investigation into his murder by the U.S. showed evidence that CIA may have either provided information to influence his murder, or was aware the Chile government felt threatened by Horman and sought him out and did not intervene.

Operation Condor

South American Assassinations

On September 21, 1976 at 9:30am Orlando Letelier, his assistant Ronni Moffitt and her husband Michael were enroot to Washington D.C. when their car exploded in front of the Irish embassy. The explosion was the result of a car bomb

placed under the driver side of the vehicle. On detonation the force of the explosion lifted the car from the ground and created a two foot diameter hole up through the driver side cutting Letelier in half below the lower torso succumbing to the injuries hours later. Although both Michael and Ronni Moffitt would escape from the vehicle, Ronni would die from internal injuries from shrapnel leaving Michael as the only survivor. Orlando Letelier's assassination was the result of orders issued by the Chilean government. Two weeks prior the Chilean government revoked Letelier's Chilean citizenship due to his interference with the Dutch government not to invest $63 million in the Chilean mining industry. The assassination was orchestrated by a former CIA asset Michael Townley. Townley was the son of a Ford Motor Company executive working in Santiago, Chile. He had attended school in Florida and worked as a mechanic in Miami along with Cuban-exiles in the 1960s. Townley returned to Chile prior to the Salvador Allende election in 1970 where he developed a relationship with CIA when operating a clandestine radio station to broadcast anti-Allende propaganda. In 1973 Townley became active with the newly formed Chilean secret police known as

DINA (Dirección de Inteligencia Nacional). DINA, which is now called CNI (Central Nacional de Informaciones), started as an Army Intelligence program in 1973. The organization was formed by General Manuel Contreras and then in 1974 became an independent entity operating separately from the military.

Townley, while working with DINA entered the United States with another Chilean secret police officer, Armando Fernandez Larios, to recruit ant-Castro Cubans to carry out the assassination. One month prior to the assassination, U.S. State Department official George Landau attempted to obtain visas for the men to enter the U.S. using false passports. Landau was told by Paraguayan intelligence that the men were in need of the visas to meet with CIA. Under suspicion, Landua investigated the claim resulting in the visas being revoked by the State Department in August of 1976. The men using assumed names and fraudulent Chilean passports were able to acquire A-2 visas and gained access to the U.S. shortly after.

The incident had marked the first act of violence against a Chilean exile on U.S. soil and prompted an immediate FBI investigation. Through a paper trail the FBI learned of Townley and Larios gaining access to the U.S. through the use of false passports and started to build their case. Townley was extradited to the U.S. from Chile in 1978 where in exchange for a lesser sentence cooperated with authorities regarding the assassination. Townley had consulted with Luis Posada Carriles and Orlando Bosch of the Coordination of United Revolutionary Organizations (CORU) to assist in recruiting five anti-Castro Cuban exiles. The CIA had employed Luis Posada Carriles, who like Townley was a demolitions expert, in 1965 to provided information on the activities of certain exile groups and continued their official relationship through 1976. The anti-Castro Cuban exiles hired were José Dionisio "Bloodbath" Suárez, Virgilio Paz Romero, Alvin Ross Díaz, and brothers Guillermo and Ignacio Novo

Sampoll. Townley, an electronics and explosives expert provided the recruited saboteurs with the plans and the bomb used to kill Orlando Letelier. In early 1979 the trial of the Novo Sampoll brothers and Díaz began in Washington, D.C., without Romero and Suárez. They were not allowed to be extradited as DINA officers on orders from General Pinochet. The three men on trail were all found guilty of murder, while Townley was released and placed into the Witness Protection Program. Larios fled Chile to the U.S. in 1987 and pled guilty to one count of acting as an accessory to Letelier's assassination and in exchange for information about the plot, authorities dropped the charges. Five years later former DINA members General Manuel Contreras and Pedro Espinoza Bravo were also convicted in Chile regarding their participation.

The Letelier investigation opened new doors and found a tie to Townley and the assassination of General Carlos Prats González. On September 30, 1974, Prats and his wife Sofia Cuthbert were killed outside their Buenos Aires apartment complex. The couple died during a car bomb which was radio controlled by Townley. The explosion was so powerful it had thrown debris nearly one hundred feet in the air. Like Letelier, the Prats assassination was also planned by DINA. Prats had been General Augusto Pinochet's predecessor as Commander-in-chief of the Chilean Army. At the time of his murder, both he and Letelier were publically vocal against Pinochet and the Chilean government.

The Letelier assassination also exposed a dirty campaign of political agenda's involving intelligence communities and assassinations implemented in South America called Operation Condor. The program was designed to eradicate social influences and exterminate political opposition with members in Argentina, Chile, Uruguay, Paraguay, Bolivia and Brazil, with Ecuador and Peru. These countries participated in covert activities including kidnappings of officials; assassinations and human rights violations. In addition, collaboration with European governments such as France also assisted in the activities by supporting Argentina and Chile's regimes. Secretary of State, Henry Kissinger was involved closely with the South American countries and knowledgeable of Operation Condor along with CIA through agreements with organizations such as Triple A (Argentine Anticommunist Alliance), an Argentine death squad active during the 1970s and linked to the military junta led by Jorge Rafael Videla. The CIA had no direct involvement with Operation Condor, yet did financially and technically support key members in exchange for intelligence. Although there have been accusations the agency was sponsoring activities of the Chilean secret police, DINA, and its chief Manuel Contreras, the CIA did pay Contreras one time for information but declined to authorize him as an asset due to concerns of his alleged human rights violations. Townley who participated in some of the assassinations was no longer officially being used by CIA during Operation Condor. The CIA did provide access to a communications installation in the Panama Canal Zone to co-ordinate intelligence information among the southern cone countries. This allowed the agency a way to accumulate information to stay informed of covert activities throughout Latin America. The program was vital to CIA for information, yet after the Letelier assassination on U.S. soil the agency looked to other options to facilitate communications to provide distance from condor participants.

In July 1976, the CIA station chief in Montevideo received information that the Uruguayan military officials threatened to assassinate US Congressman Edward Koch. The CIA took no action because the Uruguayan officers, including Colonel José Fons, who was at the November 1975 secret meeting in Santiago, Chile, and Major José Nino Gavazzo, who headed a team of intelligence officers working in Argentina in 1976, where he was responsible for more than 100 Uruguayans' deaths, had been drinking when the threat was made. In an interview with John Dingus, Koch said that George H. W. Bush, CIA's director at the time, informed him in October 1976 — more than two months afterward, and after Orlando Letelier's murder — that "his sponsorship of legislation to cut off US military assistance to Uruguay on human rights grounds had provoked secret police officials to 'put a contract out for you'". In mid-October 1976, Koch wrote to the Justice Department asking for FBI protection. None was provided for him. In late 1976, Colonel Fons and Major Gavazzo were assigned to prominent diplomatic posts in Washington, DC, but the State Department forced the Uruguayan government to withdraw their appointments, with the public explanation that "Fons and Gavazzo could be the objects of unpleasant publicity." Koch only became aware of the connections between the threats in 2001. (54)

Operation Condor ended in 1983, yet from its inception in November 1975, the leaders of the military intelligence services of Argentina, Bolivia, Paraguay, Uruguay and Chile were directly and indirectly linked to more than fifty thousand murders. In addition, Operation Condor was responsible for thirty thousand disappearances and nearly a half million Latin American people imprisoned.

In 1977 the CIA published an annual report "International Terrorism in 1976" where it concluded that Cuban exile groups operating under the aegis of a new alliance called the Coordination of United Revolutionary Organizations (CORU) were particularly active during the second half of the year and responsible for no less than 17 acts of international terrorism with at least three acts of which took place on the U.S. soil. Statistically, this matches the record compiled by the various Palestinian terrorist groups during the same period. But largely because the Cuban exile operations included the October bombing of a Cuban Airline passenger aircraft, their consequences were far bloodier.

Operation IAFEATURE
Support in Angolan Civil War

After earning their independence from Portugal in 1975, Angola embarked on the Angolan Civil War which revolved around a Cold War conflict. The war was the result of two competing factions comprised of the Communist MPLA, which was supported by Cuba, the Soviet Union, and the anti-Communist UNITA, which gained support from South Africa and the United States. In July of 1975 President Gerald Ford authorized covert aid to the UNITA group through a CIA project called Operation IAFEATURE. The operation was rolled out by DCI William Colby with an approved budget of $30 million over the course of the summer. Both the State Department and CIA were opposed to the covert operation arguing that the grand scale would be impossible to maintain U.S. secrecy. President Ford and Henry Kissinger pushed the operation believing that if MPLA succeeded the global balance of power would shift in Communisms favor. U.S. ambassador to Chile Edward Mulcahy warned the U.S. that assistance to MPLA may also cause conflict with Mobutu Sese Seko, the ruler of Zaire. Despite warnings the operation proceeded.

The budget was used mostly for funding arms to UNITA and FNLA through contacts in Zaire. The CIA flew the equipment in to Kinshasa, Zaire and then reshipped to Angolan bases aboard C-130s. In addition, CIA funded mercenaries to support both groups vs. U.S. military involvement, thus not to exposed the U.S. but to rather finance guerrillas clandestinely. Equipment provided was sanitized to avoid detection of origin and much used was supply caches from World War II. Guerillas struggled with use of the equipment which prompted CIA to employ mercs or paramilitary experts to assist in the operation. The CIA presence only fueled additional support to pro-communist groups in Angola with Soviet and Cuban involvement. Before long the resistance was armed with Soviet MiGs and 122-mm rockets and Cuban troops increased.

Operation IAFEATURE was revealed publically by New York Times reporter Seymour Hersch in December of 1975. Around the same time Dick Clark, a Democratic Senator from Iowa, became aware of the operation during a visit to Africa. Clark's findings sparked an amendment to the Arms Export Control Act, eliminating support to private groups engaged in paramilitary operations in Angola. President Gerald Ford signed the bill on February 9, 1976 forcing CIA to withdraw directly and leverage Israel to continue the support through backchannel communication. This process would prove valuable in the next few years during the Iran-Contra involvement.

In March of 1977 communist support groups invaded Shaba, Zaire from eastern Angola. The involvement of CIA most likely provoked a war with Zaire and increased covert Soviet involvement in Angola. The 27 year war officially ended in 2002 producing an estimated 500,000 deaths, thus making it the Cold War's longest and most deadly conflict.

Operation Watch Tower

Narcotic Sales for Covert Action

Ted Shackely

During the Church Committee and Select Committee on Intelligence, or Pike Committee, members of CIA realized how close the organization came to being dismantled due to questionable clandestine operations. For CIA to continue gathering reliable intelligence the agency would have to explore other avenues of funding that would be undetected by congress. In December of 1975 the CIA began a covert project between Columbia and Panama where a series of electronic beacon towers were established enabling aircraft to fly undetected. The project, known as Operation Watch Tower, was a black operation carried out by Col. Edward P. Cutolo of the 10th Special Forces Group and assigned by Col. "Bo" Baker. Cutolo worked closely with Edwin Wilson and Frank Terpil former CIA officers working on behalf of CIA as assets. By February of 1975 the CIA had flown thirty aircraft from Bogota, Columbia to Albrook Airfield in Panama transporting cocaine as the prime cargo.

The cocaine shipments were then delivered to Albrook under the security of the Panama Defense Force and overseen by Col. Manuel Antonio Noriega as well as CIA asset Wilson. Colonel Noriega, a Panamanian military official, had worked with CIA since the late 1950s. He had received intelligence and counterintelligence training at Fort Gulick in 1967, and psychological operations (Psyops) training at Fort Bragg, North Carolina. Director of Central Intelligence Stansfield Turner recognized Noriega as a valued CIA asset in the early 1970s.

Noriega leveraged a relationship with a Columbia narcotic organization known as the Medellin Cartel. The cartel was comprised of three top level individuals including Pablo Escobar, Juan David Ochoa Vazquez and Carlos Lehder. Escobar handled the production of cocaine, Ochoa managed the security and political matters within Columbia, and Lehder overseen the distribution. Although not directly associated with CIA, the Medellin Cartel assisted in providing cocaine through Operation Watch Tower that was then transferred from Columbia to Panama and then distributed through the United States to finance CIA covert activities. Noriega provided money laundering services for the cocaine traffickers through their Miami accountant Ramon Milian Rodriguez in exchange for a commission. The money was flown from Miami to Panama and placed into armored cars under the control of the Panamanian Defense Force and delivered to Banco Nacional de Panama and later Bank of Credit and Commerce International (BCCI). The relationship with Noriega and the Columbian and Panamanian drug connection became one avenue for financing covert activity against foreign governments unfriendly or deemed threatening to U.S. interests.

By 1978 Lehder had secured a Bahamian island called Norman's Cay where he grew his cocaine distribution empire. He had learned distribution techniques while serving time in a Danbury, Connecticut prison and developing a friendship with inmate George Jung, a successful marijuana smuggler. Jung educated Lehder on the use of small aircraft for transporting narcotics vs. the traditional smuggling practice of mules carrying suitcases on commercial airlines. Lehder, once released, practiced this technique to his fullest extent and by the late 1970s had built a 3,000 ft runway with radar protection and a small army on Norman's Cay to protect and operate his cocaine trafficking. Jet airliners would fly into Norman's Cay from Columbia where the cocaine would be unloaded and reloaded into smaller single engine aircraft and flown to Georgia, Florida and South Carolina for U.S. distribution. Over a short period of time, Lehder was funneling more than 6,000 kilos a day through his Norman's Cay operation and building his personal wealth in billions of U.S. dollars.

Obvious controversy has surrounded the operation because of the relationships developed between CIA, Noriega and the Medellin Cartel. It was not the first type of relationship CIA possessed in gaining illegal funding for their operations. During 1968 the Bureau of Narcotics and Dangerous Drugs were deeply involved in investigating Santos Trafficante for heroin trafficking within the United States. During sting operations arrests were made of several Cuban exiles that had been CIA assets and connected to the Bay of Pigs invasion. The BNDD investigation called Operation Eagle, had recognized a number of ex-CIA assets involved in the drug trafficking including Felix Rodriguez. Ted Shackley had been promoted to Saigon Station Chief during this period and reached out to his former Miami colleagues for assistance including Rodriguez, David Morales, Rafael "Chi Chi" Quintero and Frank Fiorini aka Frank Sturgis. These operators worked under the Civil Operations and Rural Development Support (CORDS) program, which rewarded Vietnamese people for information on Viet Cong and would eventually become Project Phoenix, or The Phoenix Program. Shackley leveraged his operators under the guidance of CIA officer Ruby Enders and CIA Base Chief Donald Gregg to conduct sabotage missions of rival drug dealers in Laos.

With Shackley in charge of the Saigon Station, Trafficante began heroin operations within the city providing narcotics to the local nightclubs visited by U.S. soldiers. Shackley also interfered with CID investigations into Vice President Nquyen Cao Ky and General Van Quang for their heroin and opium trafficking, citing their need for intelligence was far greater than their illegal narcotic activities. Shackley and Clines needed a bank to funnel their covert narcotics earnings and worked with former CIA associate Mike Hand and business partner Frank Nugan who formed the Nugan Hand Bank in 1973. The bank possessed a number of offices around the world and provided cover businesses for intelligence operations. Shackley, Clines, Gregg and William Colby could clearly see the writing on the wall regarding the exposure of covert operations to senate subcommittees. Their foreknowledge of these committees provoked the necessity to financially manipulate projects that could remain hidden from congress, thus the birth of "black operations". By sponsoring and coordinating illegal narcotic trafficking, the revenue for the venture could be funneled and remain off the books for congress to see and provide funding for valuable covert activities without congressional approval.

In 1973 Michael Hand, a decorated Green Beret who almost single-handedly held off a fourteen-hour Vietcong attack on the Special Forces compound at Dong Xaoi, and Frank Nugan, an Australian lawyer, established the Nugan Hand Bank. Another key figure in this venture was ex-CIA officer Bernie Houghton, who was closely connected to CIA officials, Ted Shackley and Thomas G. Clines. Nugan ran operations in Sydney whereas Hand established a branch in Hong Kong. This enabled Australian depositors to access a money-laundering facility for illegal transfers of Australian money to Hong Kong. According to Alfred W. McCoy, the "Hand-Houghton partnership led the bank's international division into new fields - drug finance, arms trading, and support work for CIA covert operations." Hand told friends "it was his ambition that Nugan Hand became banker for the CIA." In 1974 the Nugan Hand Bank got involved in helping the CIA to take part in covert arms deals with contacts within Angola. It was at this time that Edwin Wilson became involved with the bank. Two CIA agents based in Indonesia, James Hawes and

Robert Moore, called on Wilson at his World Marine offices to discuss "an African arms deal". Later, Bernie Houghton arrived from Sydney to place an order for 10 million rounds of ammunition and 3,000 weapons including machine guns. The following year Houghton asked Wilson to arrange for World Marine to purchase a high-technology spy ship. This ship was then sold to Iran.

By 1976 the Nugan-Hand Bank appeared to have become a CIA-fronted company. This is reflected in the type of people recruited to hold senior positions in the bank including Rear-Admiral Earl P. Yates, the former Chief of Staff for Policy and Plans of the U.S. Pacific Command and a counter-insurgency specialist, became president of the company. Other appointments included William Colby, retired director of the CIA, General Leroy J. Manor, the former chief of staff of the U.S. Pacific Command and deputy director for counterinsurgency and special activities, General Edwin F. Black, former commander of U.S. forces in Thailand, Walter J. McDonald, retired CIA deputy director for economic research, Dale C. Holmgren, former chairman of the CIA's Civil Air Transport and Guy J. Pauker, senior Republican foreign policy adviser.

Concerns over bank's questionable accounting processes began to circulate by the late 1970s as investors attending Nugan Hand AGM's were prevented from asking questions by the bank. These concerns turned into panic for bank investors in the early hours of January 27, 1980 when Nugan (who was facing charges of stock fraud) was found shot dead by a .30 caliber rifle in his Mercedes Benz 100 miles west, outside of Lithgow, New South Wales; it is said that a hand-written list was found on his body with a list of substantial loans Nugan Hand had extended to various notables, such as William Colby and Bob Wilson. The following police investigation returned a verdict of suicide. Suspicions of the bank's activities grew in subsequent days as details emerged of the contents of Nugan's car (including the business card of former CIA director William Colby) and news that Nugan's house and office had been ransacked by Hand and Yates and important company files destroyed or stolen.

Another key member was Edwin P. Wilson, who worked closely with Col. Cutolo and Frank Terpil. Wilson was born in 1928 into a poor family in Idaho. He earned a psychology degree from the University of Portland in 1953 and subsequently joined the United States Marines and fought in Korea. After being discharged in 1956, Wilson began his career with CIA until 1971 when he officially retired, yet remained loyal to the agency as a covert business asset. As a business asset Wilson managed front companies for CIA covert action teams. In the early 1970s Wilson was approached by Ted Shackley, now a CIA official, to travel to Libya and keep tabs on an international terrorist Carlos the Jackal.

At the time, a strict sanctions regime was in place against Libya and the country was willing to pay a great deal for weapons and material. Wilson began conducting elaborate dealings and guns and military uniforms were smuggled into the country. Wilson also recruited a group of retired Green Berets – decorated Vietnam veteran Billy Waugh among them to go to Libya and train its military and intelligence officers. (55)

In 1979, a gun that Wilson had arranged to be delivered to the Libyan embassy in Bonn was used to assassinate a prominent dissident. The next year, one of the Green Berets assassinated another dissident in Colorado. Wilson states that he regrets these incidents and had no prior knowledge of them. He states that he was still working for the CIA and his supplying of weapon to the Libyans was an attempt to get close to them and gain valuable intelligence. The most dramatic deal, and the one that brought Wilson to the attention from the U.S. government, was for some twenty tons of military grade C-4 plastic explosives. This was a massive quantity that was equal to the entire US domestic stockpile. Most of Wilson's connections were still under the impression that he was working for the CIA and a wide network in the United States supported his actions. The explosives were assembled by a California company and hidden in barrels of oil drilling mud. They were flown to Libya aboard a chartered jet. (56)

During an investigation by the Bureau of Alcohol, Tobacco and Firearms, Wilson was indicted by the US Justice Department for firearms and explosives violations where he stood trial on four separate occasions. Although found not guilty of trying to hire a group of Cubans to kill a Libyan dissident, he was convicted of exporting guns, including the one used in the Bonn assassination. In addition he was found guilty of shipping the explosives and sentenced to a total of 32 years.

While in prison, Wilson campaigned for his innocence and hired a new lawyer, David Adler, a former CIA officer with clearance to classified documents. Adler found eighty incidents where Wilson met on a professional basis with CIA proving the agency had indirectly used Wilson after his retirement in 1971. The CIA admitted to concealing information to prevent any compromise of additional ongoing operations at the time of the investigation. A federal judge ruled that the prosecution had acted improperly and in October 2003, Wilson's conviction was overturned after being incarcerated more than twenty years.

According to Edwin Wilson the operations were limited knowledge for several reasons including public knowledge would undermine present governmental interests. In addition, similar operations were being implemented elsewhere in the world under the "golden triangle" of Southeast Asia and Pakistan. Wilson stated in both areas of the world the CIA and other intelligence agencies are using the illegal narcotics flow to support forces fighting to overthrow communist governments, or governments that are not friendly towards the U.S. Wilson named several recognized officials of Pakistan, Afghanistan, Burma, Korea, Thailand and Cambodia as being aware and consenting to these arrangements, similar to the ones in Panama. Wilson cited the military coup in Argentina in 1976, the coup in Peru in 1976, the fall of the Somoza Government in Nicaragua in 1979, and the growing civil war in El Salvador as examples of the need for operations like Watch Tower. As these operations funded the ongoing effort to combat communism and defeat actions directed against the United States or matters concerning the U.S.

Operation George Orwell
Narcotic Sales for Covert Action

Operation Watch Tower was successful in landing at least forty aircraft safely at Albrook. When the operation was concluded Colonel Edward P. Cutolo in March of 1976 lost contact with many of the SAT (Special Activity Team) members involved. By 1978 he assumed command of the 10th Special Forces Group at Fort Devens where he recognized two soldiers that had participated in Watch Tower. The

Frank Terpil

two soldiers were Sgt. John Newby, who was assigned to a Special Forces Operational Detachment Alpha in the 3rd Battalion; and PFC William Tyree assigned to a Forward Support Team. Cutolo, under Edwin Wilson and directly ordered by the authority of FORSCOM was to implement twelve separate SATs to carry out Army Regulation 340-18-5 and execute surveillance operations on politicians, judicial figures, law enforcement agencies at the state level, and of religious figures.

"Mr. Edwin Wilson explained that it was considered that Operation Watch Tower might be compromised and become known if politicians, judicial figures, police and religious entities were approached or received word that U.S. Troops had aided in delivering narcotics from Columbia into Panama," Cutolo explained in an affidavit. "Based on that possibility, intense surveillance was undertaken by my office to ensure if Watch Tower became known of, the U.S. government and the Army would have advance warning and could prepare a defense. I was under orders not to inform Col. Forrest Rittgers, Commanding Officer of Ft. Devens. The reason for this order I was told, is that in the event Ft. Devens personnel are caught in the act of implementing the surveillance, Col. Rittger will have a margin of plausible deniability on which he may be able to downplay and defend against injuries. The surveillance was unofficially dubbed Operation George Orwell." (57)

Operation Orwell began to institute surveillance against a number of high-profile individuals including Ted Kennedy, John Kerry, Edward King, Michael Dukakis, Levin H. Campbell, Andrew A. Caffey, Fred Johnston, Kenneth A. Chandler, and Thomas P. O'Neill. The operation was geared towards more counter-intelligence focus in determining what the principles knew or didn't know. To successfully collect this information Cutolo's teams used electronic bugging equipment to record all conversations of the principles within both their residences and workplace. Surveillance was instituted at the Governors' residences of Massachusetts, Maine, New York, and New Hampshire; Catholic cathedrals of New York and Boston; and in Ft. Devens, all local police and politicians were under some sort of surveillance at various times. To compensate for the broad range of operational needs Cutolo recruited members of the 441st Military Intelligence Detachment and 402 Army Security Agency Detachment assigned to the 10th Special Forces Group to supplement the SATs tasked with carrying out Operation Orwell.

In addition Cutolo recruited a number of local state employees who worked within the ranks of local police and as court personnel as resident kites to assist in this operation. Most of these assets were veterans with previous security clearances that if caught he could simply cut the string for reasons of deniability. Cutolo was notified by Edwin Wilson that the information forwarded to Wash. D.C., was disseminated to private corporations who were developing weapons for the Dept. of Defense. Those private corporations were encouraged to use the sensitive information gathered from surveillance on U.S. Senators and Representatives as leverage to manipulate those Congressmen into approving whatever costs the weapons systems incurred. Wilson named three weapons systems associated with the private corporations receiving information from Operation Orwell. The weapons systems included an armored vehicle, an aircraft that is invisible to radar, and a weapons system that utilizes kinetic energy. Wilson indicated to Cutolo the three weapons systems would be implemented nationwide by 4 July 1980. At the time 8,400 police departments, 1,370 churches, and approx. 17,900 citizens were monitored under Operation Orwell.

On orders from Wilson, Cutolo didn't discuss Operation Orwell with staff members outside the operational participation. "The only matter discussed with Operation Orwell personnel was what the SATs needed to know in order to carry out their mission. Certain information was collected on suspected members of the Trilateral Commission and the Bilderberg group. Among those that information was collected on were President Gerald Ford and President Jimmy Carter. Edwin Wilson indicated that additional surveillance was implemented against former CIA director George Bush, who Wilson named as a member of the Trilateral Commission."

The surveillance requested on George H. W. Bush was to provide Wilson and arms dealer partner Frank Terpil leverage with carrying out their operations. Wilson grew concerned that Thomas G. Clines would sacrifice him as a fall guy if the operations were made public. Wilson and Terpil believed that surveillance on Cline's former boss and close friend Bush, who was seeking greater political ambitions, may garner intelligence they could use for immunity or a bargaining chip in ensuring their safety if both Operation Watch Tower and Operation Orwell were to be exposed.

"Wilson and myself had enough intimate knowledge of current and former CIA operations that could pose great embarrassment if found out by the American people," Frank Terpil. "It was an unspoken blackmail, if you will. There were never any overtures made to threaten the CIA with blackmail, at least on my behalf, or on my part."

Terpil, a former CIA officer like Wilson, had left the agency in the early 1970s to pursue a career as an intelligence consultant. He maintained his CIA contacts and became a very effective asset for CIA for years to come. While in Uganda, Terpil became Idi Amin's right-hand man and occupied a third floor office at Amin's infamous State Research Bureau facility. It was there Terpil used his CIA and other intelligence contacts to provide Amin with technical equipment, arms and intelligence.

Cutolo grew concerned of the nature and request made by Wilson and in March of 1980 requested Col. James N. Rowe to look into Wilson. "On 7 March 1980 Col. Rowe contacted me. During the course of our conversation Col. Rowe informed me that his initial inquiries with CIA contacts confirmed that Edwin Wilson was working for Thomas Clines at the times in question. Col. Rowe indicated that Edwin Wilson was under scrutiny by the CIA at that time but had not been given the details of the circumstances surrounding the events of that matter. Col. Rowe also indicated that there was an Israeli aspect to the matter involving Edwin Wilson and Col. Rowe provided the name of David Kimche as being the Israeli most likely to be involved with Edwin Wilson. In regards to my concerns that Edwin Wilson posed a possible threat to national security or to the inner working of the CIA, Col. Rowe indicated that off the record, that was a concern of several people to whom he had spoken. Col. Rowe also indicated that he would be in receipt of documentation by the first week of June which listed Edwin Wilson's involvement in several operations. I specifically asked Col. Rowe if he had the names of any of those operations at this time and his reply was in the negative. Col. Rowe did indicate that it was his understanding that each operation had basically the same characters involved and Col. Rowe named two other individuals involved with Edwin Wilson. Col. Rowe named Robert Gates and William Casey as officials who had been named in the documentation he would acquire prior to our scheduled meeting on June 1980." (57)

During the same month Cutolo received a photograph from U.S. Army Intelligence contacts at the Pentagon and recognized the subject as a senior Mossad agent Michael Harari. Harari began his intelligence work facilitating illegal Jewish immigration to Israel after World War II. He then spent time in the army and Shin Bet before being recruited by the Mossad in the 1960s. During his time in the Mossad he ran agents in Europe, eventually advancing to the head of the Operations Branch. It was during this time that he helped build and lead teams in Operation Wrath of God, the Israeli response to the Munich Massacre in 1972. In what became known as the Lillehammer affair, Harari led a team into Norway where they believed Ali Hassan Salameh, the chief of Black September operations was living. After identifying and assassinating the target, it was revealed that they had killed an innocent waiter, Ahmed Bouchiki, who only resembled Salameh. While authorities arrested many of Harari's team, he escaped back to Israel. A Norwegian case against him was dismissed in January 1999 because of a lack of evidence. (58)

Cutolo recognized Harari as a male Israeli national that met an aircraft which flew into Albrook Air Station during Operation Watch Tower in 1976 and provided Edwin Wilson with two briefcases containing U.S. currency. Cutolo learned from his Pentagon contacts, that Harari's activities in Latin America included drug trafficking and that Pentagon officials, on the orders of policy makers in Washington, to keep the activities of Harari a secret.

At some later point in time Harari became the Mossad station chief in Latin America based out of Israel. Although he is said to have retired after this service, it is unclear if all his Israeli intelligence connections were severed when he left for Panama, He returned to Israel just before or during the 1989 United States invasion of Panama, which deposed Noriega and installed the legitimate presidential victor Guillermo Endara. Harari later appeared on Israeli television and denied that he was ever a close advisor of Noriega, and that he had escaped by his own means. (59)

Operation Orwell came to a halt in 1980 after Edwin Wilson was indicted for his role in selling weapons to the Libyan government. Terpil fled the U.S. from Washington DC while agencies turned a blind eye. Terpil awaiting prosecution in the US on two separate terrorist charges was released on bail twice and fled to Beirut. Both Wilson and Terpil were assets of CIA and provided the agency with valuable intelligence when conducting their unsanctioned operations. Often these men worked in tandem with CIA operations as well as their own private business ventures for profit. It is due to their intelligence collecting and disseminating to CIA on their own that enabled them to work freely in the world of both narcotics and gun smuggling. It is also the reason Terpil was able to evade prosecution and flee to a country free of extradition.

Operation Eagle Claw
Iranian Hostage Rescue Effort

On November 4, 1979 at approximately 6:30am, more than 300 Iranian students, known as Muslim Student Followers of the Imam's Line, reviewed their plan to overtake the U.S. Embassy in Tehran. The intention was to invade the embassy as a way to  draw media attention for their cause and then disburse upon the arrival of police. Once the support for their actions grew and no lethal force was taken - the objective of the group changed.

As Ayatollah Musavi Khoeyniha had hoped, Khomeini supported the takeover. According to Foreign Minister Ebrahim Yazdi, when he, Yazdi came to Qom to tell The Imam about the incident, Khomeini told the minister to "go and kick them out." But later that evening, back in Tehran, the minister heard on the radio that Imam Khomeini had issued a statement supporting the seizure and calling it "the second revolution," and the embassy an "American spy den in Tehran." The occupiers bound and blindfolded the embassy soldiers and staff and paraded them in front of photographers. In the first couple of days many of the embassy staff who had snuck out of the compound or not been there at the time of the takeover were rounded up by Islamists and returned as hostages. (60)

Six American diplomats did however avoid capture and found refuge at the nearby Canadian and Swiss embassies in Tehran. The "Canadian caper" was the popular name given to the covert rescue effort between the Government of Canada and CIA of six American diplomats. The diplomats, who evaded capture during the seizure of the United States embassy in Tehran, Iran, had taken refuge within the Canadian Embassy. The caper was designed to evacuate the U.S. personnel prior to the Iranians discovering their true identity.

Once the Canadian Prime Minister Joe Clark was contacted regarding the situation it was decided to smuggle the six Americans out of Iran on an international flight using Canadian passports. Canada's Parliament convened its first secret session since World War II to grant permission for an Order-in-Council to be made for the issuance of Canadian passports to the American diplomats in Canadian sanctuary. The CIA enlisted its disguise and exfiltration expert, Antonio Mendez, to provide a cover story, documents, and appropriate clothing and materials to change their appearance. Mendez, a technical operations officer, used his artistic abilities to support clandestine and covert CIA operations.

Mendez worked closely with Canadian government staff in Ottawa, sending as much as he could in the diplomatic pouch, before flying to Tehran with an associate to assist with the rescue. There were alternate passports and identities for a variety of scenarios, but the cover story selected had the six being a Hollywood crew scouting movie locations. The elaborate back-story involved a film named Argo, for a Middle-Eastern feel, and a post office box in Los Angeles for "Studio Six", backed by display ads. (The movie scenario was considered one way to get an armed team into Tehran to retake the embassy.) (61)

Several weeks passed prior to the execution of the escape plan. The U.S. citizens were tasked with several errands to give the appearance that they were not afraid of capture as posing as Canadian citizens. On January 27, 1980, the six American diplomats, Robert Anders, Mark J. Lijek, Cora A. Lijek, Henry L. Schatz, Joseph D. Stafford, and Kathleen F. Stafford, travelling on Canadian passports boarded a flight for Zürich, Switzerland, at

Tehran's Mehrabad Airport. They arrived in the friendly nation safely. Several Canadian diplomats were recognized for their efforts in assisting the American diplomats. One notable was Canadian Ambassador Ken Taylor who became very involved in assisting the Americans and designing an escape procedure. Jean Pelletier, a writer for the Montreal La Presse newspaper, uncovered the caper and published soon after the American's European arrival, yet was unaware of CIA involvement.

The Muslim Student Followers of the Imam's Line demanded that the Shah return from the United States to Iran for trial and execution. In addition, they demanded an apology from the U.S. for the participation in the coupe of Prime Minister Mossadeq, CIA project TPAJAX, and that Iran's frozen assets totaling $8 billion in the U.S. be released. President Jimmy Carter failed in appealing to the hostage takers humanitarian aspect who gained support from many within Iran including Theocratic Islamists. Khomeini rallied many in the country under the slogan "America can't do a thing," and became apparent that the U.S. would need joint intelligence and military efforts to free the hostages.

CIA used a variety of tactics including their clairvoyance operations. Project SCANETE did project the release of hostage Richard Queen due to illness, which was later identified as MD, but wasn't sufficient enough for a full-scale rescue attempt.

President Carter, eager to have the hostages released prior to the end of his presidency, approved Operation Eagle Claw (aka Operation Evening Light). Designed as a two night mission, Eagle Claw involved establishing a staging site inside Iran, near Tabas in the Yazd Province and designated "Desert One". The site was to be used as an airstrip for the USAF MC-130E aircraft and C-130 Hercules refueling aircraft. Accompanying these planes were eight U.S. Navy RH-53D Sea Stallion helicopters flown from the USS Nimitz stationed in the Indian Ocean.

After landing the C-130s would offload Delta Force members and team up with CIA SAD teams already in Tehran, Iran. They would fly the helicopters to Desert Two for concealment. The following night the teams would then over power the hostage takers, cross the main road to the soccer stadium and await transport from the helicopters for evacuation. The CIA Special Activities Division paramilitary team was led by Richard Meadows. Major Richard J. Meadows was born on June 16, 1931 and considered the father of Delta Force. Meadows enlisted in the army at the age of 15 and served in Korea. He was trained by the British SAS and in 1953 help form the United States Army Special Forces. During Vietnam Meadows was assigned to MACV-SOG and was the team leader on Operation Ivory Coast, the daring rescue attempt at the San Tay prison. Meadows, who had retired in 1977, returned to assist CIA as a special consultant for the covert reconnaissance in Tehran under the cover of a foreign businessman. It was Meadows team who learned from an asset that the U.S. hostages were in the Embassy compound. Meadows team was to provide both intelligence as well as support to the operation.

The assault on the embassy was to occur after cutting a power grid to stall Iranian military response. AC-130 gunships were to provide additional support overhead while the helicopters transported hostages and U.S. forces from the soccer stadium to Manzariyeh Air Base. The 75th Ranger force was tasked with capturing the airfield where C-141 transports would be waiting to remove all U.S personnel.

During the execution phase of Operation Eagle Claw a haboob, an unexpected sandstorm, caused three of eight RH-53D helicopters to be inoperable. In addition, a tanker truck was destroyed by rocket fire during the securing of Desert One. With five helicopters remaining a decision was reached to abort the mission on April 25, 1980. The forces were then transported back to Masirah Island and CIA Tehran team evacuated unaware that their identities had been discovered by documents left behind in one of the downed helicopters. The following day the White House released a statement regarding the failed rescue attempt.

Ironically another Operation Ivory Coast veteran, Colonel Arthur "Bull" Simons, had his own involvement during the hostage situation. Like Meadows, Simons took part in the Son Tay raid as ground commander and was recruited by Texas billionaire Ross Perot to free two of his company Electronic Data Systems employees from an Iranian prison. Simons organized a small group funded by Perot and all involved in the private operation returned to the United States successfully and unharmed. Simons died three months later in Colorado at the age of 60 after having heart complications.

Operation Amadeus
Funding Hostage Release

Operation Amadeus was originally known as a World War II effort that assisted with covert activity in protecting Nazi scientists and intelligence officers from communist capture. The operation involved a number of countries and organizations. In the 1980's the CIA reopened Operation Amadeus as their own to leverage similar relationships built over the last four decades. The principal means of funding the original Operation Amadeus

Oliver North

activities was the profitable narcotics business. Large stocks of SS morphine had been smuggled out of Europe and into "Catholic" South America at the end of the War in accordance with the Operation Sunrise agreement between Allen Dulles, the then senior wartime OSS officer in Switzerland, and SS General Karl Wolff. The morphine was accompanied by looted SS gold and large quantities of counterfeit British banknotes, forged in concentration camps by captive but skilled counterfeiters as part of an SS scheme known as Operation Bernhardt. The escape "lines" used to move wanted men around South America, away from the prying eyes of Israeli agents, also proved ideal as smuggling routes for drugs. This was accomplished with assistance from additional organizations.

The Sovereign Military Order of Malta (SMOM) is a Roman Catholic order based in Rome, Italy. The SMOM is a sovereign subject of international law originally founded in 1099 and headquartered in Rome, Italy in 1834. The order is comprised of 12,500 members, 80,000 permanent volunteers, 13,000 medical personnel to assist the elderly, the handicapped, refugees, children, the homeless, those with terminal illness and leprosy in five continents of the world. Through its worldwide relief corps, Malteser International, the Order is also engaged to aid victims of natural disasters, epidemics and armed conflicts. In addition, the SMOM also acts as the military arm of the Vatican and is regarded as a separate State with full powers of statehood, including issuing its own diplomatic passports.

Malta knighthoods are awarded to many leading individuals who are part of the military and intelligence community. The CIA's William Casey, for example, was a Knight of Malta. Former NATO General and later US Secretary of State Alexander Haig is also a Malta Knight. Another is General Vernon Walters, the former Deputy Director of the CIA under DCI George Bush, and later appointed a roving ambassador during the Reagan Administration. The head of the OSS General William J. Donovan, CIA Chief of Counterintelligence, James J. Angleton, and CIA John McCone were also distinguished with a Malta knighthood.

In May of 1954 Prince Bernhard of The Netherlands became the founding chairman of the Bilderbergers. The Bilderbergers, named from the Bilderberger Hotel, is an annual meeting of Western power elite including regular visits from Dr Henry Kissinger, David Rockefeller, and Italy's Gianni Agnelli.

In the same year the Bilderbergers was founded, Prince Bernhard became head of the Johanitter Orde in Nederland, one of four orders that make up the Chivalric Alliance of Orders of Saint John (Alliance de Chevalerie des Hospitaliers de Saint Jean de Jérusalem). The stated purpose of these four, known as "the Alliance", which composed of northern European nations Germany, The Netherlands, Sweden and Great Britain, the latter being an ancient order known as "the Most Venerable Order" is "to reduce to silence the enemies of Christ".

On November 26th, 1963, the day after President John F. Kennedy's funeral, "the Alliance" was consolidated with the signing of a joint declaration between the Sovereign Military Order of Malta and the Most Venerable Order, at St John's Gate, London, by the Grand Chancellor of the SMOM, the Prince of Resuttano, and Lord Wakehurst, Lord Prior of the Most Venerable Order". The agreement allied both Protestant and Catholic hierarchy to a joint goal of "silencing the enemies of Christ", thus eliminate communism. (62)

Decades later, the stocks of heroin smuggled into the United States for distribution by the CIA-protected Mafia would be complemented with locally grown cocaine. CIA has always had long relationships with the Mafia, even prior to the Bay of Pigs. The OSS and ONI, the parent and sister intelligence agencies of CIA worked with Lucky Luciano and Meyer Lansky during World War II to gain intelligence from their Italian sources to prevent sabotage to the Eastern seaboard. Now in the 1980's Colonel Oliver North authorized the exchange of guns for drugs to finance Contra operations. North and CIA used contact with the New York-based Colombo family to assist in the distribution of cocaine to finance the Contra Affair. Agency relationships with Prince Bernhard and through Umberto Ortolani, a Vatican insider, the Vatican Bank, the IOR, Banco Ambrosiano and the CIA founded Nugan Hand Bank all assisted with money laundering for Operation Amadeus.

In 1980 CIA embarked on a joint venture between the United States and Iran to free 52 Americans taken hostage from the U.S. Embassy in Iran during 1979. On October 18, 1980 William Casey and Donald Gregg were flown from Washington's National Airport to Le Bourget Airfield, just north of Paris France, to attend a secret meeting. The meetings occurred on the 19th and 20th and took place at the Waldorf Florida and Crillon hotels according to Richard Brenneke, CIA asset and pilot. The meetings purpose was to establish a covert agreement between the U.S. and representatives of the Ayatollah Khomeini for the release of the 52 American hostages in Iran. Although conspiracy theorists have labeled the meeting as "October Surprise"; an agreement to not release the hostages until after the Presidential election to cement the Reagan-Bush campaign; the reality is that current  President Jimmy Carter was fully aware of the covert effort.

The agreement was based on the U.S. providing weapons to Iran and funding Contra militants in Nicaragua, in exchange for the release of the 52 hostages. The operation consisted of funneling arms through Israel to be directly delivered to Iran and leveraging relationships with drug cartels to finance the Contra rebels. The operation worked, and on January 19, 1981, with the assistance of the Algerian government the hostage crisis came to an end. The same day the 52 American hostages were released, President Ronald Reagan became the 40th President of the United States.

At the time of the arms transaction plan, Iran was in the midst of war with Iraq. The deal was brokered by National Security Adviser Robert McFarlane through the assistance of Israeli Prime Minister Shimon Peres who shipped Iran the weapons agreed upon to an Iranian group unsupportive of Ayatollah Khomeini. Global International Airways supplied one of the cargo planes used by the White House to deliver 23 tons of TOW missiles and sundry spare parts to Tehran. Among Global's clients was Southern Air Transport, once owned-and-operated by the CIA. Southern Air personnel maintain that Global ran weapons out of Dallas to the contras and cocaine back into the US. Global's biggest customer was the Egyptian American Transport and Services Corporation (EATSCO). EATSCO's board of directors included Ted Shackley and retired U.S. Air Force General Richard Secord.

Once the transactions were completed the United States replenished the Israeli military supply and earned monetary benefits. Over the relationship the transactions helped release additional hostages that had been captured after the 1979 Iran abductions. The Israeli government requested the ability to offer Iran TOW missiles to increase support, which at first was declined by President Ronald Reagan, but later approved giving McFarlane the go ahead on the trades. From August of 1985 to October of 1986, the U.S. supplied Iran with 2,500 BGM-71 Anti-tank guided missiles, commonly referred to as the TOW, Tube-launched Optically-tracked Wire-to-command-Link. In addition, the delivery of eighteen (18) Raytheon MIM-23 HAWK medium range surface-to-air missiles and numerous HAWK parts were finalized.

In 1986 the secretive scandal was revealed through a Lebanese magazine and brought to public light, which would become known as the "Iran Contra affair". Ten days after the initial exposure, President Ronald Reagan addressed the nation acknowledging the U.S. participation and involvement as being a relationship formed with Iran to replace animosity and potential acts of terrorism. Although critics viewed the participation as negotiating with terrorists, the plan bypassed Hezbollah and utilized Iran as the direct influence. Unfortunately for CIA and the Reagan Administration, the acts were in direct violation of the Boland Amendment, which consisted of three U.S. legislative amendments passed during 1982-1984 specifically limiting government assistance to the rebel Contras in Nicaragua. Later Lieutenant Colonel Oliver North, who was a key member of the National Security Council in Washington, D.C., would be charged with multiple felonies regarding the involvement. North testified he witnessed Admiral John Poindexter destroy what may have been the only signed copy of a presidential covert-action finding that sought to authorize CIA participation in the Hawk missile shipment to Iran. Public opinion was that Poindexter and North had shredded the documents to protect President Reagan in trade had convictions reversed under President Bush's Administration in 1990. Even with the evidence mounted against him, President Ronald Reagan recorded a 64% approval rating when leaving office, the highest of any President.

Although drown out by the Iran Contra affair, additional information regarding CIA involvement in drug trafficking emerged. CIA had discretion to report or not report information that came to its attention regarding potential violations of federal law by its employees, assets and other persons.

According to a 1954 memorandum from CIA General Counsel Lawrence Houston to the DCI, Houston discussed the issue of reporting Federal criminal violations to the Department of Justice (DoJ) with Deputy Attorney General William P. Rogers on February 18, 1954. Rogers and Houston agreed that CIA would be responsible for determining whether a potential violation of criminal law by persons associated with CIA would be referred to DoJ for prosecution. In the mid-1970s, this arrangement became more widely known and was subject to criticism by the Congress. Assistant Attorney General for DoJ's Criminal Division Richard Thornburgh wrote CIA General Counsel John Warner in the summer of 1975 to remind CIA of its duty to comply with 28 U.S.C. 535, a provision of law that imposes a duty on every department and agency in the Executive Branch to report promptly to the Attorney General any information, allegations, or complaints relating to possible violations of Title 18 of the United States Code by officers and employees of the U.S. Government. Warner responded that the DCI was charged under the National Security Act of 1947 with "protecting intelligence sources and methods from unauthorized disclosure" and that CIA would be seeking DoJ's advice as to fulfilling this responsibility in regard to "cases that will be reported."

In 1984 CIA received word that an asset named John Hull had been involved in smuggling narcotics. Hull was a dual United States and Costa Rican citizen residing in Muelle De San Carlos, Cost Rica during the Contra resistance. Hull's ranch possessed airstrips and storage facilities, which he allowed Contra's, CIA and United States businesses access. In 1985 the FBI started an investigation into Hull's association with Frank Castro, a known terrorist and narcotic trafficker. Hull denied any working relationship with Castro claiming he only met the man once with a group of Cuban-Americans, but was familiar with his illegal reputation. During interviews with FBI Hull claimed that Castro had been supporting Contra's financially, but denied any involvement. This was confirmed through the FBI on the following month by Moises Ruiz Nunez.

In 1986 CIA learned from the FBI that Hull was indeed using his airstrips for cocaine trafficking. According to Jack Terrell shipments were being delivered to Corn Island, Nicaragua from Colombia twice a week and that Cuban-Americans, including Rene Corvo were bringing the cocaine to Hull's ranch for shipment to the United States. The FBI report stated that both Terrell and Costa Rican authorities also believed that Dr. Hugo Spadafora, a former ARDE commander, was involved with Hull in the drug trafficking.

In an interview with CBS, Gary Betzner claimed that he had used Hull's ranch to deliver two loads of weapons, and returned with two loads totaling 1000 kilos of cocaine. Betzner stated that the cocaine was loaded from Hull's ranch and that he was present and new all about the activity. When confronted Hull claimed that it was impossible for his ranch to be used for drug trafficking and that he met Corvo several times and transported medicine and supplies to Corvo's training camps on the Northern border of Costa Rica from 1983 to 1985.

Robert Gates, who served as Deputy Director of Central Intelligence (DDCI) from April 1986 to January 1987 and May 1987 to March 1989 and ADCI from January to May 1987, said during the internal investigation that it was his position that CIA had to determine whether the Contras were involved in drug trafficking. It was "a matter of self preservation," not only for the Contra program, but for the Agency. In general, Gates said that the Agency had an obligation to terminate its relationship with any asset who was suspected by U.S. law enforcement agencies to be engaged in drug trafficking. An internal investigation into the allegations was conducted.

During the investigation CIA had numerous assets that had been accused by a number of sources including FBI and DEA as well as others of trafficking, all ended with the following response. No record has been found to indicate that the allegations received by CIA regarding Adolfo Calero, Enrique Bermudez, Stedman Fagoth, Roger Herman, Sebastian Pinel and Arnoldo Jose Arana and drug trafficking was reported to Congress.

On May 3, 1986 a U.S. Citizen airplane was forced to make an emergency landing in Tamiami, Florida. The citizen told fire department officials who responded he was carrying two large cases of top secret material and asked fire department to secure the material while he clear customs. After clearance of Customs, which made no mention of the sensitive material, he returned to the fire department, retrieved his two cases, and disappeared. As a result he was placed on a U.S. Customs watch-list. On May 15, 1986 CIA received a cable from DEA asking if CIA had any connection with the U.S. citizen. DEA reported the civilian told firemen responding to the crash that three Salvadoran passengers traveling with him were being transported to Fort Bragg, North Carolina on behalf of CIA.

On July 1, 1986, cable reported meeting with FBI and Metro Dade Police Department representatives that, when the U.S. citizen returned to retrieve two suitcases that he had left in the custody of fire officials following the crash, he was accompanied by a Metro Dade reserve police officer who also claimed connection with CIA and vouched for him. According to the report, an investigation into the matter of the Metro Dade reserve police officer was delayed by police officials fearing they would be intervening in a CIA operation. After review CIA had no association with the U.S. citizen, the Salvadorans or the reserve police officer.

DEA Special Agent Celerino Castillo alleged that Ilopango air base was used by the Contras to support Contra drug trafficking activities. Castillo served from 1985 to 1990 in the regional DEA office in Guatemala City. Castillo's responsibilities while assigned to the regional DEA office included El Salvador and Guatemala City. According to Castillo, his duties brought him into contact with CIA officials where he discussed the allegations relating to Contra drug trafficking.

On August 15 1996 Castillo stated he met with Jack McCavett, CIA station chief in El Salvador and offered evidence against the Contras. McCavett denied any connection between the CIA and the Ilopango operation. As far as William Brasher was concerned, McCavett said "He doesn't work for me. He works for the Contras and Ollie North, and we have nothing to do with that operation."

Three days later, McCavett called Castillo into his office and pulled $45,000 in cash out of his desk drawer. "I've got money left over from my budget I need to spend," he said. "Take this for your anti-narcotics group. Go buy them some cars." McCavett didn't mention the Contras, but I suspected he was trying to buy me off. The CIA, to my knowledge, had never given the DEA this kind of gift. I wrote out a receipt and handed it to him, took the stack of bills, and gave it to Adame and Aparecio. They bought three much needed vehicles for an El Salvadoran Police organization. Castillo claimed he discussed Contra drug trafficking activities with Randy Kapasar, a CIA agent in Guatemala: He knew I was investigating the Contras. I knew he was helping them. I expected him to deny my evidence of the Contras' narcotrafficking but he followed Sofi's reasoning: "Cele, how do you think the Contras are gonna make money? They've got to run dope, that's the only way we can finance this operation." (63)

According to the CIA internal report an officer who says he met former DEA Special Agent Celerino Castillo in Guatemala and, on one occasion, worked with him and others on a project unrelated to the Contras, recalls Castillo discussing suspected narcotics trafficking at Ilopango, but recalls that Castillo made no specific reference to possible Contra involvement in those activities. Contrary to Castillo's claims, this officer emphatically denies that he had any knowledge of Contra drug trafficking activities at Ilopango or elsewhere. He also denies that he made any statement to Castillo relating to such knowledge. He also denies that he ever asked Castillo to back away from any narcotics investigation.

Felix Rodriguez, former CIA officer, was an advisor to the Salvadoran military in a private capacity at Ilopango. Rodriguez worked from February 1985 until the late 1980s where he provided aid to the Contras. Rodriguez states that he has no knowledge of any alleged Contra drug trafficking activities being conducted from Ilopango or elsewhere.

In April of 1986 CIA learned that Senator John Kerry of the Senate Foreign Relations Committee had opened an investigation into the alleged drug smuggling allegations to review American involvement. The investigation found that an ongoing drug smuggling operation included the production of cocaine in Columbia, processed in Costa Rica and transported to controlled airstrips with American support for distribution to the United States.

As the Committee proceeded with its investigation, significant information began surfacing concerning the operations of international narcotics traffickers, particularly relating to the Colombian-based cocaine cartels. As a result, the decision was made to incorporate the Contra-related allegations into a broader investigation concerning the relationship between foreign policy, narcotics trafficking and law enforcement.

The Senate Committee Report on Drugs, Law Enforcement and Foreign Policy also focused on multiple businesses The State Department selected for aiding the Contra efforts. During the investigation they found that at least four businesses were owned and operated by narcotics traffickers to supply humanitarian assistance to the Contras. These companies included SETCO Air, a company established by Honduran drug trafficker Ramon Matta Ballesteros; DIACSA, a Miami-based air company operated as the headquarters of a drug trafficker enterprise for convicted drug traffickers Floyd Carlton and Alfredo Caballero; Frigorificos de Puntarenas, a firm owned and operated by Cuban-American drug traffickers; and Vortex, an air service and supply company partly owned by admitted drug trafficker Michael Palmer.

The overall conclusion from Senate Committee Report on Drugs, Law Enforcement and Foreign Policy was there were forces both inside and outside the U.S. that took advantage of the anti-communist sentiment which existed in Central America and used it for drug trafficking.

In addition to Senate hearings, the Reagan Administration found themselves in the middle of the S&L scandal. Both federal investigations and media accounts shed light on CIA involvement through covert business assets and cutouts.

After the failure of the Indian Springs State Bank in Kansas City, Missouri in 1984, federal investigators focused their attention on Farhad Azima, a major shareholder in the bank. Azima, an Iranian emigrant whose family had close ties to the Shah, was a valuable business asset for CIA. Azima was also the owner of Global International Airways. The same company whose clients included CIA supported Southern Air Transport and Egyptian American Transport and Services Corporation. The finances of Indian Springs Bank and Global were intimately intertwined. When Global filed for bankruptcy, Indian Springs was next in line. (64)

Other investigations included the First National Bank of Maryland which was used by Associated Traders, a CIA proprietary company, to make payments for covert operations. Associated traders used its accounts at First National to supply $23 million in arms for covert operations in Afghanistan, Angola, Chad, and Nicaragua. (65)

The links between the First National Bank of Maryland and the CIA were exposed in a lawsuit filed in Federal District Court by Robert Maxwell, a high-ranking bank officer. Maxwell charged in that suit that he had been asked to commit crimes on behalf of the CIA. Specifically, he charged that he was asked to conceal Associated Traders' business activities, which by law he was required to specify on all letters of credit. Maxwell alleged that he had been physically threatened and forced to leave his job after asking that his superiors supply him with a letter stating that the activities he was being asked to engage in were legal. In responding to Maxwell's lawsuit, attorneys for the bank state that "a relationship between First National and the CIA and Associated Traders was classified information which could neither be confirmed nor denied. (66)

Operation Cyclone
Soviet and Afghan Intervention

In December of 1979 Soviet forces crossed into Afghanistan in what was believed to expand their foothold on East Asia. President Jimmy Carter had enacted diplomatic policy to terminate and arranged  importation of Russian Wheat as well as prohibited American involvement in the 1980 Summer Olympics in Moscow. On July 3, 1979 President Carter authorized CIA funding for anticommunist guerrillas in Afghanistan feeling the invasion of the Soviets could threaten peace world-wide. Operation Cyclone was formed to train and arm Afghan mujahedeen and became one of the longest and most expensive covert operations in CIA history. The U.S. initially wished to simply prolong the invasion to drag the bloody conflict out for as long as possible. "We now have the opportunity of giving to the Soviet Union its Vietnam War," Carter's national security advisor, Zbigniew Brzezinski.

By 1980, under President Ronald Reagan, the operations annual budget was approximately $20 million to use CIA SAD teams to both train and provide arms. Under the leadership of CIA regional head Gust Avrakotos and former green beret and CIA SAD officer Michael G. Vickers, the operation consisted of secretly training guerrilla fighters to use more modern weapons that could not be traced to the United States in their struggle against the Soviets. Avrakotos was born on January 14, 1938 in Aliquippa, Pennsylvania. The son of a Greek American soft drink manufacturer, he graduated valedictorian from Aliquippa High School in 1955 and later attended the University of Pittsburgh graduating summa cum laude with a degree in economics. Avrakotos joined CIA in 1962 where he was assigned to Greece and worked in anti-terrorism. By the 1980s, while stationed at Langley, he was assigned to work with Congressman Charlie Wilson. Avrakotos retired in 1989 but returned as a contractor to CIA in 1997-2003. Two years later he died on December 1, 2005 after suffering a massive stroke at the age of 67.

The program funding was increased yearly due to lobbying by prominent U.S. politicians and government officials, such as Charles Wilson, Gordon Humphrey, Fred Ikle, and William Casey. Under the Reagan administration, U.S. support for the Afghan mujahedeen evolved into a centerpiece of U.S. foreign policy, called the Reagan Doctrine, in which the U.S. provided military and other support to anti-communist resistance movements in Afghanistan, Angola, and Nicaragua.

By the mid-1980s Texas Congressman Charlie Wilson built relationships with Pakistani Inter-Services Intelligence (ISI) as an intermediary for funds distribution, passing of weapons, military training and financial support to Afghan resistance groups. Along with funding from similar programs from Britain's MI6 and SAS, Saudi Arabia, and the People's Republic of China, the ISI armed and trained over 100,000 insurgents. They encouraged the volunteers from the Arab states to join the Afghan resistance in its struggle against the Soviet troops based in Afghanistan. A Pentagon senior official, Michael Pillsbury, successfully advocated providing Stinger missiles to the Afghan resistance. Once the mujahedeen was armed with the Stinger Missile (man-portable air-defense system), they were able to shoot down hundreds of combat helicopters, thus removing their greatest Soviet threat. The Soviet troops completely pulled out of Afghanistan on February 15, 1989. President Reagan's Covert Action program has been credited with assisting in ending the Soviet occupation of Afghanistan.

Prior to CIA operations in Afghanistan opium production was limited to small territories or regions. CIA used assets to require peasants to grow opium as a revolutionary tax, where it was transferred across the Pakistan border under security of the ISI to heroin laboratories of local drug lords. According to former CIA director of Afghan operations Charles Cogan, the CIA sacrificed the drug war to fight the Cold War. "I don't think that we need to apologize for this. Every situation has its fallout... There was fallout in terms of drugs, yes. But the main objective was accomplished. The Soviets left Afghanistan."

In the wake of the Cold War, Central Asia was prosperous due to oil reserves, but also 75% of the world's opium production. According to the United Nations, the "Golden Crescent" drug trade funds business syndicates, financial institutions, intelligence agencies and organized crime with an annual turnover of $200 billion.

After the Soviets fled Afghanistan in 1989 the United States slowly limited their support and aid to the country. Civil war eventually broke out producing an imbalance in governmental control and years of bloody conflict between combative factions. In 1996 the Taliban, a political-religious group seized the province of Kabul and within four years controlled Afghanistan. During the Taliban rule it was illegal for Afghans to grow hashish and poppy because the illicit drug production of opium. Poppy's also produced opium derivatives, morphine and heroin. By 2001 the Taliban had effectively wiped out almost all opium production in the country, which was responsible for one third of Afghanistan's GDP (gross domestic product).

Operation Queens Hunter
El Salvador Civil War

The FMLN (Farabundo Martí National Liberation Front) is a Socialist political party of El Salvador that was formerly a revolutionary guerrilla organization. The FMLN formed as an umbrella group on October 10, 1980 from the left wing guerilla organizations: the Fuerzas Populares de Liberación Farabundo Martí (FPL), Ejército Revolucionario del Pueblo (ERP), the Resistencia Nacional (RN), the Partido Comunista Salvadoreño (PCS) and the Partido Revolucionario de los Trabajadores Centroamericanos (PRTC).

In December of the same year, the Salvadoran branch of the Partido Revolucionario de los Trabajadores Centroamericanos broke away from its central organization and affiliated itself to FMLN. After the formation of the FMLN, they organized to launch their first major military offensive on January 10, 1981. During this offensive, the FMLN established operational control over large sections of the departments of Morazán and Chalatenango, which remained largely under guerrilla control throughout the rest of the civil war. Revolutionaries ranged from children to the elderly, both male and female, and most were trained in FMLN camps in the mountains and jungles of El Salvador to learn military techniques.

The "Woerner Report," a secret Pentagon document produced in 1981 by Brig. Gen. Fred F. Woerner, provided an early, critical blueprint for U.S. assistance to the Salvadoran armed forces, recommending support for a "strategic victory" against the guerrillas. General Woerner's report included the creation of twenty-five battalions with training to improve command control, intelligence, communication, combat support, and military training. The second part of the report was the strategy on fighting the war. Woerner believed tactically to use both day and night operations with small units to fight the insurgents. With eight battalions strategically located in key positions of the country for supply and support, Woerner felt this plan would provide both aggression as well as protection for the country's economic structure.

The plan was approved by President Ronald Reagan and thrust support through the use of U.S. Army Special Forces, Delta Force and CIA NOCs to coordinate training to Salvadorian soldiers. Woerner's strategy called for additional military support fearing the El Salvadorian military was too small to combat the rightwing guerrillas. This prompted the U.S. to recruit combat contractors or mercenaries to assist in the offensive and increased training to include counterinsurgency tactics on bases in Honduras, Panama and the United States. The current El Salvadorian forces were poorly equipped and trained and lacked motivation for combat. CIA had overseen the U.S. military involvement through the use of Operations, Plans, and Training (OPAT) with assistance of U.S. Special Forces. Although only fifty-five U.S. military personnel were approved to participate through Congress, CIA leveraged three month rotations of mobile infantry teams that were not required to be accounted for during the operations to conceal exact numbers.

The training objective was to win the "hearts and minds" of the El Salvadorian people and limit collateral damage, thus gaining support for democratic elect President Duarte and sway negativity towards the FMLN. OPAT created smaller teams to work round the clock in providing defense to El Salvador villages and communities to limit FMLN involvement. Because of increased attacks from FMLN members the country's fear increased and their support for Duarte decreased. CIA leveraged NSA resources from Fort Meade to provide technical assistance to increase their intelligence on FMLN members. This provided knowledge that the FMLN was leveraging Sandinista assistance through transporting supplies across the Nicaraguan borders and providing logistics for border attacks. President Reagan grew concerned that if the FMLN took control of El Salvador, U.S. interests such as the Panama Canal, oil supplies, and sea lanes may be disrupted.

The NSA involvement accompanied by additional intelligence sources proved effective in gathering and locating a number of FMLN supply routes and hideouts through the use of Beech craft King Air 100s crisscrossing overhead. The secretive ISA (Intelligence Support Activity), also known as "Activity", were the prime overseers of the operation. The ISA came to light in the mid 1980s during the Vietnam POW topic. Former Special Forces Lt. Col. "Bo" Gritz claimed he was tasked by the organization to conduct a covert rescue mission to free Vietnam POWS. In reality, CIA was meeting with Gritz to gather knowledge on his alleged Laos sources for an operation, which would be called Operation Velvet Hammer. After learning he was not credible, the operation was disbanded. The ISA today works under a variety o different code names which are changed every two years. Some past code names include CENTRA SPIKE, TORN VICTOR, CEMETERY WIND and GRAY FOX. Originally formed as a signal intelligence division the 250-275 strong group now works in both SIGINT and HUMINT. Often overseen by CIA SAD, the ISA primarily provides intelligence for tactical Delta and DEVGRU (elite SEAL team, formerly SEAL Team 6 or ST6) operators.

The NSA and ISA operation, known as Operation Queen Hunter, succeeded gathering vital intelligence for the El Salvador affair and by the end of 1982, U.S. Special Forces was able to prevent numerous FMLN ambushes and also provide the Contras with Sandinista intelligence collected from FMLN prisoners. This was crucial in chartering the ISA to engage in "special activities" reserved for CIA under Presidential Executive Order 12333, which was passed by President Ronald Reagan on December 4, 1981. The success enabled the ISA to participate in clandestine operations with the direct communication to both CIA and DIA knowledge.

Unfortunately with other priorities throughout the world, the U.S. focus on El Salvador was minimal and the objective to strengthen the El Salvador government to overrun the guerrillas failed. In January of 1984 Vice-President George Bush requested CIA to report on the progress of the El Salvador government in dealing with the rightwing violence in the country. CIA acknowledged that the action by El Salvador government and military was primarily verbal through denouncing the death squads in the local press, but has not taken any action regarding the situation. For years the death squads would instill havoc on El Salvador through the eruption of a civil war. Over the course of the next five years the unstable government would eventually reach a peace agreement in 1992.

CIA learned of many factors that impacted the survival of the guerrilla fighters that were from sources unexpected to the military tactical planning. On February 5, 1990 CIA reported "The catholic church has played the most important political role of all the churches in El Salvador. Many government officials believe that the frequent attempts by Catholic leaders to mediate talks between the FMLN and the government have boosted the guerrillas' political legitimacy both domestically and abroad, catholic leaders in El Salvador also served as intermediaries between the guerrillas and government officials, are known to meet privately with rebel leaders, and often work to expedite the evacuation of wounded insurgents or make other requests on their behalf. The government is very sensitive to charges of persecution of religious workers, especially in the wake of international outrage over the arrest and deportation of foreign church workers.

As a result, President Cristiani ordered that all searches of church property must be approved by the Army High Command. Although no serious incidents have occurred since early in the offensive, relations between the churches and the security forces are likely to remain uneasy as the government continues to monitor closely church activities. Because the FMLN's November offensive the level of popular support for the insurgents, the military probably is even more convinced, in our judgment, that foreign support, especially from religious and humanitarian organizations, is crucial to the FMLN's survival."

During the offensive the agency was aware that Catholic churches had assisted the FMLN through a variety of situations including:

- Hiding FMLN fighters
- Caring for wounded FMLN
- Funding FMLN fighters through church donations
- Recruit outside clergy to raise funding

On numerous occasions--including during the recent FMLN urban offensive members often hid in churches, and, usually posing as civilians, sought refuge in church-run shelters. CIA learned that international humanitarian aid workers told that various churches provided charitable contributions and food donations to known FMLN insurgents. This included the Lutheran Church who coordinated the return of Salvadoran refugees planning to participate in the FMLN offensive, and that Baptist Church members' were stockpiling food, medicines, and supplies, which speculates they may have supported the FMLN during the pending urban offensive.

On February 19, 1991 Ambassador William Walker sent a secret cable to Assistant Secretary of State, Bernard Aronson on the Salvadoran military's stonewalling of investigations into the

1989 murders of six Jesuit priests. According to Walker the El Salvador military is "committed to protecting their own at whatever cost." The pleas and threats made by the U.S. to investigate the murders have produced no results. Walker concluded that the El Salvador government was controlled by a flawed leader.

After the ceasefire established by the 1992 Chapultepec Peace Accords, the FMLN became a legal political party. The FMLN has since participated in elections from 1994 - 2009. The FMLN is currently, along with ARENA, one of the two dominant political parties in El Salvador. Since 2000, the FMLN and ARENA have traded off in elections with controlling the largest number of Legislative Assembly seats.

Operation Panama 3 & 4
Overthrowing Manuel Noriega

Operation Panama 3 and 4 were a covert Central Intelligence Agency program to support political opponents of General Manuel Antonio Noriega during 1988 and 1989. The operations were basically unresponsive from the start. Both alternatives CIA selected to replace Noriega fell apart during operations. In Panama 3, the Senate Intelligence Committee objected to

Manuel Noriega

the operation, which intended to support a military coup led by Col. Eduardo Herrera Hassan. Hassan, an anti-Noriega military officer, was CIAs first choice since he was appointed to lead the Panama Defense Force by the new Government. The committee believe there was little chance for success with the coup and had concerns that the action could bring the United States dangerously close to violating a Presidential ban on supporting political assassinations. During Operation Panama 4, CIA selected a Panamanian, Carlos Eleta Alamaran. Eleta's role in the covert program for the elections was to distribute money to others involved in opposition political activities. Unfortunately for CIA, Eleta on April 6, 1989 was arrested in Macon, GA on charges of conspiracy to import cocaine and money laundering. Much of the operation would be at ground level and rely on assets and cutout operatives CIA officers could recruit on the fly.

Jose A. Rodriguez, Jr. was born in Puerto Rico in 1948, Rodriguez attended the University of Florida, earning both a bachelor's and law degree and joined the CIA in 1976. He was assigned to the Directorate of Operations in the Latin America division working in Peru and Belize. Over time he was promoted to Chief of Station (COS) in Panama, Mexico and the Dominican Republic. (60) Rodriguez was assigned the task of overseeing Operation Panama 3 and Operation Panama 4. For many years Noriega was a CIA collaborator, but by 1988 the U.S. government turned against him and his increasingly oppressive and corrupt regime. Much of Noriega's involvement was made public during the Iran-Contra scandal just a few years earlier. By removing Noriega from power the agency could distance themselves from association. The CIA was ready to assist those Panamanians who wanted to bring an end to Noriega's dictatorship. One big challenge was Noriega himself. The CIA was cautious in their covert activity because of Noriega's inside knowledge of the CIA and how their covert activities play out. Noriega had been an asset of CIA since the 1960s and was even trained by the U.S. in intelligence and counterintelligence techniques.

Rodriguez and CIA had learned of an American named Kurt Muse, who along with some friends had been operating a clandestine radio station that overrode government frequencies and broadcast anti-Noriega messages. "We were not a very expensive operation to run," Muse recalls. "But we had some apartments that we rented, and basically we were just running out of money. And elements of the U.S. government contacted us and wanted to know if we needed any help." It was a tense time, according to Muse, a U.S. citizen who grew up in Panama and became involved in the anti-Noriega opposition. "You could not broadcast anything," Muse says. "You couldn't print anything offensive to the government. The freedom of assembly was severely curtailed. In our own meetings of our group of five, we seldom had an opportunity to actually get together, the five of us, without risk of being compromised." (61)

This knowledge was beneficial for covert activity and the CIA's objective in overthrowing the Noriega regime. Rodriguez was significant in recruiting and funding Muse's underground radio effort and other covert anti-Noriega operations. Rodriguez worked freely in Panama as a NOC and at high risk to his own safety. Noriega was infuriated by the underground radio operation and soon Kurt Muse was located by the PDF and imprisoned awaiting execution. Muse was imprisoned for several months, threatened repeatedly with execution and finally rescued by the U.S. military in the first hours of the December 1989 U.S. invasion of Panama, Operation Just Cause. Muse rescue was known as Operation Acid Gambit and conducted by a small team of Delta Force operators that in the middle of the night landed a helicopter on the roof of the prison and under the cover of smoke grenades and plastic explosives made their way to Muses cell where they were able to evacuate him. Under heavy fire from the PDF their helicopter crashed shortly after lifting off from the prison. The crash left Delta Force operators Pat Savidge, James Sudderth, and Kelly Venden wounded, while Muse and both pilots were uninjured. Shortly after the crash an armored personnel carrier from the 5th Infantry Division extracted Muse and the retrieval team.

In addition to the rescue mission, Operation Nifty Package was a United States Navy SEAL-operated plan designed to apprehend or prevent the escape of Noriega. Executed in tandem with Operation Just Cause, this operation was handled by SEAL Team 4 and tasked with destroying Noriega's private jet on the ground at the Punta Paitilla Airport, a coastal airport in Panama City. A firefight ensued during the team being ambushed by Panamanian military forces, which resulted in the death of four SEAL members. The mission was a strategic success with the launch of a AT4 rocket that destroyed Noriega's plane. Another Navy SEAL group, consisting of four divers and teams in Zodiac attack boats, was assigned to sabotage Noriega's heavily armed gunboat while it was tied to a pier on the canal. The divers swam in the canal while being attacked with Panamanian grenades. Two of the divers descended to the bottom of the canal, beyond the maximum operating limit of their breathing units, and with two bombs successfully destroyed Noriega's gunboat.

Five days after the launch of Operation Just Cause, and a demonstration by thousands of Panamanians demanding he stand trial for human rights violations, Noriega surrendered on January 3, 1990. He was tried on eight counts of drug trafficking, racketeering, and money laundering in April 1992. His trial was held in Miami, Florida, in the United States District Court for the Southern District of Florida. The United States Attorney negotiated deals with 26 different drug felons, including Carlos Lehder, who were given leniency, cash payments, and allowed to keep their drug earnings in return for testimony against Noriega. Several of these witnesses had been arrested by Noriega for drug trafficking in Panama. Noriega was found guilty and sentenced on September 16, 1992, to 40 years in prison for drug and racketeering violations. His sentence was reduced to 30 years in 1999.

Operation Gothic Serpent
Covert Action in Mogadishu

In early 1991, after intense and bloody fighting, Ali Mahdi Muhammad of the United Somali Congress took control of Mogadishu and the rest of southern Somalia. The Somali National Movement gained control of the north, the old British Somaliland, and proclaimed  it the independent Somaliland Republic. In 1992, civil war between the two Somalia's, internal clan-based fighting, and the worst African drought of the century created devastating famine, which threatened one-fourth of the Somali population with starvation. In response, troops from the United States and other U.N. nations occupied Somalia in late 1992 to ensure distribution of food aid and to suppress Somalia's warring factions. Although many of the U.N.'s temporary humanitarian aims were achieved, the military operation was largely unsuccessful. In 1993, a national cease-fire was signed, but no central government was formed, and fighting erupted again later in the year.

Somalia was a nation in need of rebuilding. A revolt against the country's sitting dictator in 1991 had left the capital in anarchy; the ensuing civil war ravaged southern Somalia. Along the way, the U.S. Embassy and the CIA's Mogadishu station were evacuated by helicopter. The United Nations suspended its efforts at famine relief because of thievery and fighting. In late 1992, President George H. W. Bush sent 25,000 U.S. troops to Somalia for the express purpose of assuring the delivery of U.N. food, medicine and other supplies. As soon as Operation Restore Hope was unveiled, the CIA sent advance teams to Somalia to assess conditions on the ground before the troops arrived. The first American killed in Somalia, in fact, was a CIA operative whose vehicle hit a mine outside Bardera on December 23, 1992. "The U.S. military was going into Somalia knowing nothing about Somalia," William R. Piekney, then chief of the CIA's Africa division. "We were their eyes and ears on the ground."

By May 1993 relief supplies flowed and the country was relatively peaceful, the U.S. withdrew most troops and turned Somalia over to U.N. peacekeeping forces. The Clinton administration strongly supported this more aggressive stance and the United Nations named retired U.S. Navy Adm. Jonathan Howe, who had been President Bush's deputy national security adviser, as its senior representative in Somalia. The head of the Somali National Alliance, Gen. Mohamed Farah Aideed, became the dominant force in Mogadishu and was unpleased with both the United Nations and U.S. involvement. Aideed increased his armed presence in Mogadishu and started a propaganda campaign of anti-U.N. rhetoric on Radio Mogadishu. In early June, twenty-four Pakistani peacekeepers were killed in an ambush just after they had inspected Aideed's radio transmission center. Howe issued an arrest warrant for Aideed and offered a $25,000 reward, turning U.N. peacekeepers into a posse. Aideed denied involvement in the ambush and asked for a commission of inquiry. Howe reported to U.N. headquarters in New York but also had direct access to senior officials in the Clinton White House. Howe lobbied the U.S. officials to send in the Delta Force to apprehend Aideed. Instead, the U.S. took a more aggressive approach launching a missile attack against the Somali National Alliance (SNA) command center killing several of Aideed's high ranking militants. The result of the attack included the SNA declaring war on the United States.

Any chance the peacekeepers had of negotiating with Aideed disappeared in mid-July, when a unit of the U.S. Army's

10th Mountain Division — the American component of the U.N. peacekeeping force — launched a ferocious missile attack on the Somali National Alliance's command center, killing at least 20, and perhaps as many as 50, Aideed lieutenants and operatives. The attack, approved at the highest levels of both the United Nations and the Clinton administration, was supposed to remove Aideed and the SNA as an obstacle to nation building in Somalia.

The CIA needed more in-depth intelligence for future military assistance. In August of 1993 Garret Jones and John Spinelli stepped off of a DC-3 onto an airstrip in Mogadishu. Jones had just finished a year's study at the Army War College in Carlisle, Pa., where he'd written a paper on U.N. peacekeeping missions. At the time CIA was closing stations all around the world, and Jones who had African knowledge, volunteered for the operation. There to meet him was his deputy, Spinelli, who had been reassigned from CIA's Rome station and sent to Somalia. He knew nothing about Africa, but he spoke Italian, and the Italians in the U.N. peacekeeping force weren't getting along with their American counterparts. Spinelli took Jones, the new CIA Station chief to the compound which was like nothing Jones had ever seen. The entire building was unsecured in an area that contained burned out wreckage scattered with litter and combatants all around.

The CIA requested Jones to assist the military in gathering intelligence on the SNA as well as relocate the CIA base of operations from the airfield to the United Nations compound. Relations between the CIA and U.N.'s special envoy Robert Gosende were strained. The country was basically in turmoil outside the U.N. compound with no true official authority. The CIA's electronic snoops tried to monitor Aideed's radio traffic from a tent on the sand dune overlooking the airstrip, but all the high-tech wizardry was of little value; Mogadishu had sunk to what might be called a pre-electronic state. If Jones's band of spies were going to help the military arrest Aideed, they would have to do it by working those streets.

The agency's primary asset was a minor sub clan leader from north Mogadishu left over from before the U.S. government pulled out in 1991. He controlled approximately 350-400 men, which was small but rentable for the CIA and had extensive knowledge of logistics valued for seeking out Aideed. The CIA even brought in an operations officer who was the Warlord's previous controller to run him for the current operations. The officer, code-named Condor, had distinguished himself as a military officer in Vietnam and become a stellar CIA operator. Condor had another critical attribute: He was African American, which allowed him to blend into the scenery in a way that Jones and Spinelli, both white men, never could. With Condor on the scene, the CIA's Office of Technical Services back in Langley implanted a homing beacon into an ivory-handled walking stick and hatched a plan straight out of Hollywood. The Warlord would give Aideed the walking stick as a token of friendship. After that, tracking Aideed would be a simple matter of following the beacon's signal.

In late August Jones met a C-141 Starlifter, carrying an advance team of security guards, communications technicians and logistics officers, told Jones all he needed to know: The Delta Force was being sent in to take down Aideed. "With you in town, I work for you," Jones told the man with the cigar. He was Maj. Gen. William F. Garrison, Delta's commander, traveling under cover. "Okay," Jones remembers Garrison replying, "I need intelligence." Delta Force worked out the communications between Delta and CIA station while on the airstrip and wasted no time in developing a plan in seeking out Aideed. Unfortunately their asset the Warlord would be unavailable for the purpose of the capture. The evening before, he shot himself in the head during a game of Russian roulette. Garrison assigned a

Delta officer code named Gringo II as a liaison between Delta and CIA.

On August 26 thirteen Delta Force operators, a company of U.S. Rangers and 16 helicopters touched down under a barrage of mortar attacks on the airstrip. Garrison wished to hit Aideed hard and after a failed kidnapping attempt at a local hangout called Lig-Ligato, resulting in the capture of U.N. officials vs. Aideed and his people, he requested Jones to put together a Tier One List of Aideed's top lieutenants. If you can't find the head, attack the body. The plan was code named Operation Gothic Serpent.

Through military intelligence Jones learned there had been a list composed but was severely outdated, thus leaving Delta with alternative targets. Condor suggested taking over the dead Warlords men to track down Aideed. Since the initiative was both bold and dangerous Jones arranged for him to carry this out and Garrison added four Navy SEAL snipers to protect him from a distance. Condor's team was flown in to an abandoned soccer stadium in Mogadishu where they were then transported to a safe house.

In addition, Spinelli had been contacted to arrange a meet with some of Aideed's bodyguards who were looking to collect the $25,000 reward. After mapping out Spinelli's meeting point, Spinelli and a CIA SAT team headed to meet with the bodyguards but were caught in crossfire. Spinelli had been shot in the neck He was flown first to Germany and then the U.S. to Fairfax Hospital where he recovered from his surgery. After two weeks of success, Condor was retrieved by Garrison's Delta Force team after Jones got word that Aideed was suspicious of his origins.

The CIA left a couple surveillance teams in the area for gathering intelligence, but no more undercover work was active.

Towards the end of September, and pressure from President Bill Clinton, the CIA got a break when an asset through Condor's team advised he would produce the whereabouts of Osman Ato, the number two of Aideed. Osman was a money man and key in providing Aideed arms for his fighters. The CIA team used the cane with the radio beacon during the meet and was able to track Ato's movements. Within minutes, a Delta team in a Little Bird helicopter located the vehicle and fired three sniper rounds disabling the vehicle. Delta Force then handcuffed Alto and evacuated with him from the area. Jones contacted his CIA supervisor; Africa division chief Piekney offering, "Things are bad and they're getting worse," Jones began. "Howe didn't know what he was doing, Jones wrote, and the Delta Force was being misused — capturing Aideed would do little to solve Somalia's problems as a nation."

On October 3 the CIA gained a tip from a newly formed asset top Aideed lieutenants, including two from the Tier One list — Omar Salad Elmi and Mohamed Hassan Awale — would be meeting that afternoon near the Olympic Hotel and the Bakara market. The Delta Force intelligence chief instructed the asset to drive to the target building, pull up out front and open the hood of his car. Once the asset reached the location, an Orion spy plane and surveillance helicopters recorded the exact location and streamed back to the Delta Force command center.

Both Jones and Garrison were in the command center when the general gave the order for assault and watched it unfold in real time across a bank of video screens. Delta Force commandos roped down from helicopters and blew open the doors of the target house. Rangers roped down from helicopters and secured the perimeter. Within minutes, Jones heard a radio call from a commando inside the target building: "Precious cargo." The commandos had 24 Somali prisoners in cuffs. At 4:20 p.m., Jones heard radio from the Delta Force command center that a Blackhawk helicopter had been shot down and the convoy bearing the "precious cargo" had been redirected to the crash site. Soon after Condor called in from his tent on a dune near the airstrip, "There's another Blackhawk going down right now." On its way to the first crash site, the convoy got lost in Mogadishu's labyrinthine streets, blasted at every intersection with machine guns and grenade launchers. About 90 minutes after the first Blackhawk went down, the convoy made its way back to the airstrip — without ever reaching the crash site. Nearly half of those on board — 50 U.S. soldiers and their 24 Somali prisoners — had been shot or hit by shrapnel.

The Somali incident was popularized in mainstream media through books and film, "Blackhawk Down", but the operation by the CIA that initiated the assault was not. Both the execution of the operation and the intelligence aspect proved to be a failure. Jones believed the rushed process due to a sense of urgency pressured by Congress was a leading factor.

Operation DBACHILLES

CIA backed Saddam Hussein Military Coup

Beginning in 1980, the CIA militarily and monetarily assisted Iraq during the Iran–Iraq War. This was the province of the South Asia Operations Group headed by Gust Avrakotos. There was little the Agency could do directly against Khomeini. But indirectly it was doing tremendous damage by providing covert assistance to Saddam Hussein and the Iraqis for their bloody war with Iran. As explained by Ed Juchniewicz – Avrakotos's patron and

Saddam Hussein

the number two man in the Operations Division at that time -- they were just leveling the playing field: "We didn't want either side to have the advantage. We just wanted them to kick the shit out of each other". By 1989-1990 the CIA withdrew all support of Saddam Hussein after his 1990 invasion into Kuwait. (62) Prior to Saddam's invasion, Mohammed Abdullah Shahwani fled Iraq and defected to London, England. Shahwani, a Sunni from Mosul and a charismatic commander who made his reputation in 1984 with a helicopter assault on Iranian troops atop a mountain in Iraqi Kurdistan. His popularity made him dangerous to Saddam Hussein, and he was arrested and interrogated in 1989. (63) Shahwani was key to the CIA in building relationships with strategic Iraqi Military officials. At the time, CIA was providing intelligence support to the U.S. Military for Desert Storm and Desert Shield, but Shahwani added a new spin for the agency. In 1991, Shahwani began efforts to organize a military coup utilizing former members of the Iraq Special Forces, which Hussein had disbanded. Shahwani soon returned to Jordan to collect intelligence on Iraq during the Gulf War.

Operation DBACHILLES began in the fall 1994 as the concept of the CIA's Near East Division Chief, Stephen Richter, who believed that a military coup against Hussein was possible with the help from Shahwani. Shahwani began planning a coup against Saddam Hussein with the support of his three sons then serving in the Republican Guard. Al-Shahwani also brought in Iraqi National Accord leader Ayad Allawi, who in turn informed MI6, and consequently the CIA. (64) As the CIA was drafting its plans, the British encouraged the agency to contact an experienced Iraqi exile named Ayad Allawi, who headed a network of current and former Iraqi military officers and Baath Party operatives known as Wifaq, the Arabic word for "trust."

Complicating the CIA's coup planning was a similar effort in northern Iraq by Ahmed Chalabi's Iraqi National Congress. A CIA officer named Bob Baer was dispatched in January 1995 to coordinate the various covert efforts, but they only got more tangled. Chalabi launched his unsuccessful coup in March 1995, and Baer was suddenly summoned home to Washington. The 1995 fiasco only reinforced the CIA's belief in the traditional military coup approach of DBACHILLES. But an Iraqi source argues that by late 1995, some of Shahwani's and Allawi's operatives were already controlled by Iraqi intelligence. (65)

In March of 1996 Chalabi visited Washington and CIA Director John Deutch and Deputy Director George Tenet to express concern that the operation had been compromised and any attempt at a military-coup would be disastrous. Chalabi advised that the Iraqi military had intercepted an Inmarsat satellite phone from an Egyptian courier while in route to Baghdad. The secure phone was meant to be delivered to one of Shahwani's sons. Both men, Deutch and Tenet, didn't seem too concerned over the interception and the coup continued as planned.

"I moved in and out of northern Iraq, as well as the countries bordering Iraq," says Rick Francona, Air Force lieutenant colonel assigned to both the Defense Intelligence Agency, and CIA. "We were involved in what was known inside the Agency as 'DBACHILLES' – the overthrow of Saddam Hussein. We at CIA had tried to contact and co-opt as many Iraqi military officers as we could, hoping to convince them that they should not fight when and if an invasion or coup attempt occurred. That program had some successes." Francona was uniquely equipped for the duty. Fluent in Arabic, Francona had worked out of the defense attaché office in Baghdad at the end of the Iran-Iraq War. As a Defense Intelligence Agency official, he had worked as America's liaison officer to Iraq's Directorate of Military Intelligence.

The agency set him up in Kurdistan, the northern section of Iraq no longer under Saddam's control. Working out of a heavily sandbagged house in Sal-ah-din, Francona worked with Kurdish officials and ran several operations, training Kurdish pershmerga militants, extricating the family of an Iraqi nuclear scientist who had defected and meeting regularly, even daily, with Kurdish leaders, including Talabani. At the time, Talabani was head of the PUK, the Patriotic Union of Kurdistan, the main Kurdish opposition group. He is now President of Iraq.

"I met with Talabani on numerous occasions. I was a guest in his home, we had professional meetings almost daily," says Francona. "In 1996, we were involved in supporting the Kurds and other opposition groups operating out of northern Iraq, also other countries in the region. (66)

In late June of 1996 Operation DBACHILLES came to a bloody end with Iraqi military arresting more than 200 coup participants and executing at least 80 of the plotters. The CIA

blamed Chalabi for exposing the plot. Shahwani was able to escape but his three sons, Major Anmar al-Shahwani, Captain Ayead al-Shahwani, and Lt. Atheer al-Shahwani were among the 80 operatives killed.

In the run-up to war, both Allawi and Shahwani played important roles in the coalition's effort to encourage Iraqi officers to surrender or defect. It was, in essence, the same strategy that had been tried unsuccessfully in the mid-1990s, but intelligence operatives moved ahead, regardless. The anticipated defectors included a top Iraqi Defense Ministry official and a top Republican Guard commander. Among the few who were dubious from the start, it's said, was Defense Secretary Donald Rumsfeld. "Rumsfeld always said that you need to be wary of people who say they'll flip for you, because they're probably playing, at a minimum, both sides and saying similar things to Saddam," recalled Deputy Defense Secretary Paul Wolfowitz. (65)

Between 1996 and 2003 Shahwani continued building an opposition network in Iraq with the help of the CIA, and although a planned military uprising was vetoed by the Pentagon, Shahwani used his influence to try and convince Iraqi security forces not to resist the American led invasion. He himself participated in covert American missions in western Iraq in the lead-up to the 2003 invasion of Iraq.

On December 13, 2003 during Operation Red Dawn, a U.S. military operation conducted in the town of ad-Dawr, Iraq, Task Force 121 located and captured Iraq President Saddam Hussein. Hussein was hiding in a spider hole and armed with a pistol, AK-47 and hundreds of thousands of dollars in U.S. currency.

In Bad Company

Operation JAWBREAKER
The Hunt for Osama Bin Laden

After the 9/11 attacks President George W. Bush turned to CIA for answers and a response. The CIA's planning efforts had put them in a better position to respond after the attacks. As CIA Director George Tenet put it, How could [an intelligence] community without a strategic plan tell the president of the United States just four days after 9/11 how to attack the Afghan sanctuary and operate against al Qaeda in ninety-two countries around the

Osama bin Laden

world? On September 15th, 2001 President George W. Bush held a special meeting at Camp David. The meeting was a secretive *war council* with select members of the National Security Council. Representatives from CIA included George Tenet and Joseph "Cofer" Black. Tenet proposed firstly to send CIA teams into Afghanistan which would collect intelligence and mount covert operations. The teams would act jointly with military Special Operations units. "President Bush later praised this proposal, saying it had been a turning point in his thinking." (67) Because of his past knowledge of al-Qaeta and Osama bin Laden, Cofer Black was in attendance. "When we're through with them they will have flies walking across their eyeballs" he said. It was an image of death that left a lasting impression on a number of war cabinet ministers. Black became known in Bush's inner circle as the "flies on the eyeballs guy"…Black's enthusiasm was infectious …Colin Powell, for one, saw that Bush was tired of rhetoric. The President wanted to kill somebody. (68)

On September 26, 2001 CIA sent seven operators of the SAD into the Hindu Kush, Afghanistan by an unmarked helicopter to seek out Osama Bin Laden and kill him. The SAD (Special Activities Division) team was led by Gary C. Schroen. Schroen had planned to retire but was recalled to lead the mission. Schroen had been with CIA for 30 years starting as a case officer and at the time of the mission was Deputy Chief, Near East Division, Directorate of Operations. Schroen was the logical selection because of his experience serving in the Middle East. He served in numerous posts including Station Chief in Kabul, Afghanistan and Islamabad, Pakistan, and possessed numerous relationships with the Mujahideen commanders who fought the Soviets in the Soviet-Afghan War. Another team member was William "Billy" Waugh. Waugh, a highly decorated Vietnam War hero served in the U.S. Army as a Green Beret in 1954 and the CIAs Special Activities Division since 1961. Waugh retired from both the Army and CIA in 1972, yet worked as a contractor periodically when requested. At the age of 71, Waugh joined Schroen as one of the seven SAD members entering Afghanistan. Schroen sought Waugh's experience with Osama bin Laden since he had conducted surveillance and intelligence gathering on bin Laden in Khartoum, Sudan during the 1990s.

The SAD team was code named "Operation Jawbreaker" and tasked with taking out Afghanistan's oppressive Taliban regime, eliminate al-Qaeda, and kill Osama Bin Laden for his role in downing four passenger planes, leveling the World Trade Center towers and leaving the Pentagon in flames. In August of 1998 a bombing of two U.S. Embassies in Dar es Salaam and Nairobi, Africa were attributed to Osama bin Laden and his terrorist network, thus placing him at the top of CIA's watch list. Bin Laden, sheltered by Taliban support, had overseen terror training camps with young jihadists for more than seven years in Asia, Africa, and the Philippines. CIA was limited with human intelligence due to lack of al Qaeda infiltration and was not given authorization by then President Bill Clinton to use lethal force.

The goal of the infiltration was to lay the intelligence groundwork for military action. Henry Crumpton, Deputy Chief of Operations, CIA Counterterrorism Center assembled the first early response team led by Schroen two days after the 911 attacks. "The team leaders we picked were just that, they were leaders. We didn't have time for them to come back and say 'Should I do this' or 'Should I do that'. We expected them to make decisions and they did. The CIAs mission was to determine among the strata of tribal leaders who could we bring to our side."

"Intelligence is the key to this," Crumpton. "All most all of the military participation were ex special forces and had worked within the CIA blending their paramilitary skills with intelligence and covert action." Regarding 911 - "I was watching it on television at the time and suspected it was an al-Qaeda attack given the information we had collected over the years. But once I say the second plane hit I knew immediately it was al-Qaeda. On 911 we had more than 100 sources throughout the various tribal entities, within Afghanistan. And I immediately thought of how do we get into Afghanistan, how do we collect intelligence, how do we recruit allies and how do we engage and kill the enemy. After 911 the president turned to the director of the CIA and said - you have lead...execute. At that point they called me and said, you been wanting to get into Afghanistan for these years past, organize the teams, go." (30)

"We had a major problem with terrorist safe haven in Afghanistan, and given the fact that - that terrorist element inside Afghanistan was dependent upon the support of the Taliban, it seemed to me that it was extremely important for us to penetrate the Taliban as thoroughly as we possibly could," Robert Grenier, CIA Station Chief, Islamabad. "Prior to 911 our role in Afghanistan was simply collecting intelligence. Once 911 happened simply collecting intelligence on the problem wasn't sufficient. We had to do something about it." (30)

The seven man SAD team established landing and operational command in the Panjshir Valley of Afghanistan. Once on the ground the team checked equipment including AK-47s, 9mm pistols, GPS systems, laptops, and millions of dollars to buy support from locals for manpower and logistical assistance for CIA to build the plan for war. Their first step was to build alliances through recruiting Northern tribal forces. The teams location at the upper mountains of Northern Afghanistan left them surrounded by al-Qaeda and Taliban forces in trenches within the valleys below. The SAD team gathered intelligence through the allied Afghans to gain specific knowledge of Taliban and al-Qaeda locations and strongholds. Many allies were former tribal groups CIA sponsored a decade prior to fight of the Soviet invasion during Operation Cyclone. The group was known as the Northern Alliance. CIA had continued relations with the Northern Alliance for years trading information and was leveraging them to piggy back on their civil war against the Taliban. Weeks prior the Northern Alliance leader and CIA asset Ahmad Shah Massoud was assassinated when al-Qaeda terrorists posing as journalists detonated a bomb in his tent. Massoud was a hero among Afghans from his fighting against the Soviets in the 1980s. The CIA quickly reached out to Massoud's senior command and again rebuilt relations. The first meeting between the SAD team and Northern Alliance was with Aref Sarwari, Massoud's head of intelligence. Sarwari agreed to a $500,000 down payment from CIA in exchange for his cooperation. This included the Northern Alliance keeping tabs on positions of the

Taliban and al-Qaeda as well as logistical support in mapping a point of attack.

The next step was recruiting tribal war lords by offering large sums of cash for logistical support. The SAD team remained housed in a Spartan safe house while relying on intelligence from paid assets. In addition these allies were also the SADs lifeline to key essentials such as food, water and other necessities. Without their assistance and trust - the SAD team would not survive for long. The Northern Alliance had struggled since the Taliban takeover of Afghanistan in 1996 to maintain the Northern section of the country called the Panjshir Valley. Similar to World War I, a thousand Northern Alliance soldiers were trying to fend off a Taliban offensive. During the CIAs covert action a conventional war was also being fought.

On October 1st two members of the SAD team journey to the front. Their mission is to map out the battlefield for logistical support for U.S. Bombing campaigns against Taliban defensive positions. The team followed pencil markings to guide them to the front and then used GPS to record their coordinates all while just a few hundred yards from enemy positions. The data was then sent back to the compound where it is then relayed through intelligence cables to Langley, Virginia.

Days went by and there was no U.S. action. CIA officers grew concerned over the loyalty of their Northern Alliance allies and the team was also in a transitional phase. Schroen who had faced mandatory retirement exited the SAD team as leader and was replaced by Gary Berntsen, CIA Senior Operations Officer. "I was told to find Bin Laden, kill him, cut his head off and bring it back to the President," Berntsen. "I said fine, got that." (30)

Berntsen was accompanied by Crumpton, Deputy Chief of Operations and followed up by assisting in seeking those who possess native language skills such as Dari, Farsi, Pashtun, or Arabic. In addition seek out those who possess military skills.

The teams were comprised of officers with paramilitary skills and those operational intelligence and language skills and cultural knowledge of the specific region.

"The CIA. The Directorate of operations does two things: it conducts what we call the (FI) Mission, the Foreign intelligence mission that is collecting intelligence, and it does covert action. Covert action is the taking of any step that the U.S. Government wants to conceal. So if you want to conceal support to some local security forces, to fight some terrorist organization, want to do it secretly, CIA are the people who have the mandate to do that." "The afghans are tribal, they don't get along with one another, and when they do cooperate it's usually against foreign invaders. This is what makes it difficult. It's their territory, it's their ground, they know the ground very well. And they are prepared to fight on it."

On October 7th, 2001 the air assault on the Taliban and al-Qaeda locations began. In addition, U.S. Army Special Forces teams ODA 555 were deployed from the air. These groups immediately took over positions in the front line and laser guided strategic targets for numerous bombing campaigns flown by both bombers and drones.

The bombing campaigns were a success and on October 13th, 2001 - the Taliban had fled Kabul as CIA SAD teams and Special Forces soldiers swept the town. The small U.S. force of 110 CIA officers and 300 Special Forces officers on the ground had been responsible for the evacuation of 60,000 Taliban forces and killed more than 10,000. While sweeping Kabul, the teams located numerous safe houses with intelligence left behind - including weapons, cell phones, manuals and laptop computers. After submitting the raw intelligence to Langley, analysts were able to determine bin Laden's ultimate goal was to obtain nuclear weapons. "The intelligence collected by CIA teams in Afghanistan after 9/11 was truly breathtaking both its scope and its quality for CIA for U.S. Military and for the national command authority to make decisions about where to go next," Crumpton. "With approximately 110 CIA personnel and 300 Special Forces officers on the ground 25% of the Taliban's leadership had been killed.

With the threat of the Taliban removed the CIA focused next on their primary target...Osama bin Laden. Intelligence gathered placed bin Laden heading towards a mountain region known as Tora Bora. CIA SAD teams were concerned that if bin Laden evaded capture too long he could sneak across the border into Pakistan. Berntsen organized a group of his team and headed to Jalalabad and code named Jawbreaker Juliet. Following was a Special Forces unit headed by 20 year veteran Delta Force operator alias Dalton Fury. "Well Delta Force came in to do a target hunting," Fury. "I was specifically asked if I wanted to go after Osama bin Laden or if I wanted to go after Mullah Omar, the Taliban leader. After some consultation with my senior sergeants, we decided to go after Osama bin Laden. We received the orders there to kill bin Laden and the unofficial order to bring back proof."

As they made their way towards Tora Bora, Berntsen's team discovered bin Laden's tracks and moved up the steep mountain terrain trying to avoid the company size factions of al-Qaeta resistance. At approximately 11,000 feet they located a base with hundreds of al-Qaeta soldiers. Berntsen radioed the coordinates for an air strike and within minutes the location was devastated with U.S. Bombs from B52s. Hours after the bombing team Juliet rifled through the debris from the strike including manuals, weapons and even the pockets from dead al-Qaeta soldiers. During the intelligence gathering the team located a radio and began monitoring al-Qaeta traffic. Before too long a CIA translator intimately knowledgeable with bin Laden's voice confirmed him as a party speaking on the radio.

Berntsen sent Fury's team of Special Forces to advance up the mountain and locate bin Laden. "The footing of the mountains on Tora Bora is very unsure," Fury. "It's very rugged. You are talking about terrain go from 4,000 feet at the base up to 10,000 in the battlefield area. You could take a step on a rock and it would give away, and you are worried about stepping on land mines." (30)

By early December the CIA had been tracking bin Laden through his satellite phone. They detect movement through GPS and closed in on the target through ground forces. When they intercept a truck they find the phone with bin Laden's bodyguard as a decoy. This prompted bin Laden to use only human intelligence vs. Technology to avoid detection.

5000 pound laser guided bunker blaster bombs were dropped whenever Fury's team located al-Qaeta soldiers in trenches or caves in Tora Bora. On December 11, 2001, Fury receives word from local tribal CIA assets that they're within hours of bin Laden's camp. When preparing to laser guide a bomb to the destination, the Eastern Alliance announce bin Laden wishes to surrender. The Delta team felt that this was a technique to stall and decided to move in but their allies turn on them holding the team hostage. The group referred to as the Eastern Alliance was not as loyal to CIA as the Northern Alliance. Many revered bin Laden or viewed him and his activities as that of a hero. Once disengaged Berntsen requested addition Special Forces assistance due to the vast terrain. Crumpton, his superior, agreed but was denied by the White House who decided to rely on Pakistan to intercept bin Laden during any border crossing attempt.

On December 15, 2001 CIA spots bin Laden at an al Qaeda cave. They knew this may be their last chance to kill him prior to him fleeing Afghanistan. Almost immediately bombers began blasting the site which continued for nearly three hours. The amount of devastation left the SAD teams to believe that bin Laden had been buried in the cave from the bombing attack. Later reports confirmed that just prior to the bombing Osama bin Laden escaped and disappeared across the border into Pakistan.

The CIA continues to seek out Osama bin Laden and nullify the al Qaeda terrorist network by removing safe havens and identifying resources that are exploited for terrorist gain.

In April of 2002 CIA contracted a private security firm called Blackwater USA, Blackwater Worldwide, which has changed its name in 2009 to Xe Services, and is based in North Carolina, to assist with seeking out Osama bin Laden and his hierarchy. The $5 million contract consisted of Blackwater recruiting and training a small elite special operations team to be deployed inside Afghanistan working out of the CIA station in Kabul, which the mud hut earned the nickname "The Alamo". The primary responsibility at the time for the Blackwater operators was to provide CIA security and the company was selected because their ability to be on the ground faster than other private security firms. The relationship between CIA and Blackwater formed shortly after the September 11th, 2001 attacks, between the company's CEO Erik Prince and CIA Executive Director, Alvin Krongard. Prince was a former intelligence specialist and Navy SEAL who had applied previously to work for CIA, but was rejected.

By 2004 the relationship had expanded with Blackwater leveraged to provide surveillance and additional support. Speculation has grown that Blackwater may have also been under the agreement to work as an assassination team to eliminate al-Qaeta operatives. Operational planning grew for Blackwater to use inactive CIA operators with paramilitary experience to recruit and train assassins for unsanctioned CIA operations from their Mt. Carroll facility in Northern Illinois. According to the New York Times, when CIA Director Leon Panetta found out about the assassination team he called an emergency meeting in June 2009 to advise congress of the hidden operation and had authorized the immediate cancelation of the program. After a review of the assassination program, White House and the Congressional intelligence committees stated that Mr. Panetta's predecessors did not believe that they needed to tell Congress because the program was not far enough developed.

Opposed to their involvement was Jack Rice. Rice, a former CIA field officer who worked on CIA paramilitary operations, showed disfavor at CIA for ceding their authority to a privatized company to simply provide the agency with deniability. Rice has shared the CIA was using Blackwater to carry marching orders out as a way to shield the CIA from accountability similar to orchestrating torture through the Syrians or the Egyptians for U.S. gain. In recent years Blackwater has hired numerous CIA personnel in key positions including Alvin Krongard, Enrique Prado, Robert Richer, and Cofer Black. Prince has also created a private sector CIA service called, "Total Intelligence", ran by Richer and Black.

In 2007 Prince was asked to testify regarding the deaths of seventeen Iraqi civilians during a Blackwater private security detail (PSD) escort of US State Department vehicles in western Baghdad. In addition, Federal prosecutors were investigating into whether Blackwater employees illegally smuggled weapons to the Kurdistan Workers Party (PKK), a Kurdish nationalist group designated a terrorist organization by the US, North Atlantic Treaty Organization and the European Union. In 2009 Prince stepped down at the CEO.

Capturing Abu Zubaydah
Waterboarding Controversy

During the hunt for bin Laden and additional al-Qaeta heads, one name kept populating CIA reports. Abu Zubaydah. Born in Saudi Arabia, in 1971, Zubaydah moved to the West Bank as a teenager where he joined in Palestinian demonstrations against the Israelis. Later in 1991, he

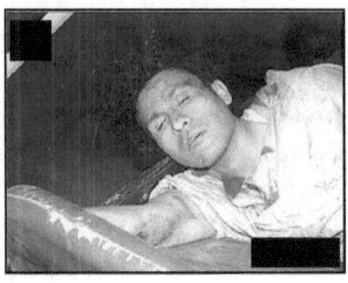

Abu Zubaydah

moved to Afghanistan where he assisted the Mujahideen in their fight against the Afghan and Soviet Communists. In 1992, while fighting for the Mujahideen Abu Zubaydah was injured from a mortar shell blast which left shrapnel in his head and caused severe memory loss, as well as the loss of his ability to speak for over one year and eventually became involved in the jihad training camp known as the Khalden Camp. Internationally Abu Zubaydah was convicted in absentia by a Jordanian court for his alleged role in plots to bomb U.S. and Israeli targets in Jordan. In addition, CIA received reports from Middle East security officials Zubaydah had directed the Jordanian cell and he was part of Osama bin Laden's inner circle.

In an August 6, 2001 classified FBI report entitled "Bin Laden determined to strike in U.S.", revealed that the foiled millennium bomber, Ahmed Ressam, had confessed that Abu Zubaydah had not only encouraged him to blow up the Los Angeles airport, but had facilitated the operation and that that Zubaydah was planning his own separate attack on America.

To mount terrorist operations al-Qaeta needed individuals to handle logistics and supply terrorist cells with supplies and moving them across borders. This was a job of Abu Zubaydah. Zubaydah was responsible for all of al-Qaeta's major terrorist logistical planning, which included funding the September 11th hijackers and provided their visas. Zubaydah was identified by CIA in 1998 as a plotter in the Millenium terrorist plan to blow up the Los Angeles International Airport. As the Station Chief in Islamabad, Grenier and his officers tracked movements of Zubaydah from Pakistan to Afpganistan. Through an asset the agency learned that Zubaydah was somewhere in Pakistan and the U.S. order came down to capture him alive. Unfortunately where in Pakistan was not known. A tip from a source in detention shared that Zubaydah often travelled through Faisalabad when entering Pakistan.

In March of 2002, CIA assigned John Kiriakou, who had been assigned to Pakistan since 1998, to locate Abu Zubaydah. "You need a perfect storm of intelligence an element of luck, maybe a good walk-in," Kiriakou. "Someone who walks in off the street and says 'I've got some information, I don't know what it means but if you give me $10 I let you have it,' which happens, and in many cases it's the best ten dollars you've ever spent." (30)

The CIA stepped up their efforts by rendering new photographs of Zubaydah to assist in seeking out any physical changes to his appearance that may be helpful in locating him. Kiriakou and associate posed as textile barons and purchased a large home in Faisalabad to set up an operational base. They began the operation by exploiting the terrorist's cell phone traffic through high tech intercept and monitoring equipment. All calls intercepted where then reviewed by analysts and interpriters and tracked by GPS. The CIA then used the raw data to select reference points of each phone call and created relationships among each phone intercept to begin to map out the terrorist network.

Kiriakou requested a targeting officer, Deuce Martinez, who happened to be a top CIA analysts to assist in focusing the manhunt. According to Kiriakou - once Martinez arrived in Faisalabad, he rolled out a sheet of butcher block paper onto the floor and started writing down addresses. The analyst assisted Kiriakou in narrowing down the hundreds of potential locations that Abu Zubaydah could be hiding to a few dozen. With these addresses in hand Kiriakou and team physically drove around the city to gather more information on the addresses and possible subjects and activity around them. After discounting several, Kiriakou and his team were able to narrow the locations to fourteen specific addresses which may be housing Zubaydah. The challange was how the CIA was going to initiate action on fourteen locations at one time. Kiriakou requested manpower from his supervisor Robert Grenier, who knew that they would have to simutainiously hit the fourteen targets at once to prevent Zubaydah from escaping and going underground. Grenier requested additional manpower and Kiriakou created fourteen teams consisting of at least one CIA officer, FBI agent and ISI officer per team. The raid was the largest the CIA had ever conducted. Kiriakou even made the teams syncronize their watches since the strike was based on time vs. communication.

All fourteen teams spread out accross Faisalabad to locate their strike target. Kiriakou's team found an abandoned lot which concerned them considering they were on a timed strike operation. Through his Pakistan counter-part, he learned that the phone number attached to the land parcel was actually being stolen and rewired to a second floor building close by. At 2am on March 28, 2002, the strike began breaking into fourteen separate locations across the city of Faisalbad. Although many were private residences, the address with the stolen telephone system was not. After breaking through a steal door and entering the room, one subject fled to the roof to avoid capture. Outside a Pakistan strike force detects the subject and fires three shots striking the man. The subject was Abu Zubaydah. Both Grenier and Kiriakou were aware of the valuable intelligence source they just captured but now run the risk of bleeding out from the severity of his wounds. They rushed Zubaydah to a nearby hospital and after surgeries the doctors were able to care for the critical wounds he received. He was taken to Faisalabad Hospital nearby and treated for his wounds, where the attending doctor admitted to John Kiriakou, he had never before seen a patient survive such severe wounds. In addition, CIA flew in a doctor from Johns Hopkins University to ensure Zubaydah would not succumb to his wounds during transit out of Pakistan.

Abu Zubaydah was transferred to CIA operated prisons in Pakistan, Thailand, Afghanistan, Poland, Northern Africa, and Diego Garcia. Historically renditions to countries which commit torture have been illegal, however, a U.S. Department of Justice memo issued on March 13, 2002, just days before Abu Zubaydah's capture, provided President George W. Bush and CIA with legal efforts for renditions to places such as Thailand.

After September 11th, Cofer Black played a leading role in many of the CIA's more controversial programs, including rendition and interrogation of al-Qaeda suspects and the detention of some of them in secret prisons outside the U.S. CIA uses covert aircraft leased by front or agency sponsored shell companies to fly subjects to countries including Egypt, Jordan, Morocco, Pakistan, Saudi Arabia and Syria. Most of the states to which the U.S. transfers these individuals are known to use torture and other ill-treatment in interrogations, thus CIA often will use disinformation with detainees to gain cooperation prior to actually transferring. If the need arises, CIA will assign the subjects to a specific 'black site' for interrogation. Due to certain laws within the United

States, CIA often uses black sites, which are covert detention centers strategically placed in countries that do not participate or come under scrutiny of U.S. guidelines. These facilities tend to be used in rotation, with detainees transferred from site to site together, rather than being scattered in different locations. Subjects are often moved several times, but always held in complete isolation, always in cells with blank walls, no floor coverings, no windows, no natural light. There is no contact with anyone other than their interrogators. Depending on the facility there is often a constant low-level hum of "white noise" and artificial light kept on 24 hours a day. Detainees are held sometimes for as little as 3-5 days or as long as years depending on the success of the information gathered.

Renditioning had been brought to light through the media with the help of Amnesty International and alleged victims of the program including Muhammad Abdullah Salah al-Assad, Salah Nasser Salim 'Ali, Muhammad Faraj Ahmed Bashmilah, and Maher Arar. In addition Eurpoean heads of state have also expressed their concern regarding the practice, yet were not aware that their own governments often assisted in the practice. Speaking to the BBC, Colin Powell said: "Well, most of our European friends cannot be shocked that this kind of thing takes place...The fact is that we have, over the years, had procedures in place that would deal with people who are responsible for terrorist activities, or suspected of terrorist activities, and so the thing that is called rendition is not something that is new or unknown to my European friends." (69)

On a visit to some European capitals, Secretary of State Condoleezza Rice had said that "extraordinary rendition" was used when a state could not detain or prosecute a suspect, and traditional extradition was not an option. In such cases, she said, the state could choose to cooperate in a "rendition", adding that "the United States has fully respected the sovereignty of other countries that cooperate in these matters". She further noted that: "Some governments choose to cooperate with the United States in intelligence, law enforcement, or military matters. That cooperation is a two-way street. We share intelligence that has helped protect European countries from attack, helping save European lives." (70)

Zubaydah became the first test case for a simulated drowning technique known as "waterboarding", but the critical intelligence from Zubaydah was gained when CIA conducted a false-flag operation against Zubaydah by tricking him to think he had been turned over to Saudi Arabian Secret police, when in reality he was with Arab-American CIA officers posing as Saudi interrogators and threatened him with brutal punishment. The CIA controllers then were surprised to learn that Zubaydah was not afraid, but rather relieved and volunteered a private cell phone number that belonged to a member of the Saudi Arabian Royal Family. Zubaydah explained that the contact would then demand his release and urged the CIA to contact the individual. The phone number belonged to Prince Ahmed bin Salman bin Abdul Zies the nephew to the King of Saudi Arabia. In addition Zubaydah named two other royal family members as well as the chief of the Pakistan Air Force and were all associates of his and al-Qaeta and were privy to the September 11th prior to the attack.

Within months the three princes Zubaydah named were all dead. On July 22, 2002 Prince Ahmed bin Salman bin Abdul Zies, 44 years-old died of a heart attack; July 23, 2002 Prince Sultan bin Faisal bin Turid, 41 years-old died while in a single car accident; and July 29, 2002 Prince Fahd bin Turki bin Saud Al-Kabeer, 25 years-old died of thirst while stranded in a desert.

Abu Zubaydah admitted in his CSRT testimony that he recommended to the leader of Khalden Camp that Ahmed Ressam be allowed to train there. Abu Zubaydah further testified that he facilitated Ahmed Ressam's travel to the camp as well as to

Algeria once Ressam's training was complete. Abu Zubaydah admitted he attempted to procure Canadian passports for Ahmed Ressam and other trainees, but not for "terrorist-related activities." Zubaydah denied ever having participated in the planning of the Millennium Plot or encouraging Ahmed Ressam to attack American targets or civilians. (71)

The U.S. Government alleges, in Abu Zubaydah's summary of evidence, that Ahmed Ressam identified Abu Zubaydah as the leader of the Khalden camp and an associate of Osama Bin Laden "equal to and not subordinate to UBL." The U.S. Government further alleges that Ahmed Ressam stated that Abu Zubaydah had "known of Ahmed Ressam's operation, although not specifically the date and exact target" and that Abu Zubaydah wanted Ressam to acquire "fraudulently-obtained Canadian passports" for himself and five others, in order to facilitate their travel into the United States to "possibly bomb several cities." Abu Zubayda is currently in U.S. custody in Guantanamo Bay, Cuba, as a detainee in the war on Terror.

Neutralizing Terrorism
Hunting al-Qaeta Terrorist Plotters

The search for terrorists changed the rules and the entire atmosphere of CIA. Unlike the cold war, terrorists, although often political, do not have a country and leverage transient protocol to evade or elude authorities. The function of CIA is to collect

intelligence on any threat to national security, and terrorist groups, especially al-Qaeta, have topped the CIA most-wanted list.

"September 11th changed everything for the CIA," John Kiriakou, CIA Counterterrorism officer. 'It changed the way we looked at threats around the world. Instead of being reactive, we became proactive. We had a mandate from the White House to go out and target terrorist groups to disrupt future attacks and neutralize those groups." (30)

In November of 2002, a RQ-1 Predator fired a Hellfire missile at a car in Yemen killing al-Qaeda leader Qaed Senyan Abu Ali al-Harithi; January 2006 a RQ-1 Predator airstrike on Damadola, Pakistan killed seventeen, and targeted al-Qaeda's number two Ayman al-Zawahri; May 2008 missile attack against a target in the Dhuusamarreeb region in central Somalia against Islamist militant group al-Shabaab killed eleven; and the October 26, 2008 raid in Abu Kamal, Syria killing high ranking terrorist Abu Ghadiyah was for smuggling foreign fighters into Iraq as part of an attack responsible for the deaths of eleven Iraqi policeman in the spring.

The biggest challenge CIA faced was not having enough human intelligence within the regions that the terrorists resided. After the escape of Osama bin Laden, CIA focused their hunt in Bahawalpur, Pakistan.

On August 9, 2006 Pakistan's ISI (Inter-Service Intelligence Agency) had executed a snatch and grab mission retrieving Rashid Rauf. Immediately CIA was contacted to update their ongoing operational status. The information regarding the capture was implemented into the PDB (Presidents Daily Brief) and also shared with MI6.

"These are the nation's most sensitive secrets that people put their lives at risk to acquire," Fran Townsend, Homeland Security Advisor to the President. (30)

Western Intelligence identified the subject as a vital link to the global terrorist group al-Qaeta. The tip came from MI5, British Domestic Intelligence, whom been working on piecing together the players within a terror cell in London, England. With assistance from the NSA, the CIA was able to intercept communications and other sensitive intelligence to learn al-Qaeta was attempting to once again down passenger airliners. CIA had learned that Jihadists were developing a bomb that was liquid-based that could be easily smuggled onto any airline through security. The bomb materials could be brought onboard in containers including toothpaste or shampoo bottles and then assembled once the terrorists boarded.

"It's not that liquid explosives were anything new," Townsend. "It was how the developed it and the ability to break it down to component pieces to understand otherwise non-threatening appearing items could be constructed in a way to make an explosive device." (30)

"When you have a political entity like al-Qaeta, seeking to attack us in the home land yet again, that's not a criminal enterprise, or a law enforcement issue, it is war." Rober Grenier, CIA Station Chief, Islamabad (30)

The immediate concern was not enough intelligence on when or where the attack would originate or take place. CIA was also uncertain as to how many terrorist cells were involved and where they were all located. Timing is critical and for CIA the practice is to hold off on any interception for as long possible to gather as much intelligence from wire taps, surveillance, and other espionage techniques. Once CIA gathers all vital intelligence, such as the players involved, targeted dates, times and locations of planned attacks, etc., then they can take action. If executed too soon the agency would have run the risk of missing key information that may result in an additional terrorist attack.

The CIA and MI6 learned that al-Qaeta was behind the planning, funding of resources, and individuals involved whom had all originated from Pakistan. Rauf was a key player acting as the go between for the high level al-Qaeta leadership and the terrorist cell operatives. With ISI removing Rauf from the picture, the communication from al-Qaeta and the British cell was cut - leaving the terrorists without direction for the time being. Rauf acted as a broker of terrorism operating in the open, unlike high level al-Qaeta leadership. Their responsibility is to provide any and all support needed to terror cell members, such as money, passports, and equipment needed to execute the bombings.

Once Rauf was in ISI custody, MI5 and MI6, along with British police closed in on the London terrorist cell and arrested the suspects to prevent them from fleeing or carrying out their objective. Foreign Intelligence services need to work together closely to ensure operational communication is conducted in a timely fashion to secure terrorist cell activity. The CIA would not be allowed to question Rauf - because he was able to flee from his Pakistan captures during prayer in December of 2007. Shortly after Rauf's escape, the Pakistan government dropped all charges against him regarding the Hethrow Airport Bomb Plan.

In Fall of 2008 the CIA was able once again to pick up the trail of Rauf, who was planning to attend a terrorist conference in a Pakistan training camp. The CIA used a predator drone to enable and secure communications from the sites location. Transmission from the drone was gathered and funneled to CIA headquarters in Langley, Virginia for analysts and translation monitoring to collect intelligence. Once the CIA was able to confirm high level al-Qaeta participants at the conference - an order was given to lock on with the predator drones missile guidance system and fired three hellfire missiles, which resulted in destroying the target. Although his body was never located, CIA confirms Rashid Rauf as being one of the dead terrorists killed by the missile attack.

"Everything is transnational. Weapons is transnational, drugs are transnational, and terrorism is transnational," Peter Earnest, CIA Senior Clandestine Services officer. "It's like slaying a dragon that represents the Soviet Union, and now replacing with poisonoius snakes [al-Qaeta]. In some way the dragon was easier to keep track of." (30)

After a press report during the initial hunt for bin Laden it was made public globally that CIA was using cellular telephone traffic as a way to locate his whereabouts. Since that time bin Laden, as well as senior al-Qaeta leadership have gone back to stone age communication. By seeking refuge in what is most likely the tribal area of Pakistan, bin Laden and his al-Qaeta leadership are protected by the most lawless residents of the country. The territory does not possess a police force and even the Pakistan military is afraid to enter the dangerous region. It makes the location perfect for bin Laden to find a safe haven from U.S. and other allies seeking his capture.

The situation poses a non-government entity who is a considerable threat to the United States because of the global terrorist capability. On the ground CIA officers continue efforts in recruiting spies to steal secrets. Their primary task is seeking out the al-Qaeta operatives that communicate with the outside world, thus leaving them vulnerable.

Extraordinary Rendition
The Milan Fiasco

Hassan Mustafa Osama Nasr, also known as Abu Omar, was an Egyptian cleric and member of al-Gama'a al-Islamiyya, an Islamic organization focused on overthrowing the government of Egypt. The radical group had been suspected to be behind the assassination of Anwar Sadat in 1981 and other terrorist campaigns. Once the group was classified as a terrorist organization by Europe and the United States, Omar sought asylum in Italy.

In 2003, at the age of forty, Omar was living in Milan, Italy. On February 17th of the same year Omar, while walking to his mosque for his noon prayers was abducted. Omar had left his flat at A18 Conte Verde Street on his way to pray at the mosque of Islamic Culture College at Viale Jenner when an American male, posing as a policeman, approached him asking him for proof of permission to be in Italy. At approximately noon during this conversation, a white minivan pulled up behind Omar in broad daylight in the streets of Milan and he was dragged from behind into the van where he was then drugged and restrained. The CIA van then drove to Aviano airbase, a USAF facility in northeastern Italy 15 kilometers from Pordenone. Omar was then taken to Ramstein airbase, a USAF facility in the German state of Rheinland-Pfalz. Ramstein serves as headquarters for the United States Air Forces in Europe (USAFE) and is also a North Atlantic Treaty Organization (NATO) installation. From Germany, Omar, accompanied by CIA officer, Robert Seldon Lady, was flown to Alexandria, Egypt and turned over to the Egypt's State Security Intelligence (SSI) in the Lazoghli section of Cairo as part of the extraordinary rendition. The SSI has been accused of torture by Human Rights Watch and Amnesty International who claim SSI involvement in sexual abuse and targeted persecutions of homosexuals, Islamists, and Christians. Omar would be held by the SSI at Cairo's Torah Reception Prison.

After being stripped and then placed in a blue prison jumpsuit, Omar was placed into a room and questioned by Egyptian Minister of Interior, Al Habib al-Adli and the CIA's Lady. The intention was to try and flip Omar to spy for the United States, with the understanding that if he agreed he would then be returned to Milan, Italy, but Omar refused. At this point Lady returned to Italy, and Omar was held in SSI custody as a ghost detainee.

According to an article in the Italian Corriere della Serra, Omar allegedly smuggled out a statement of his experiences. The statement describes the conditions he underwent during his captivity and alleged torture:

Here I briefly describe what went on inside the interrogation room:

1. At first they used to curse and swear at Italy and the Italian government for granting me asylum. They told me that the Italians handed me to Egypt and no one from Italy would come to take me out of this living hell. They also ordered me to sign a document given up my political asylum in Italy.

2. At the beginning of the interrogation a guard enters my room blindfolds my eyes and ties my hands at my back, so I cant remove during interrogation and see the face of the officer doing the interrogating and the torturing. My feet also stay tied up before I get drugged to the interrogation room where I they striped me naked before they take me to the officer who orders the guard to initiate the torture by indecently touching my sexual organs to humiliate me. This followed by savage torture which continued for the seven and half months in state security

3. My feet hanged me from the ceiling and my head down, my hands tied to my back my feet tied up. I was subjected to electric shocks all over my body specially in my head, nipples, testicles, and penis. My testicles where also beaten with a stick and squeezed tightly if I refused to answer their questions or suspected of telling lies.

4. They fixed my body to an iron door and on a wooden instrument they call the bride, where my hands where tied over my head from behind and my legs tied together or sometimes each leg in a different sides. The torture that takes place during this is electric shocks, beating with a shoe, cables.

5. All forms of media were strictly prohibited as well as radio and televisions. We were not allowed to talk to the guards. Once got severe punishment when I dared to ask a guard to bring me a copy of the Koran. They did so because I dared to look through the hole and have the energy to hold and read the Koran, so they doubled the amount of torture. Even if they brought me a copy, I wouldn't be able to read it because cell was in total darkness, but I wanted kiss it and hold it for few seconds to get some comfort that would make me forget for few seconds some of the humiliation, suffering and pain.

6. I lost hearing in one ear after being hit so badly on it.

7. I was tortured in what they call the mattress. They placed a wet mattress connected to an electric mains in the floor tie me up and put me over it, while one person would sit on a wooden chair places between my shoulders while at the other end someone would sit on another wooden chair between my legs. They would turn the power on so my body would rise up but the

chairs prevent me from going high up. Then they turn the electricity off, this followed by electric shocks in on my testicles and penis and would curse me and say let Italy help you.

8. They prevented me from sleeping and made me stand on my feet for long hours. I was allowed to wash my body once ever four months. I also couldn't cut my hair or facial hair, the state I was in when they eventually release me in April 2004, reminded of how Saddam Hussein looked like when he was found at his famous pet.

9. They made me listen for long hours to the torture of others inside the interrogation room. I could hear people's pleas, screaming and crying, this made me breakdown and get fits and lose consciousness.

10. They sexually assaulted me and raped me. This was the worse thing that happened to me, physical torture can be overcome with times, but the psychological impact of rape and the feeling of humiliation stay for good. I was raped twice. My hands were tied to my back and naked face down, while someone lay on top of me attempting to rape me. I screamed so hard till I lost consciousness and I don't know if he it was for real or just threats.

11. When they took me to State Security building in March and April 2004, they used to torture me before I and tell me to remember what I should say front of the state attorney. I was told to say that I came to Egypt at my own accords and that I purchased a ticket from Egypt Air and landed in Cairo's international Airport and went to the security office at the airport and handed in my Italian passport, and explained my situation. Every time I go the state attorney, they questioned me about what I said there and if I said what I was ordered to say. They told me

they would know if I am saying the truth or not. In fact I did what I was told to say front of the attorney general. Who never asked me there about reasons for the wounds on my face and the state of my head and facial hair?

Just six days shy of serving nearly four years in captivity Abu Omar was released on February 11, 2007 after an Egyptian court ruled he had been wrongfully imprisoned. The involvement of both the CIA and the Italian intelligence community had come under increased scrutiny as the situation became apparent to the public eye. The CIA's former head of counter-terrorism, Cofer Black, predicted that the agency would be in court for the actions taken involving the extraordinary renditions yet felt the program necessary to gather intelligence. The Milan operation had failed to remain covert on many levels including the players and the planes. During the investigation Italian police officials were able to easily track CIA personnel through their Virginia PO boxes, hotels and frequent flyer miles as well as identify planes used in rendition operations. Richard Stolz, a former CIA DDO, "It's not only bad tradecraft, but it's stupid."

The common practice for rendition is to have the host country make the arrest and turn the suspect over to CIA, but in the Milan case that didn't happen. In Milan the CIA ran the operation and was directly involved in the abduction of Abu Omar. Some speculated that both Lady and Castelli were acting alone as a way of increasing their notoriety within the agency. "If I had taken a plan to my bosses to kidnap someone in Europe, it better have been Osama himself, and I doubt I would have gotten permission even then," said Michael Scheuer, former head of the CIA program.

On November 4th, 2009 twenty-three Americans were convicted of the kidnapping of Abu Omar by an Italian court. Topping the list was Robert Seldon Lady, the former chief of the

CIA's Milan station, whose sentence consisted of imprisonment for eight years. Former CIA Milan station chief Jeff Castelli, and two other American's were acquitted under the protection of diplomatic immunity. Along with Lady, Italy convicted the following American citizens as being CIA operatives that violated Omar's rights, Joseph Romano, Sabrina De Sousa, Lorenzo Gabriel Carrera, Ben Amar Harty, Anne Lidia Jenkins, James Robert Kirkland, Eliana Isabella Castaldo, Brenda Liliana Ibanez , Victor Castellano, John Thomas Gurley, Gregory Asherleigh, George L. Purvis, Lorenzo Carrera, Benamar Harty, Raymond Harbaugh, Pilar Rueda, Joseph Sofin, Monica Courtney Adler, Cynthia Dame Logan, John Kevin Duffin, Drew Carlyle Channing, and Michalis Vasiliou.

"Of course it was an illegal operation," explained Lady. "But that's our job. We're at war against terrorism". Since the Italian government has declined to seek the extradition from the U.S. of the convicted American's, it is unlikely any will serve their prison sentences.

Sabrina De Sousa, employed in the US consulate offices in Milan at the time of the abduction, and one of the American's convicted offered, "Everything I did was approved by Washington... and we are paying for the mistakes right now, [of] whoever authorized this."

"I think these people have been hung out to dry," complained Republican congressman Pete Hoekstra of the House Intelligence Committee. "They're taking the fall for a decision that was made by their superiors."

The judge ruled that neither the former head of Italy's military intelligence service Nicolo Pollari nor his deputy could be convicted because the evidence against them was subject to official secrecy restrictions. But two other Italian intelligence officials were each given three-year prison terms.

CIA New Domestic Involvement
Assessing Terrorist Threats at Home

Although the Central Intelligence Agency has long kept their intelligence gathering techniques secret for national security reasons, they have since 2001 increased their domestic involvement in surveillance and intelligence gathering within the U.S. Due to very stringent rules and legal safeguards in protecting the rights of U.S. citizens, conventional law enforcement and FBI are limited to their involvement in these types of intelligence gathering processes. The CIA created the domestic division in 1963 as means of gathering intelligence through clandestine operations in the United States against foreign spies or organizations. These operations were cut significantly in 1973 by introducing a stricter oversight review of covert activities. Because of the methods of collecting information are legally quite different, the FBI in the past has had to reject much information offered by CIA.

With the formation of the USA Patriot Act, government agencies, both law enforcement and intelligence, now share vital information to assist in preventing terrorist attacks. In 1941 during Pearl Harbor, as in 2001 with the September 11th attacks, the U.S. continued the same path of domestic and foreign intelligence being shared on a piece by piece basis. This flaw in collaboration contributed to the success of both attacks on U.S. soil. The U.S. government believes now that the new information sharing process will better prepare the country from terrorism. The USA Patriot Act allows the CIA, FBI, INS, and the Border Patrol to share information broadly and has also created liaison positions with CIA officers and assets assisting FBI on a domestic level.

The USA Patriot Act also increases federal investigation powers by leveraging CIA to assist in conducting secret searches of homes and businesses with wiretaps through their authorized access under the Foreign Intelligence Surveillance Act. This practice empowers both local law enforcement and federal agencies with methods of gaining more intelligence to prevent terrorist activities at home. Although levels of information shared must be controlled as CIA is an intelligence apparatus, thus providing a higher level of clearance for their sensitive information, it is inconceivable that they not share information when U.S. interests domestically can be threatened. The domestic division also receives valuable data from new technologies not offered in the 60s, 70s, or 80s, which includes email and text message intercepts, and soon social media communication. In-Q-Tel, the independent investment arm of the U.S. government, has sponsored Visible Technologies to build a platform that will enable the CIA to read blogs, forums, YouTube, and Twitter across the Internet. This technology will prove vital for CIA in collecting information and review potential threats that could become vital to U.S. national security.

Currently CIA is providing officers and assets to FBI offices all over the U.S. in an advisory role. Their identities are often kept secret and act under the guise as special federal positions, business owners, informants, or other non-law-enforcement positions. While working in federal buildings in the U.S. they may take on the role of a sales representative for an outside company, or information technology employee. In this role their identity is protected and only shared with the highest FBI authority assigned to the location. The FBI now depends on their CIA advisors to help analyze information gathered and rely on their expertise in suggesting additional directions of surveillance, or action. Although direct action may be suggested by CIA, they do not accompany FBI or local law enforcement in the process since they possess no arrest powers on a domestic level. As one FBI special agent in the Midwest stated, "We now let them call the shots because of their knowledge in the intelligence world." In an interview with the Washington Post in 2002, Ellen Knowlton, the special agent in charge of the FBI's Las Vegas field office, called the CIA officers in her office "full and active participants" in day-to-day operations. The exchange of ideas among the FBI, the CIA and local law enforcement "is very interactive," she said. In the same article, "You balance how you use them" with the potential for compromising officers still under cover, said Joseph Billy Jr., special agent in charge of the FBI's New York field office. "We reserve the right for the CIA to make that call." In Oregon, Portland Police Chief Mark Kroeger said there remains a deep distrust toward giving law enforcement or the CIA expanded powers. Although he approves of the CIA presence, he said he purposefully stays clear of the CIA officers. "I know very little about them and I chose to keep it that way," he said. "The CIA is not a dirty word," he said. "They have roles and responsibilities that certainly have shifted. I have a lot of admiration for the organization."

The USA Patriot Act now provides CIA with overt access to testimony collected by federal grand juries, phone records and credit cards statements to profiles of suspected terrorists. Critics who oppose the joint venture fear that CIA's domestic involvement will repeat similar activities as in Operation CHAOS, where CIA conducted spying on US citizens including antiwar protesters, black militant groups and even congressmen. They also fear that to combat global terrorism barriers between covert intelligence operations and by-the-book law enforcement investigations will create a blurred line for U.S. citizens and their rights. The CIA's Domestic Contact Service (DCS) has long been awarded authority over domestic affairs on a secretive level. Under Executive Order 12333, signed by President Ronald

Reagan, the CIA is permitted to secretly collect "significant" foreign intelligence within the United States if the collection effort is not aimed at the domestic activities of U.S. citizens and corporations. The CIA's domestic field offices are secretly located throughout the United States and can at times be under the disguise as a legitimate business or organization. These offices are responsible for recruiting foreigners who are temporarily residing in the United States. These foreigners could be diplomats, scientists, business executives, and even students. The domestic objective of the CIA is to recruit these individuals while they are in the U.S. as assets to then provide intelligence later when they return to their foreign home. Other tasks of the domestic CIA personnel include debriefing Americans returning from abroad, and counterintelligence assessments of defectors. In 2001 there were less than twenty offices located throughout the United States, but since September 11th, the National Resources Division increased by thirty percent in 2002 and has grown consistently since then to an undisclosed number by 2009.

Reference Section

Central Intelligence Agency Terminology

Asset: A person with a formal relationship characterized by a witting agreement and a degree of commitment and control and who provides information or services

CCE: Continuing Criminal Enterprise

CI: Counterintelligence

CoS: Chief of Station

Cutout: A mutually trusted intermediary, method or channel of communication, facilitating the exchange of information between agents.

DCD: CIA DO/Domestic Collection Division

DCI: Director of Central Intelligence

DDCI: Deputy Director of Central Intelligence

DDO: CIA Deputy Director for Operations

Dead drop: A container not easily found to to store sensitive information for assets and agents.

DIA: Defense Intelligence Agency

Disinformation: Deliberately misleading information announced publicly or leaked by a government or especially by an intelligence agency in order to influence public opinion or the government in another nation.

DO: CIA Directorate of Operations

DoD: Department of Defense

DoJ: Department of Justice

DoJ/OIG: Department of Justice/Office of Inspector General

DoS: Department of State

Double Agent: A counterintelligence term for someone who pretends to spy on a target organization on behalf of a controlling organization, but in fact is loyal to the target organization.

False Flag Operation: A covert operation conducted by governments, corporations, or other organizations which are designed to deceive the public in such a way that the operations appear as though they are being carried out by other entities.

FBI: Federal Bureau of Investigation

Front Organization: Like a Shell Company, is any entity set up by and controlled by another organization, such as intelligence agencies, organized crime groups, banned organizations, religious or political groups, advocacy groups, or corporations.

Graymail: Threat to disclose classified or sensitive information to preclude prosecution

HAC: House Appropriations Committee

HUMINT: A syllabic abbreviation of the words HUMan INTelligence, refers to intelligence gathering by means of interpersonal contact, as opposed to the more technical intelligence gathering disciplines such as SIGINT, IMINT and MASINT.

IG: Inspector General

IRO: CIA DO/Information Review Officer

Mole: A spy who works for an enemy nation, but whose loyalty ostensibly lies with his own nation's government.

National Clandestine Service (NCS): Is the main United States intelligence agency for coordinating human intelligence (HUMINT) services. The organization absorbed the entirety of the Central Intelligence Agency (CIA)'s Directorate of Operations, and also coordinates HUMINT between the CIA and other agencies, including, but not limited to, the FBI, the DSS, DIA, and all military intelligence organizations.

NSC: National Security Council

OGC: Office of General Counsel

OIC: Office of Independent Counsel

OIG: Office of Inspector General

Puppet State, or Puppet Government: A nominal sovereignty controlled effectively by a foreign power.

SAD: Special Activities Division

Safehouse: Is a hidden and secretive location unknown to opposing intelligence agencies or opposition.

SFRC: Senate Foreign Relations Committee

Sleeper Cell: A cell, or isolated grouping of sleeper agents that belong to an intelligence network or organization. The cell "sleeps" (lies dormant) inside a target population until it receives orders or decides to act.

Tradecraft: A general term that denotes a skill acquired through experience within the Intelligence Community as a collective word for the techniques used in modern espionage.

TSD: Technical Services Department

Military Phonetic Alphabet

ALFA, BRAVO, CHARLIE, DELTA, ECHO, FOXTROT, GOLF, HOTEL, INDIA, JULIETT, KILO, LIMA, MIKE, NOVEMBER, OSCAR, PAPA, QUEBEC, ROMEO, SIERRA, TANGO, UNIFORM, VICTOR, WHISKEY, X-RAY, YANKEE, and ZULU.

Department of Defense Definitions

black list: An official counterintelligence listing of actual or potential enemy collaborators, sympathizers, intelligence suspects, and other persons whose presence menaces the security of friendly forces.

burn notice: An official statement by one intelligence agency to other agencies, domestic or foreign, that an individual or group is unreliable for any of a variety of reasons.

clandestine operation: An operation sponsored or conducted by governmental departments or agencies in such a way as to assure secrecy or concealment. A clandestine operation differs from a covert operation in that emphasis is placed on concealment of the operation rather than on concealment of the identity of the sponsor. In special operations, an activity may be both covert and clandestine and may focus equally on operational considerations and intelligence-related activities. See also covert operation; overt operation.

counterintelligence: Information gathered and activities conducted to protect against espionage, other intelligence activities, sabotage, or assassinations conducted by or on behalf of foreign governments or elements thereof, foreign organizations, or foreign persons, or international terrorist activities. Also called CI. See also counterespionage; countersabotage; countersubversion; security; security intelligence.

covert operation: An operation that is so planned and executed as to conceal the identity of or permit plausible denial by the sponsor. A covert operation differs from a clandestine operation in that emphasis is placed on concealment of the identity of the sponsor rather than on concealment of the operation. See also clandestine operation; overt operation.

direct action: Short-duration strikes and other small-scale offensive actions conducted as a special operation in hostile, denied, or politically sensitive environments and which employ specialized military capabilities to seize, destroy, capture, exploit, recover, or damage designated targets. Direct action differs from conventional offensive actions in the level of physical and political risk, operational techniques, and the degree of discriminate and precise use of force to achieve specific objectives. Also called DA. See also special operations; special operations forces.

domestic intelligence: Intelligence relating to activities or conditions within the United States that threaten internal security and that might require the employment of troops; and intelligence relating to activities of individuals or agencies potentially or actually dangerous to the security of the Department of Defense.

espionage: The act of obtaining, delivering, transmitting, communicating, or receiving information about the national defense with an intent, or reason to believe, that the information may be used to the injury of the United States or to the advantage of any foreign nation. Espionage is a violation of 18 United States Code 792-798 and Article 106, Uniform Code of Military Justice. See also counterintelligence.

foreign intelligence: Information relating to capabilities, intentions, and activities of foreign powers, organizations, or persons, but not including counterintelligence, except for information on international terrorist activities. See also intelligence.

guerrilla force: A group of irregular, predominantly indigenous personnel organized along military lines to conduct military and paramilitary operations in enemy-held, hostile, or denied territory.

host country: A nation which permits, either by written agreement or official invitation, government representatives and/or agencies of another nation to operate, under specified conditions, within its borders.

insurgent: Member of a political party who rebels against established leadership. See also antiterrorism; counterinsurgency; insurgency.

intelligence community: All departments or agencies of a government that are concerned with intelligence activity, either in an oversight, managerial, support, or participatory role. Also called IC.

interrogation (intelligence): Systematic effort to procure information by direct questioning of a person under the control of the questioner.

joint intelligence operations center: An interdependent, operational intelligence organization at the Department of Defense, combatant command, or joint task force (if established) level, that is integrated with national intelligence centers, and capable of accessing all sources of intelligence impacting military operations planning, execution, and assessment. Also called JIOC.

laundering: In counterdrug operations, the process of transforming drug money into a more manageable form while concealing its illicit origin. Foreign bank accounts and dummy corporations are used as shelters.

military intelligence: Intelligence on any foreign military or military-related situation or activity which is significant to military policymaking or the planning and conduct of military operations and activities. Also called MI.

national intelligence: The terms "national intelligence" and "intelligence related to the national security" each refers to all intelligence, regardless of the source from which derived and including information gathered within or outside of the United States, which pertains, as determined consistent with any guidelines issued by the President, to the interests of more than one department or agency of the Government; and that involves (a) threats to the United States, its people, property, or interests; (b) the development, proliferation, or use of weapons of mass destruction; or (c) any other matter bearing on United States national or homeland security.

overt operation: An operation conducted openly, without concealment. See also clandestine operation; covert operation.

paramilitary forces: Forces or groups distinct from the regular armed forces of any country, but resembling them in organization, equipment, training, or mission.

political intelligence: Intelligence concerning foreign and domestic policies of governments and the activities of political movements.

private sector: An umbrella term that may be applied in the United States and in foreign countries to any or all of the nonpublic or commercial individuals and businesses, specified nonprofit organizations, most of academia and other scholastic institutions, and selected nongovernmental organizations.

propaganda: Any form of communication in support of national objectives designed to influence the opinions, emotions, attitudes, or behavior of any group in order to benefit the sponsor, either directly or indirectly. See also black propaganda; grey propaganda; white propaganda.

psychological operations: Planned operations to convey selected information and indicators to foreign audiences to influence their emotions, motives, objective reasoning, and ultimately the behavior of foreign governments, organizations, groups, and individuals. The purpose of psychological operations is to induce or reinforce foreign attitudes and behavior favorable to the originator's objectives. Also called PSYOP. See also overt peacetime psychological operations programs; perception management.

rules of engagement: Directives issued by competent military authority that delineate the circumstances and limitations under which United States forces will initiate and/or continue combat engagement with other forces encountered. Also called ROE.

sabotage: An act or acts with intent to injure, interfere with, or obstruct the national defense of a country by willfully injuring or destroying, or attempting to injure or destroy, any national defense or war materiel, premises, or utilities, to include human and natural resources.

security classification: A category to which national security information and material is assigned to denote the degree of damage that unauthorized disclosure would cause to national defense or foreign relations of the United States and to denote the degree of protection required. There are three such categories. a. top secret--National security information or material that requires the highest degree of protection and the unauthorized disclosure of which could reasonably be expected to cause exceptionally grave damage to the national security. Examples of "exceptionally grave damage" include armed hostilities against the United States or its allies; disruption of foreign relations vitally affecting the national security; the compromise of vital national defense plans or complex cryptologic and communications intelligence systems; the revelation of sensitive intelligence operations; and the disclosure of scientific or technological developments vital to national security. b. secret--National security information or material that requires a substantial degree of protection and the unauthorized disclosure of which could reasonably be expected to cause serious damage to the national security. Examples of "serious damage" include disruption of foreign relations significantly affecting the national security; significant impairment of a program or policy directly related to the national security; revelation of significant military plans or intelligence operations; and compromise of significant scientific or technological developments relating to national security. c. confidential-- National security information or material that requires protection and the unauthorized disclosure of which could reasonably be expected to cause damage to the national security. See also classification; security.

signals intelligence: A category of intelligence comprising either individually or in combination all communications intelligence, electronic intelligence, and foreign instrumentation signals intelligence, however transmitted. Intelligence derived from communications, electronic, and foreign instrumentation signals. Also called SIGINT.

special activities: Activities conducted in support of national foreign policy objectives that are planned and executed so that the role of the US Government is not apparent or acknowledged publicly. They are also functions in support of such activities but are not intended to influence US political processes, public opinion, policies, or media and do not include diplomatic activities or the collection and production of intelligence or related support functions.

special forces group: A combat arms organization capable of planning, conducting, and supporting special operations activities in all operational environments in peace, conflict, and war. It consists of a group headquarters and headquarters company, a support company, and special forces battalions. The group can operate as a single unit, but normally the battalions plan and conduct operations from widely separated locations. The group provides general operational direction and synchronizes the activities of subordinate battalions. Although principally structured for unconventional warfare, special forces group units are capable of task-organizing to meet specific requirements. Also called SFG.

special operations: Operations conducted in hostile, denied, or politically sensitive environments to achieve military, diplomatic, informational, and/or economic objectives employing military capabilities for which there is no broad conventional force requirement. These operations often require covert, clandestine, or low visibility capabilities. Special operations are applicable across the range of military operations. They can be conducted independently or in conjunction with operations of conventional forces or other government agencies and may include operations through, with, or by indigenous or surrogate forces. Special operations differ from conventional operations in degree of physical and political risk, operational techniques, mode of employment, independence from friendly support, and dependence on detailed operational intelligence and indigenous assets. Also called SO.

subversion: Action designed to undermine the military, economic, psychological, or political strength or morale of a regime. See also unconventional warfare.

torture: As defined by Title 18, US Code, Section 2340, it is any act committed by a person acting under color of law specifically intended to inflict severe physical or mental pain or suffering (other than pain or suffering incidental to lawful sanctions) upon another person within his custody or physical control. "Severe mental pain or suffering" means the prolonged mental harm caused by or resulting from: (a) the intentional infliction or threatened infliction of severe physical pain or suffering; (b) the administration or application, or threatened administration or application, of mind-altering substances or other procedures calculated to disrupt profoundly the senses or personality; (c) the threat of imminent death; or (d) the threat that another person will imminently be subjected to death, severe physical pain or suffering, or the administration or application of mind-altering substances or other procedures calculated to disrupt profoundly the senses or personality.

unconventional warfare: A broad spectrum of military and paramilitary operations, normally of long duration, predominantly conducted through, with, or by indigenous or surrogate forces who are organized, trained, equipped, supported, and directed in varying degrees by an external source. It includes, but is not limited to, guerrilla warfare, subversion, sabotage, intelligence activities, and unconventional assisted recovery. Also called UW.

weapons of mass destruction: Weapons that are capable of a high order of destruction and/or of being used in such a manner as to destroy large numbers of people. Weapons of mass destruction can be high-yield explosives or nuclear, biological, chemical, or radiological weapons, but exclude the means of transporting or propelling the weapon where such means is a separable and divisible part of the weapon. Also called WMD.

CIA Cryptonym

The Central Intelligence Agency uses cryptonym which contain a two character prefix called a digraph. The digraph usually designates a specific geographic location or operational area. The second part of the cryptonym is usually a dictionary word. Cryptonyms can be seen as one word or separated by a "/", e.g. ZRRIFLE or ZR/RIFLE. Cryptonyms will often designate a "-" followed by a number "1,2,3,etc." to identify persons involved in the operation, e.g. AMICE-27. Below are some examples of CIA Cryptonym usage from past operations.

Organizations

CATIDE: Bundesnachrichtendienst
KUBARK: CIA Headquarters
KUCAGE: CIA Overseas Paramilitary / Propaganda Operations
KUCLUB: Office of Communications
KUDESK: Counterintelligence department
KUDOVE: Office of the director
KUFIRE: Intelligence
KUGOWN: Propaganda
KUHOOK: Negotiations/Logistics (unsure)
KUSODA: CIA Interrogators
LNWILT: US Counterintelligence Corps (CIC)
ODACID: United States Department of States/U.S. embassy
ODEARL: United States Department of Defense
ODENVY: Federal Bureau of Investigation
ODOATH: United States Navy
ODOPAL United States Army Counterintelligence Corps
ODUNIT: United States Air Force
ODYOKE: Federal Government of the United States
QKFLOWAGE: United States Information Agency
SKIMMER: The "Group" CIA cover organization supporting Castillo Armas.
SGUAT: CIA Station in Guatemala
SMOTH: Secret Intelligence Service (MI6)

SYNCARP: The "Junta," Castillo Armas' political organization headed by Cordova Cerna.
UNIFRUIT: United Fruit Company

Individuals

AEBARMAN: Soviet officer Yuri Ivonovich Nosenko
AEBURBLE: Stateside Soviet double-agent Guenter Schulz.
AEDONOR: Soviet officer Yuri Ivonovich Nosenko
AEFOXTROT: Soviet officer Yuri Ivonovich Nosenko
AEGUSTO: Yuriy Loginov, a KGB officer who became an in-place double agent for the CIA
AELADLE: Anatoliy Golitsyn, a Soviet defector
AMLASH: Rolando Cubela Secades
AMQUACK: Che Guevara, Argentinian guerrilla leader
AMTHUG: Fidel Castro, president of Cuba
ESQUIRE: James Bamford, author of "The Puzzle Palace"
GPFLOOR: Lee Harvey Oswald
GPIDEAL: John F. Kennedy, US president
GRALLSPICE: Pyotr Semonovich Popov, Soviet defector
JMBLUG: John S. Peurifoy, U.S. Ambassador to Guatemala
KUMOTHER: James Jesus Angleton, head of the CIAs counter intelligence
PANCHO: Carlos Castillo Armas, President of Guatemala, also RUFUS
POCAPON: Taketora Ogata, Japanese politician in 50s
PODAM: Matsutarō Shōriki, Japanese businessman and politician
RUFUS: Carlos Castillo Armas, President of Guatemala, also PANCHO
SKILLET: Whiting Willauer, U.S. Ambassador to Honduras.
STANDEL: Jacobo Arbenz, President of Guatemala

Locations

BOND: Puerto Barrios, Guatemala
DTFROGS: El Salvador
HTKEEPER: Mexico City
HTPLUME: Panama

JMMADD: CIA airbase near city of Retalhuleu, Guatemala
JMTIDE: CIA airbase in Puerto Cabezas, Nicaragua
JMTRAX: CIA covert airbase/training camp in Guatemala
JMWAVE: CIA station in Miami
KMFLUSH: Nicaragua
KMPAJAMA: Mexico
KMPLEBE: Peru
LCPANGS: Costa Rica
LIONIZER: Guatemalan refugee group in Mexico
PBPRIME: the United States of America
PBRUMEN: Cuba
SARANAC: Training site in Nicaragua
SCRANTON: Training base for radio operators near Nicaragua.
WSBURNT: Guatemala
WSHOOFS: Honduras

MISC

BGGYPSY: Communist
ESCOBILLA: Guatemalan national
FJHOPEFUL: military base
LCFLUTTER: Polygraph.
LIENVOY: Wiretap or Intercept Program
RYBAT: Indicates that the information is very sensitive
SLINC: Telegram indicator for PBSUCCESS Headquarters in Florida.

Offices of Central Intelligence Agency

The Directorate of Intelligence (DI), where incomplete and sometimes contradictory information is transformed into unique insights that inform US policy decisions. Members of the DI help provide timely, accurate, and objective all-source intelligence analysis on the full range of national security and foreign policy issues to the President, Cabinet, and senior policymakers in the US government.

The National Clandestine Service (NCS) serves as the clandestine arm of the Central Intelligence Agency (CIA) and the national authority for the coordination, de-confliction, and evaluation of clandestine operations across the Intelligence Community of the United States.

The Directorate of Science and Technology (DS&T) is one of four major components whose employees carry out the CIA's mission. The DS&T brings technical power and expertise to clandestine collection and analysis on the most pressing intelligence problems.

The Directorate of Support (DS) provides everything the CIA needs to accomplish its critical mission of defending our nation. Serving side-by-side with our mission colleagues from the Directorate of Intelligence, the Directorate of Science & Technology, and the National Clandestine Service, our job is to ensure that all our mission elements have everything they need for success.

The CIA Office of General Counsel (OGC) is an independent office of the CIA that is headed by the General Counsel and assists the General Counsel in carrying out his statutory and other responsibilities. On behalf of the General Counsel, OGC provides legal advice and guidance to the Agency and to the Director of the CIA.

The Director of OPA serves as spokesperson for the CIA. He reports to the Director of the CIA, providing public affairs support and acting as senior adviser for media and public policy issues. He oversees the daily operations of communicating with the media, the general public, and CIA's workforce.

In Bad Company

Rear Admiral U.S. Navy
Roscoe H. Hillenkoetter
1947-1950

General U.S. Army
Walter Bedell Smith
1950-1953

Allen W. Dulles
1953-1961

John McCone
1961-1965

Vice Admiral U.S. Navy
William Raborn
1965-1966

Richard M. Helms
1966-1973

James R. Schlesinger
1973

William Colby
1973-1976

George H. W. Bush
1976-1977

Admiral U.S. Navy
Stansfield Turner
1977-1981

William J. Casey
1981-1987

William H. Webster
1987-1991

Robert M. Gates
1991-1993

R. James Woolsey
1993-1995

John M. Deutch
1995-1996

George J. Tenet
1997-2004

Porter J. Goss
2004-2005

Michael Hayden
2006-2009

Leon Panetta
2009

(top left) The new entrance to CIA headquarters. *(top right)* Kryptos sculpture by American artist Jim Sanborn located on the grounds of the Central Intelligence Agency in Langley, Virginia. *(bottom left)* CIA Wall of Honor *(bottom right)* 16 foot seal of the Central Intelligence Agency.

Specific Medals of the Central Intelligence Agency

(from left to right) DISTINGUISHED INTELLIGENCE CROSS: For a voluntary act or acts of extraordinary heroism involving the acceptance of existing dangers with conspicuous fortitude and exemplary courage. DISTINGUISHED INTELLIGENCE MEDAL: For performance of outstanding services or for achievement of a distinctly exceptional nature in a duty or responsibility, the results of which constitute a major contribution to the mission of the Agency. INTELLIGENCE STAR: For a voluntary act or acts of courage performed under hazardous conditions or for outstanding achievements or services rendered with distinction under conditions of grave risk. HOSTILE ACTION SERVICE MEDAL: For direct exposure to a specific life-threatening incident in the foreign field or in the U.S. where the employee was in close proximity to death or injury, but survived and sustained no injuries. INTELLIGENCE COMMENDATION MEDAL: For the performance of especially commendable service or for an act or achievement significantly   above normal duties which results in an important contribution to the mission of the Agency. EXCEPTIONAL SERVICE MEDAL: For injury or death resulting from service in an area of hazard. AGENCY SEAL MEDAL: For non-Agency personnel, to include U.S. Government employees and private citizens, who have made significant contributions to the Agency's intelligence efforts.

Bibliography

1. **Mitrokhin, Christopher Andrew and Vasili.** *The Mitrokhin Archive, Volume 1: The KGB in Europe and the West.* 1999.

2. *Chef Julia Child, others part of WWII spy network.* [Television] Atlanta : CNN, 2008.

3. **Goudsmit, Samuel.** *Alsos.* New York : Henry Schuman Inc., 1947.

4. **Bernstein, Jeremy.** *Hitler's Uranium Club: The Secret Recordings at Farm Hall.* New York : Copernicus Books, 2001.

5. **Forman, Paul and Sánchez-Ron, José Manuel.** *National Military Establishments and the Advancement of Science and Technology.* s.l. : Kluwer Academic Publishers, 1996.

6. **Phayer, Michael.** *The Catholic Church and the Holocaust .* 2008.

7. **Loftus, Aarons &.** Unholy Trinity: The Vatican, The Nazis, and the Swiss Bankers. s.l. : St Martins, 1991, p. 36.

8. **Sereny, Gitta.** Into That Darkness . s.l. : Picador, 1977, p. 289.

9. **Lyon, Paul B. IB Operating Officer.** *History of the Italian Rat Line.* Austria : 430th Counter Intelligence Corps, 1950.

10. **Walker, Andrew.** Project Paperclip: Dark side of the Moon. *BBC News.* November 21, 2005.

11. Operation Paperclip. [Online] [Cited: September 14, 2009.] http://www.operationpaperclip.info/arthur-rudolph.php.

12. **Taylor, R.** *Memo from Helms to Shepardson.* s.l. : Record Group, 1944.

13. *Stella Polaris' and Postwar Europe.* **Aid, Matthew.** Journal of Intelligence and National Security, pp. Vol 17, No 3.

14. **O'Donnell, Patrick K.** *Operatives, Spies and Saboteurs: The Unknown Story of WWII's OSS.* New York : Kensington Publishing, 2004.

15. **Warner, Robert Louis Benson and Michael.** Venona: Soviet Espionage and the American Response, 1939-1957.

16. **Mahl, Tom E.** *Espionage's most wanted: the top 10 book of malicious moles, blown covers.* Virginia : Brasseys, Inc. , 2003.

17. **BBC.** *CIA: Shocking Stories Behind the Headlines.* 2004.

18. **Fischer, Benjamin.** Hitler, Stalin & Operation Myth. s.l. : CIA History Staff.

19. CIA Ties With Ex-Nazis Shown. *The Washington Post.* June 7, 2006.

20. **Vulliamy, Ed.** Secret agents, freemasons, fascists... and a top-level campaign of political 'destabilisation'. *The Guardian.* December, 1990, Vol. 5.

21. **Willan, Philip.** US 'supported anti-left terror in Italy'. *The Guardian.* July, 2004, Vol. 24.

22. **Rowse, Arthur.** GLADIO: THE SECRET U.S. WAR TO SUBVERT ITALIAN DEMOCRACY. *Covert Action Quarterly.* December, 1994.

23. **Moore, Malcolm.** US envoy admits role in Aldo Moro killing. *The Telegraph.* March, 2008, Vol. 16.

24. **Manr, Saviona.** *A murder still fresh. Haaretz.* s.l. : Haaretz, 2008.

25. **Irvine, Ian.** George Blake: I spy a British traitor. *The Independent People.* October 1, 2006.

26. **Constantine, Alex.** Mockingbird: The Subversion Of The Free Press By The . 2000.

27. **Braden, Thomas.** *The Rise and Fall of the CIA.* [interv.] Granada Television World in Action. 1975.

28. **Lee, Christopher.** CIA Ties With Ex-Nazis Shown. *The Washington Post.* June 7, 2006.

29. **Bernstein, Carl.** The CIA and the Media. *Rolling Stone.* October 20, 1977.

30. **Geographic, National.** *CIA Confidential.* [Video] s.l. : National Geographic, 2009.

31. **Helms, Richard.** [interv.] David Frost. May 23, 1978.

32. **Colby, William.** *Honorable Men: My Life in the CIA* . pages 425-426 : Simon and Schuster, 1978.

33. **Kinzer, Stephen.** All the Shah's Men. An American Coup and the Roots of Middle East Terror. s.l. : John Wiley and Sons, 2003, p. 209.

34. **Nagorski, Andrew.** The Greatest Battle. 2007, pp. 196-198.

35. **Andrew, Christoper & Mitrokhin, Vasili.** *The Mitrokhin Archive: The KGB in Europe and the West.* s.l. : Gardners Books, 2000.

36. **Seth, Jacobs.** Cold War Mandarin: Ngo Dinh Diem and the Origins of America's War in Vietnam 1950-1963. s.l. : Rowman & Littlefield, 2006, pp. 45,53.

37. *King of the Mountain: The Nature of Political Leadership.* **Ludwig, Arnold M.,.** 2004, University Press Kentucky, p. 150.

38. *Engineers of Happy Land: Technology and Nationalism in a Colony.* **Mrazek, Rudolf.** 2002, Princeton University Press.

39. **Friend, Theodore.** *Indonesian Destinies.* Boston : The Belknap Press of Harvard University, 2003.

40. **Evans, Thomas.** *The very best men: four who dared : the early years of the CIA* . New York : Simon & Schuster, 1995.

41. June. *Time Magazine.* 1958.

42. **Ehrlich, Richard.** Death of a dirty fighter . *Aisan Times.* 2003.

43. **Leary, William M.** [interv.] James Lair. July 3, 1993.

44. **Van Es, Hubert.** Thirty Years at 300 Millimeters. *The New York Times.* April 29, 2005.

45. **Rodríguez, Félix I.** Shadow Warrior. s.l. : Simon and Schuster, 1989, p. 148.

46. —. *Executive Action.* [interv.] BBC Documentary. 1992.

47. *CORDS/Phoenix.* **Willbanks, Dale Andrade and Lieutenant Colonel James H.** 2006, Military Review, p. March.

48. **Halperin, Moron H.** *The Lawless State.* New York : Penguin, 1976.

49. **Powers, Thomas.** The Man Who Kept the Secrets. New York : Knopf, 1979, p. 246.

50. **Security, Center for National.** *Operation Chaos.* Washington D.C. : Center for National Security, 1972.

51. **McMoneagle, Joseph.** *Memoirs of a Psychic Spy: The Remarkable Life of U.S. Government Remote Viewer 001.* s.l. : Hampton Roads Publishing Co, 2002, 2006.

52. **Butler, Allen.** Project SCANATE: The CIA and the Birth of Remote Viewing. *Associated Content, Inc. .* March 15, 2006.

53. **Waller, Douglas.** The Vision Thing. *Time Magazine.* December 11, 1995, p. 45.

54. **Dingus, John.** *The Condor Years: How Pinochet and His Allies Brought Terrorism to Three Continents.* s.l. : The New Press, 2004.

55. **Waugh, Billy and Keown, Tim.** *Hunting the Jackal.* s.l. : Avon Books, 2005.

56. **Carlson, Peter.** International Man of Mystery. *Washington Post.* June, 2004, Vol. Page C01.

57. **Edward P. Cutolo, Colonel, Infantry Commanding.** *Affidavit.* 1980. March 11.

58. **Burea of Democracy, Human Rights, and Labor.** *Norway Report on Human Rights Practices.* s.l. : US State Department, 2000.

59. Israeli Denies He Served as Noriega Adviser. *The New York Times.* January, 1990, 7.

60. **Bowden.** *Guests of the Ayatollah.* 2006.

61. *CIA Goes Hollywood: A Classic Case of Deception.* **Mendez, Antonio J.** 1999-2000, Studies in Intelligence.

62. **Guyatt, David G.** The Mafia, The CIA, & The Vatican's Intelligence Apparatus. *Nexus Magazine Volume 7, Number 5.* October 11, 2000.

63. **Castillo, Celerino & Harmon, Dave.** *Powderburns: Cocaine, Contras & the Drug War.* s.l. : Sundial, 1994.

64. **Brewton, Pete.** *Houston Post.*

65. **Bainerman.** *Covert Action.* 1990, Vols. 276-277, 35.

66. —. *Washington Business Journal.* 5, 1990, Vol. February.

67. Ex-Spymaster in the Middle. *New York Times.* February, 2008, Vol. 20.

68. **Engelberg, Stephen.** Drug Arrest Disrupted C.I.A. Operation in Panama . *New York Times.* January, 1990, Vol. 14.

69. **Crile, George.** *Charlie Wilson's War.* s.l. : Grove Press, 2003.

70. **Ignatius, David.** A Sectarian Spy Duel In Baghdad. *Washington Post.* June, 2007, 14.

71. **Hiro, Dilip.** *Neighbors, Not Friends: Iraq and Iran After the Gulf Wars.* s.l. : Routledge, 2004. p. 102.

72. **Ignatius, David.** CIA And the Coup That Wasn't. *Washington Post.* 2003, Vol. May, 16.

73. **Windrem, Robert.** Ex-Saddam defense minister set to be executed. *NBC News.* October, 2007, Vol. 12.

74. **Congress, U.S.** *9/11 Commission Report.* Washington, D.C. : USA, Chapter 10.

75. **Woodward, Bob.** *Bush At War.* pp. 53.

76. **Frost, David.** *Interview with Colin Powell.* [TV] s.l. : BBC, 2005.

77. **Rice, Condoleezza.** 2005. *Departure for Europe.* [December 5] s.l. : US Department of State, 2005.

78. **Zubaydah, Abu.** *Combatant Status Review Tribunal.* s.l. : Department of Defense, 2007.

X

Z